CHILTON'S GUIDE TO AUTO ELECTRONIC ACCESSORIES

Sound • Security • Safety

Vice President and General Manager JOHN P. KUSHNERICK
Managing Editor KERRY A. FREEMAN, S.A.E.
Senior Editor RICHARD J. RIVELE, S.A.E.
Contributing Editor IVAN BERGER (Auto Sound Section)

CHILTON BOOK COMPANY
Radnor, Pennsylvania
19089

SAFETY NOTICE

Proper service and repair procedures are vital to the safe, reliable operation of all motor vehicles, as well as the personal safety of those performing repairs. This book outlines procedures for servicing and repairing vehicles using safe, effective methods. The procedures contain many NOTES, CAUTIONS and WARNINGS which should be followed along with standard safety procedures to eliminate the possibility of personal injury or improper service which could damage the vehicle or compromise its safety.

It is important to note that repair procedures and techniques, tools and parts for servicing motor vehicles, as well as the skill and experience of the individual performing the work vary widely. It is not possible to anticipate all of the conceivable ways or conditions under which vehicles may be serviced, or to provide cautions as to all of the possible hazards that may result. Standard and accepted safety precautions and equipment should be used when handling toxic or flammable fluids, and safety goggles or other protection should be used during cutting, grinding, chiseling, prying, or any other process that can cause material removal or projectiles. Some procedures require the use of tools specially designed for a specific purpose. Before substituting another tool or procedure, you must be completely satisfied that neither your personal safety, nor the performance of the vehicle will be endangered.

Although information in this guide is based on industry sources and is as complete as possible at the time of publication, the possibility exists that the manufacturer made later changes which could not be included here. While striving for total accuracy, Chilton Book Company cannot assume responsibility for any errors, changes, or omissions that may occur in the compilation of this data.

PART NUMBERS

Part numbers listed in this reference are not recommendations by Chilton for any product by brand name. They are references that can be used with interchange manuals and aftermarket supplier catalogs to locate each brand supplier's discrete part number.

ACKNOWLEDGMENTS

Auto Sound Section prepared by Electronic Industries Association/Consumer Electronics Group (EIA/CEG).

Copyright © 1983 by Chilton Book Company
All Rights Reserved
Published in Radnor, Pennsylvania 19089 by Chilton Book Company

Manufactured in the United States of America
1234567890 2109876543

Chilton's Guide to Auto Electronic Accessories: Sound, Safety & Security
ISBN 0-8019-7322-8 pbk.
Library of Congress Catalog Card No. 82-72906

Contents

CONTENTS

The Electronic Industries Association/Consumer Electronics Group

The Electronic Industries Association/Consumer Electronics Group is a Washington, D.C.-based trade association of more than 500 manufacturers of electronic products that has served the industry and consumers for nearly 60 years.

The EIA was founded in 1924 as the Radio Manufacturers Association (RMA). As electronics expanded dramatically, so did the scope of the trade association. The Consumer Electronics Group (CEG) represents a wide variety of electronic products for the consumer and is actively involved with government and consumer affairs, marketing statistics, engineering and industry development.

One of its primary industry development functions is to provide consumers with up-to-date information about the broad range of consumer electronics product available to them and to increase their awareness of how these products contribute to the quality of their lives. This book on car audio is just one of many publications that the EIA/CGA has participated in publishing. Other consumer guides available directly from the EIA cover audio, video, personal computers, audio safety, and television.

1

Electronics

Like other facets of our lives, electronics are gradually being integrated into the automobile. From engine controls to stereo radios, electronics are making components more versatile, reliable and convenient.

The U.S. is generally the world leader in transportation electronics, but vehicle manufacturers worldwide are turning to the power of the on-board computer (microprocessor) to perform and control more and more functions of the vehicle. It's estimated that electronics will represent about $900 of the average domestic vehicle's content by 1985. By 1990, that figure should rise to nearly $1400.

A look at the new 1983 car models *reveals that virtually all of the nearly 700 models contain complex on-board computers which do everything from controlling engines to actually talking to the motorists.*

There are cars that talk—not only in English but in Spanish or French. There are cars that listen and respond to oral commands. There are cars that translate gallons to liters, miles to kilometers, or vice versa, and tell drivers when they need service, and cars that let their drivers know where they are—in case they forgot where they parked their wheels.

This dramatic change has been subtle. At first there was the introduction of the electronic ignition which was a herald of things to come. Next was the introduction of electronic engine controls. Cadillac led the way by offering the first trip computer in its '78 Seville, as an option. The pathway to the electronic age began broadening.

Now, with the introduction of the 1983 cars from the leading makers of the U.S., England, Brazil, Germany, France, Italy, Japan, Sweden, there isn't a single model that doesn't have microprocessors or electronic memory chips to either control engine operations, exhaust emissions, or transmissions.

For example, American Motors now has an electronics package known as "Systems Sentry" that monitors all fluid levels—from engine oil to brake fluid, from coolant to window washer fluid, from power steering fluid to transaxle liquid. There's a readout on the dashboard that tells the driver if any of these fluids are low and need attention.

AMC is offering an electronic door opener-and-locker. It's a small sending unit, on a key chain, about the size of an oldtime silver dollar. Pressing a button on the sending unit locks or opens the car doors electronically.

Chrysler's latest marvel, "Electronic Voice Alert," is capable of monitoring 11 mechanical or safety functions, compiling and processing information, and actually giving the driver voice-reports. If there are no problems, for example, when the

Module with "chip" exposed (center)

car is started, EVA says "All monitored systems functioning." EVA is also extremely polite. After the driver has paid attention to the message and taken appropriate action, EVA says "Thank You." To top it off, EVA is available in several languages, including English, French and Spanish.

Ford's version of a talking car, available as an option on the new Thunderbirds and Cougars, tells the driver whether the key is left in the ignition before he departs, or if the headlights are on, or if a door isn't properly closed.

Many of the new car models have versions of electronic travel computers. Display screens on the instrument panels tell drivers the departure time, accumulated mileage, average speed, fuel consumption, and estimated time of arrival.

Ford also has an electronic anti-theft system, an electronic mirror that changes from day to night position, a dashboard TV screen that reveals the car's location on a display map, and a hand-held transmitter that pinpoints the car's location in a parking lot.

Buick, as still another illustration, has an electronic dashboard, an electronic climate control, and General Motors' on-board computer which regulates engine operation and emissions. Cadillac, meanwhile, has added an electronic in-and-out-of-the-car dashboard readout that interfaces with the car's heating and cooling system. Oldsmobile's electronic innovations now include a bar graph on the dash showing the amount of fuel in the tank.

Pontiac's 6000STE (Special Touring Edition) comes with a standard driver's information center which does almost everything—even regulating the car's load weight riding condition.

In addition to on-board computers and electronic fuel injection systems, other "little black box" marvels include such passenger pleasure achievements as, for example, the Delco-GM/Bose Music System which is lauded as the first car stereo whose speakers and receiver are customized to the car's interior for maximum acoustics. The system consists of four speaker/amplifier units designed and made by Bose. The tonal response of each of the four modules is adjusted to match the

Composite photo taken through a microscope and assembled shows thousands of circuits on a single ⅛″ square "chip"

individual acoustics of a particular car. The new system is optional on 1983 Cadillac Sevilles and Eldorados, Buick Rivieras and Olds Toronados.

Ford is also the developer of a voice recognition system that makes it possible for the car to respond to the driver's voice commands. "Turn on the headlights," you say. Or "Open the trunk." Through the genius of super electronics, the car listens, and follows orders.

The accompanying table shows the speed with which electronic applications are taking place on cars and trucks. As early as 1974, automotive electronics experts predicted that 55 automotive functions would be controlled by electronics in 1990. Two-thirds of them have reached production by 1982.

Automotive electronic applications are not limited to vehicle manufacturers either. Aftermarket and component manufacturers have been quick to take advantage of the technology afforded by electronics. Manufacturers of car stereo systems, security systemns, radar detectors, CB radios, cruise control and a host of other convenience and safety products routinely apply the latest space-age technology to their products.

Automotive Electronic Applications

Predicted Automotive Electronics - 1974	Actual 1982	Projected 1985	1990
AUTOMATIC DOOR LOCKS	•		
ALCOHOL DETECTION SYSTEMS			•
FLASHER CONTROL SYSTEMS		•	
PROGRAMMED DRIVING CONTROLS	•		
HIGH SPEED WARNING	•		
HIGH SPEED LIMITING		•	
LAMP MONITOR SYSTEMS	•		
ELECTRONIC HORN			•
CRASH RECORDER			
TRAFFIC CONTROLS	•		
TIRE PRESSURE MONITOR	•		
TIRE PRESSURE CONTROL			
AUTOMATIC SEAT POSITIONER	•		
AUTOMATIC MIRROR CONTROL		•	
AUTOMATIC ICING CONTROL	•		
ROAD SURFACE INDICATOR		•	
4 WHEEL ANTI-LOCK	•		
VEHICLE GUIDANCE	•		
STATION KEEPING			
AUTOMATIC BRAKING			•
PREDICTIVE CRASH SENSORS	•		
ELECTRONIC TIMING	•		
MULTIPLEX HARNESS SYSTEMS		•	
ELECTRONIC TRANSMISSION CONTROL	•		
ELECTRONIC COOLING SYS. CONTROL			•
CLOSED DOOR EMISSION CONTROL	•		
ACCESSORY POWER CONTROL		•	
CRUISE CONTROL	•		
THEFT DETERRENT SYSTEMS	•		
ON BOARD DIAGNOSTIC SYSTEMS	•		
OFF BOARD DIAGNOSTIC SYSTEMS	•		
LEVELING CONTROLS	•		
RADIO FREQUENCY DISPLAY	•		
DIGITAL SPEEDOMETERS	•		
DIGITAL TACHOMETERS	•		
ELAPSED TIME CLOCK	•		
ELECTRONIC ODOMETER	•		
TRIP ODOMETER	•		
DESTINATION MILEAGE	•		
MILES PER GALLON	•		
MILES TO GO	•		
ESTIMATED ARRIVAL TIME	•		
TRIP FUEL CONSUMPTION	•		
AVERAGE SPEED	•		
AVERAGE MILES PER GALLON	•		
DIGITAL FUEL GAGE	•		
SERVICE INTERVAL	•		
DIGITAL TEMPERATURE GAGES	•		
DIGITAL PRESSURE GAGES		•	
DIGITAL VOLTMETER	•		
DIGITAL METRIC CONVERSIONS	•		
ACCELERATION GAGE			
DRUNK DRIVERS		•	
EKG			
SLEEP DETECTORS		•	
TOTAL 55	37	9	4
CUM. % OF TOTAL	67%	84%	91%

Whether you're installing a stereo system or trying to figure out why your lights won't work, you're going to be dealing with the vehicle's electrical system. It will be worth your time to understand why and how it works.

BASIC ELECTRICITY

Atoms and Electrons

At one time the atom was considered to be the smallest particle of matter. Today, we know that the smallest particle of matter is the electron, a part of the atom.

The atom is a complete electrical system, also partially composed of a nucleus which is made up of positively charged particles called protons, and neutrons which are neither positive, nor negative—they have no polarity. All matter is made up of atoms, so it follows that all matter is made up of electricity. A study of the makeup of each atom will give the clue to the type of material it will become.

The hydrogen atom is the simplest in atomic structure. It is composed of one proton and one electron. The metal copper is composed of unnumbered billions of copper atoms. Take just one of these copper atoms and examine its construction. It consists of 29 protons and 34 neutrons; these are surrounded by 29 electrons. As with all atoms the protons always equal the electrons in number.

Static Electricity

For centuries, it was known that certain materials when rubbed together produced some odd effects. One example of this was the reaction of glass rods and sealing wax. When two clean dry glass rods are first rubbed with silk and then brought near each other repulsion will result. That is, they will move away from each other. When two clean dry sticks of sealing wax are rubbed with wool and then brought near each other, repulsion will likewise occur. However, should the glass rod and the sealing wax stick be brought together, they will attract towards each other.

This reaction resulted in applying the names positive and negative; a charge like that found on glass was called positive, and a charge like the one on the sealing wax was called negative.

The explanation is that some of the external electrons on the surface of the material were removed. The positive and negative charges within the atoms of the

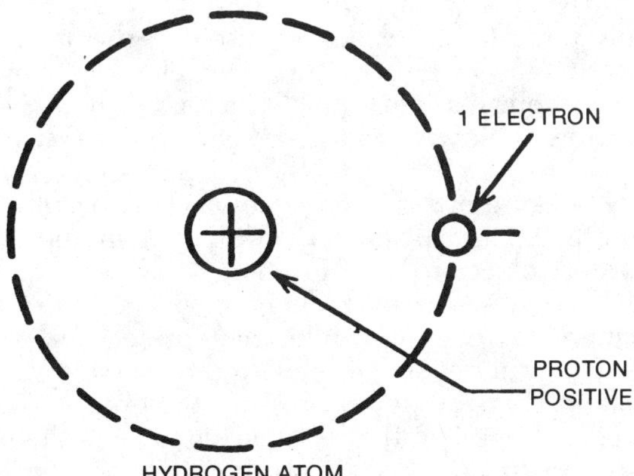

Atomic structure of our simplest atom, the gas Hydrogen. It is composed of one positive proton and one negative electron

material are no longer equal. This removal of free electrons would give the nucleus of the atom an excess of positive protons and thus the atom would have a positive charge. Allowing the electrons to return to the atom produces a neutral atom again. Thus a positive charged atom is one having an excess of protons and a negative charged atom is one having an excess of electrons.

What happened was that a glass rod rubbed with silk became positive. This was because some of the electrons in the outer surface of the glass were picked up by the atoms of the silk. Now with the sealing wax becoming negative; when its surface was rubbed with the wool cloth, electrons from the wool were left upon the wax, thus making the wax negative as a result of the excess electrons. It would follow then, should the wool be tested, it would be positive because it would have more positive protons than negative electrons. This discovery then indicated that when a material has an excess of electrons, it is negatively charged, and when it has a lack of electrons, it is positively charged.

What Is Electricity?

Electricity is the flow of free electrons. Some materials allow the electrons to flow and others do not. The material that allows the electrons to flow is called a conductor. The material that resists or stops the flow of free electrons is called an insulator.

The difference between conductors and non-conductors is the way that free electrons are bound to the nuclei. In non-metallic materials, such as glass, rubber and plastics, the outer ring of electrons are held securely to the nucleus. This condition prevents the electrons from flowing easily and resisting this flow of electrons, forms an effective electrical insulator. With metallic materials such as iron, copper, silver, aluminum and mercury, the electrons are not securely bound to the nuclei. The free electrons in the atom's outer orbit can flow easily away from the atom. All atoms having less than four electrons in their outer orbit are good conductors of electricity. Atoms having four or more electrons in their outer orbits are good insulators.

If we take a piece of copper wire and a light bulb, connect these to an automotive battery, the lamp will light when all connections are made. When the end of the wire is connected to the positive post of the battery the free electrons at the end of the wire will be attracted to the positive post of the battery. They will bump the electrons from the positive post through the battery electrolite to the negative post and so cause a flow of electrons through the circuit. This flow of free electrons is called an electric current.

The flow of electrical current, or free electron flow, is measured in amperes (amps). Compare this term to the gallon as used in the measure of water flow. Amperes indicate the amount of electricity or free electrons flowing in the circuit. One ampere may not seemn like very much current. But when you consider that it takes more than 6 billion electrons to make one ampere, it's a tremendous flow of free electrons.

Free electrons flow because of a difference in electron balance in a circuit. When there are more electrons in one part of a circuit than in another, the electrons move from the area of greatest electron concentration to the area of least electron concentration. This difference in electron accumulation is called voltage or difference in potential. The higher the voltage or difference in electrical pressure the greater the electron flow. Voltage can be compared with the pressure developed by a pump in a water system. The higher the pump pressure the greater the water flow. However, the resistance of the pipe like the resistance or size of the wire in an electrical circuit also affects the flow of current or water. The larger in diameter the wire, the more surface area it has, and the more current it can carry. Conversely, the smaller the wire, the less current it can carry. The effect of length is similar; the longer the wire, the more resistance to electrical flow.

OHM'S LAW

The resistance of a wire varies depending upon its length, its cross-sectional area, or diameter, its composition and its temperature. Even a copper wire offers resistance to the flow of free electrons. This resistance to flow is expressed in Ohms. The name was derived from the scientist who first expressed the relationship known as Ohm's Law. The law states that; voltage is equal to amperage times ohms. With this basic law all electrical calculations have been made. The law can be used to find any one of the three electrical factors:

$$\text{volts} = \text{amperes} \times \text{ohms},$$

$$\text{or amperes} = \frac{\text{volts}}{\text{ohms}}$$

$$\text{or ohms} = \frac{\text{volts}}{\text{amperes}}$$ sometimes this formula is expressed as follows:

E = Volts	$E = I \times R$
I = Amperes	$I = \frac{E}{R}$
R = Resistance	$R = \frac{E}{I}$

By covering up the factor to be found, the formula is easily determined. As an example: to find volts (E), cover the E and the formula shows that ohms (R) must be multiplied by amperes (I). How many volts will it take to push 2 amperes through 6 ohms of resistance? I = 2 Amperes × R – Resistance 6 ohms equals E or 12 volts.

THEORY APPLICATION

This formula is a valuable one to remember because it makes understandable many of the things that happen in an automotive electrical circuit. As an example: If the voltage remains constant, the current will go down if the resistance increases. Take the case of an automobile with a 12 volt system. The light switch has dirty and loose connections, the switch contacts are oxidized, some of the wiring is only hanging on by a strand or two. All of these conditions increase the resistance of the circuit. With increased resistance, less current will flow in the circuit. Using the same voltage as the problem above, the voltage will remain at 12 volts. The resistance has now gone up to 8 ohms as a result of the bad connections and wiring. This increased resistance now cuts the amperes flowing in the lighting circuit to 1.5 amperes so the lights will dim.

Automotive electrical troubles are multiplied by the gradual increase of resistance in the electrical circuits. Loose and dirty connections, burnt contacts, oxidized terminals and couplings all contribute to increasing electrical resistance which reduces the current flow.

Resistance can remain normal in an automotive electrical circuit but an increase in voltage can also cause trouble. The increased voltage forces more current through a given circuit and thus can burn out such items as the light bulbs, alternator, radio and instruments in the dash. A decrease in voltage can result in not enough current reaching the device to be operated. The starter cannot turn the engine if the correct voltage isn't present at the battery, all other things being normal. Clean, tight (mechanical and electrical) connections are a must for the successful functioning of any electrical circuit.

ELECTRO-MAGNETISM

When an electric current is passed through a wire a magnetic field is set up around the wire. The lines of force set up around the wire form concentric circles about

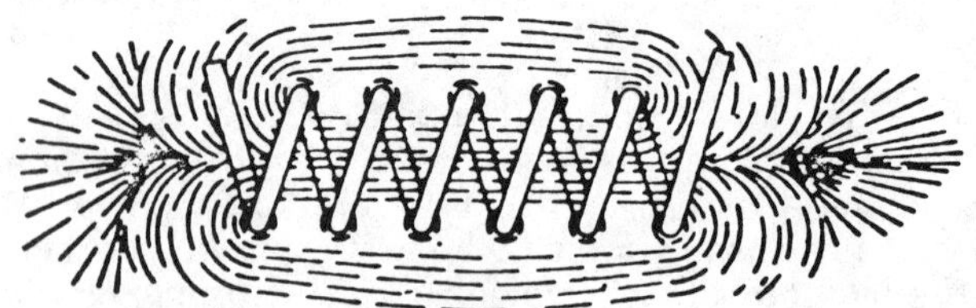

This diagram shows an electromagnet. Direct current passing through the wire creates lines of force similar to that of a bar magnet. An electromagnet can be made stronger by inserting a laminated iron bar through the core or center of the coil of wire

the axis of the wire. The direction of magnetic flux (name given to magnetic field) in circling around the wire is determined by the direction of the direct current flow in the wire. Current flows from negative to positive. To determine the direction of magnetic flux around a wire the "left hand rule" has been devised. Place the left hand around a wire with the thumb pointing in the direction of current flow; the fingers will then be curled around the wire in the direction of magnetic flux flow around the conductor.

NOTE: *Don't do this while the component is operating.*

If this wire were wound into a number of turns of wire and the same amount of current passed through the wire, the lines of force would increase. This is because the individual lines of force around each wire now combine to increase their number. Thus, electro-magnets can be strengthened by either increasing the current flow or the number of turns of wire in the electro-magnet. Because magnetic lines pass easily through iron, an iron core is sometimes inserted into the electro-magnet to strengthen the magnetic field. These cores are always of a laminated nature to offset the effects of eddy currents which detract from the effectiveness of the iron core.

ELECTRO-MAGNETIC INDUCTION

A current can be produced in a wire by moving the wire through a magnetic field. If the wire is held stationary and the field moved across the wire, a current will also be produced. Also, both the field and the wire can be held stationary, but turn the current on and off in the wire and this causes the field to collapse across the wire cutting the lines of force and inducing an electric current in the wire. This principle of Electromagnetic Induction is the basis for the operation of the automotive generator, alternator and the high tension ignition coil.

TROUBLESHOOTING ELECTRICAL SYSTEMS

There are two rules to remember. First, voltage, no matter how large or small, is a force and, to function, must flow from its source to a destination, usually ground.

Second, electricity has an annoying habit of taking the path of least resistance, through "open" or "short" circuits.

Grounding

For any electrical system to operate, it must make a complete circuit. This simply means that the power flow from the battery must make a complete circle. When an electrical component is operating, power flows from the battery to the component, passes through the component causing it to perform its function (lighting a light bulb), and then returns to the battery through the ground of the circuit. This

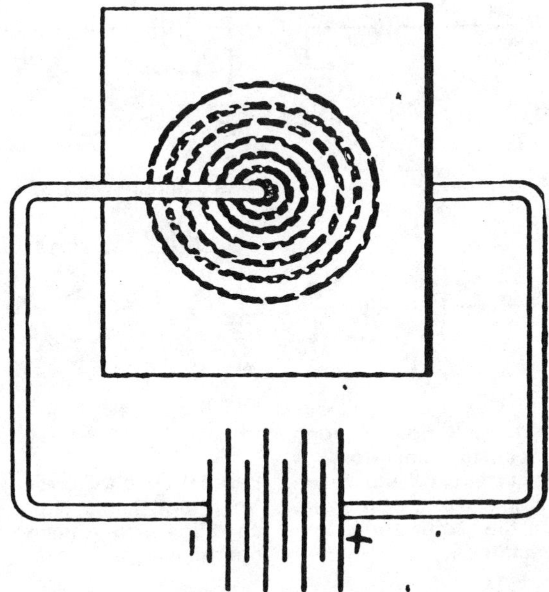

When direct current from a battery is passed through a wire, magnetic lines of force will form concentric circles around the axis of the wire

ground is usually (but not always) the metal part of the car on which the electrical component is mounted.

Most passenger cars use a negative ground electrical system. This means that the negative terminal of the battery is grounded. By "ground" we mean that the metal chassis of the car (or parts attached to the chassis) are used to complete the electrical circuits, rather than many return wires running back to the source of power (battery). This "common ground" method is used in all automotive electrical systems so that all that is needed is a single wire to conduct electrical power to the load—motor, bulb, relay, whatever.

Perhaps the easiest way to visualize this is to think of connecting a light bulb with two wires attached to it to your car battery. The battery in your car has two posts (negative and positive). If one of the two wires attached to the light bulb was attached to the negative post of the battery and the other wire was attached to the positive post of the battery, you would have a complete circuit. Current from the battery would flow out one post, through the wire attached to it and then to the light bulb, where it would pass through causing it to light. It would then leave the light bulb, travel through the other wire, and return to the other post of the battery.

The normal automotive circuit differs from this simple example in two ways. First, instead of having a return wire from the bulb to the battery, the light bulb returns the current to the battery through the chassis of the vehicle or through a wire to the chassis. Since the negative battery cable is attached to the chassis and the chassis is made of electrically conductive metal, the chassis of the vehicle can serve as a ground wire to complete the circuit.

Secondly, most automotive circuits contain switches to turn components on and off as required. There are many types of switches, but the most common simply serves to prevent the passage of current when it is turned off. Since the switch is a part of the circle necessary for a complete circuit, it operates to leave an opening in the circuit, and thus an incomplete or open circuit, when it is turned off.

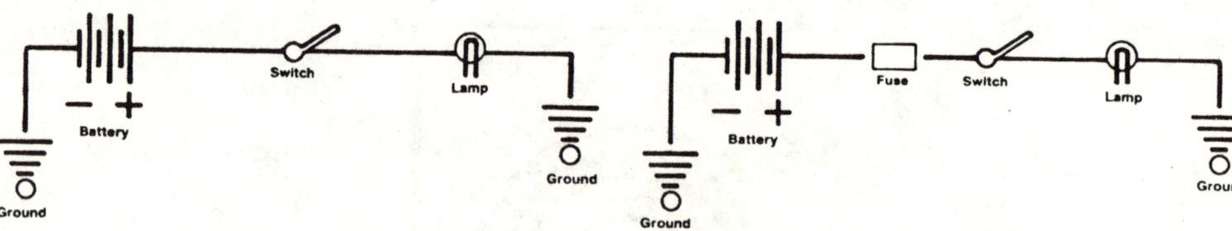

Basic unfused switched circuit

Basic fused switched circuit

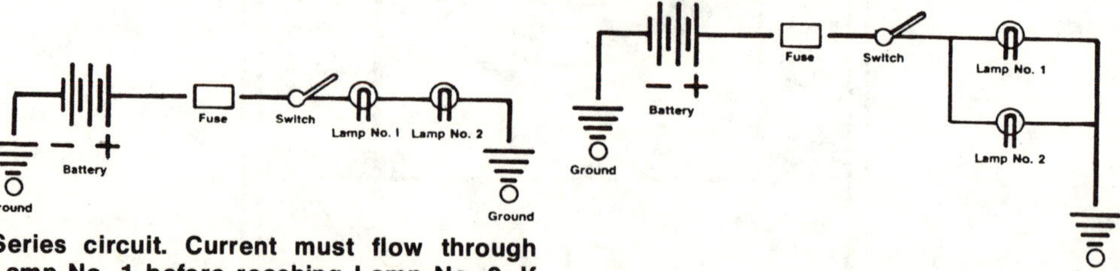

Series circuit. Current must flow through Lamp No. 1 before reaching Lamp No. 2. If first lamp burns out, current will not reach the second lamp. If Lamp No. 2 burns out, current will not reach the Ground and neither lamp will be illuminated

Parallel circuit. Current flows through Lamp No. 1 and Lamp No. 2 independently. The condition of one lamp has no effect on the operation of the other

Some electrical components which require a large amount of current to operate also have a relay in their circuit. Since these circuits carry a large amount of current, the thickness of the wire in the circuit (gauge size) is also greater. If this large wire were connected from the component to the control switch on the instrument panel, and then back to the component, a voltage drop would occur in the circuit. To prevent this potential drop in voltage, an electromagnetic switch (relay) is used. The large wires in the circuit are connected from the car battery to one side of the relay, and from the opposite side of the relay to the component. The relay is normally open, preventing current from passing through the circuit. An additional, smaller, wire is connected from the relay to the control switch for the circuit. When the control switch is turned on, it grounds the smaller wire from the relay and completes the circuit. This closes the relay and allows current to flow from the battery to the component. The horn, headlight, and starter circuits are three which use relays.

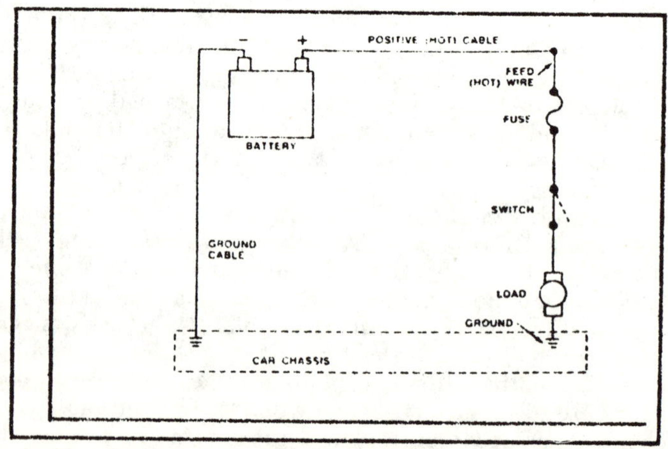

Simple electrical circuit that forms the basis of more complicated circuits in modern cars and trucks

Open and Short Circuits

In many cases, the load or component itself may be grounded to the chassis through its connection. As an example, many light bulbs are grounded to the chassis through their sockets, which are connected to sheet metal, which is in turn connected to the frame by bolts, (all conductors).

Open circuits are caused by poor ground connections, or by breaks in the wires or other open conditions. Electricity flows when the circuit is closed or completed. An open point in the circuit could be a switch in the OFF position, a bulb that does not operate or a break in the wire at some point.

A short circuit is a path for electricity that was not intended. Ground wires do not have to be insulated from contact with other conductive elements because the common ground is not insulated. However, all "hot" wires (those that supply current) must be insulated. If the insulation breaks or wears through to bare wire, and the wire touches a metal part of the vehicle, a short circuit is created. This removes the load from the circuit and allows the electricity to flow directly to ground, overloading the circuit.

Fuses, Circuit Breakers, and Fusible Links

Fuses are replaceable electrical conductors sealed in small glass cylinders for protection against dust and corrosion. The conducting portion of the fuse is made of a metal with a low melting point. The fuse is designed so that if the amperage passing through it exceeds its rated capacity, the conducting material will melt and interrupt the flow of current through the circuit.

Circuit breakers are electrical switches that employ bimetallic elements to open the circuit whenever current exceeds a specified level. The heat from the passage of current through the unit bends the bimetallic arm to open the contacts of the switch. After a short period of cooling, the contacts close again.

Circuit breakers are usually used to protect heavy-duty electric motors that can be operated only intermittently. These motors power such auxiliaries as power windows, convertible tops, and tailgates.

Fusible links are sections of vehicle wiring designed to protect the wiring itself, as well as individual accessories. The links consist of wiring sections about four gauges smaller (larger numerically) than the regular wiring. If a severe overload occurs, the link will burn out entirely before the regular vehicle wiring is damaged.

Did you ever notice how your instrument panel lights get brighter the faster your car goes? This happens because your alternator (which supplies the battery) puts out more current at speeds above idle. This is normal. However, it is possible for larger surges of current to pass through the electrical system of your car. If this surge of current were to reach an electrical component, it could burn it out. To prevent this from happening, fuses are connected into the current supply wires of most of the major electrical systems of your car. The fuse serves to head off the surge at the pass. When an electrical current of excessive power passes through the component's fuse, the fuse blows out and breaks the circuit, saving it from destruction.

The fuse also protects the component from damage if the power supply wire to the component is grounded before the current reaches the component.

Let us here interject another rule to the complete circle circuit. *Every complete circuit from a power source must include a component which is using the power from the power source.* If you were to disconnect the light bulb (from the previous example of a lightbulb being connected to the battery by two wires) from the wires and touch the two wires together (please take our word for this; don't try it), the result would be shocking. You probably haven't seen so many sparks since the

Fourth of July. A similar thing happens (on a smaller scale) when the power supply wire to a component or the electrical component itself becomes grounded before the normal ground connection for the circuit. To prevent damage to the system, the fuse for the circuit blows to interrupt the circuit—protecting the components from damage. Because grounding a wire from a power source makes a complete circuit—less the required component to use the power—this phenomenon is called a short circuit. The most common causes of short circuits are: the rubber insulation on a wire breaking or rubbing through to expose the current carrying core of the wire to a metal part of the car, or a shorted switch.

Some electrical systems on the car are protected by a circuit breaker which is, basically, a self-repairing fuse. When either of the above-described events takes place in a system which is protected by a circuit breaker, the circuit breaker opens the circuit the same way a fuse does. However, when either the short is removed from the circuit or the surge subsides, the circuit breaker resets itself and does not have to be replaced as a fuse does.

The final protective device in the chassis electrical system is a fuse link. A fuse link is a wire that acts as a fuse link. It is connected between the starter relay and the main wiring harness for the car. This connection is under the hood, very near a similar fuse link which protects the engine electrical system. Since the fuse link protects all the chassis electrical components, it is the probable cause of trouble when none of the electrical components function, unless the battery is disconnected or dead.

Locating Problems

Electrical problems generally fall into one of three areas:

1. The component that is not functioning is not receiving current.
2. The component itself is not functioning.
3. The component is not properly grounded.

Problems that fall into the first category are by far the most complicated. It is the current supply system to the component which contains all the switches, relays, fuses, etc.

Troubleshooting Tools

TEST LIGHT

A test light is a 12-volt bulb with two test leads used for voltage checks or to check short circuits.

SELF-POWERED TEST LIGHT

The self-powered test light is a light, battery, and set of test leads wired in series, used for continuity and ground checks. When connected to two points of a continuous circuit, the light glows.

CAUTION: *Be sure power is off in circuit during testing.*

JUMPER WIRE

This is a length of wire with clips, used to connect two points of a circuit. A jumper wire can complete a circuit by bypassing an open.

CAUTION: *Never use a jumper wire across high-resistance loads (motors, etc.) connected between hot and ground. This direct battery short may cause injury or fire.*

VOLTMETER

A DC voltmeter measures circuit voltage. Connect negative (– or black) lead to ground, and positive (+ or red) lead to voltage measuring point.

OHMMETER

An ohmmeter shows the resistance between two connected points. IT SHOULD ONLY BE USED ON DE-ENERGIZED CIRCUITS. Hot circuits can cause meter damage and false readings.

Basic Troubleshooting

VOLTAGE CHECK

Connect one lead of test light to a known good ground, or the negative (–) battery terminal. Test for voltage by touching the other lead to the test point. The bulb will light when the test point has voltage.

SHORT CHECK (SHORT TO GROUND)

A blown fuse is usually caused by a short to ground in that circuit. Check as follows:

1. Turn off everything powered through the fuse.
2. Disconnect all loads powered through the fuse.

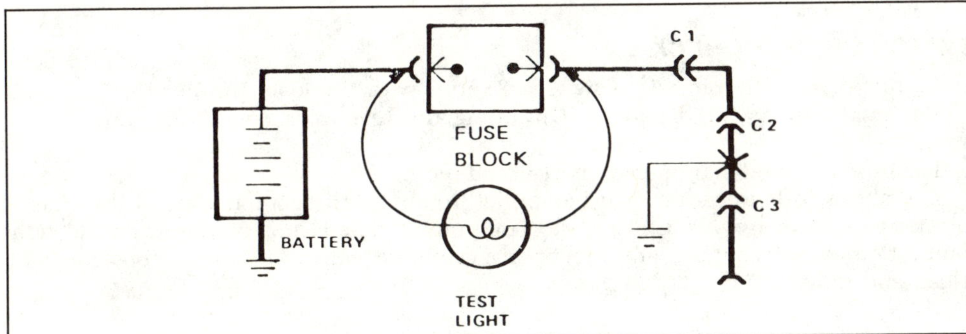

Short check

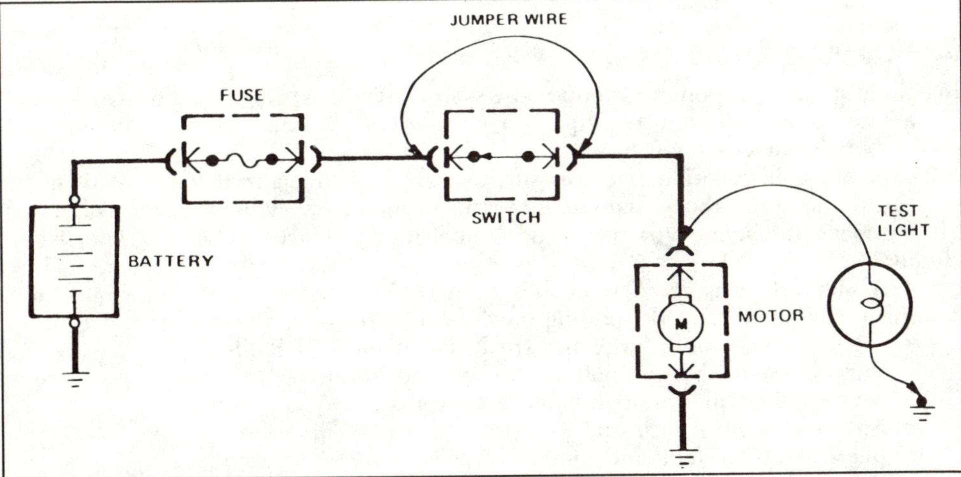

Switch circuit and voltage check

—motors: disconnect motor connector
—lights: remove bulbs

3. Turn ignition switch to RUN (if necessary) to power fuse.
4. Connect one test light lead to hot end of blown fuse. Connect other lead to ground. Light should glow showing power to fuse.
5. Disconnect ground lead and connect to load side of fuse.
   a. Test light OFF: the short is in the disconnected equipment.
   b. Test light ON: short is in wiring. Find short by disconnecting circuit connectors one at a time. In the example with a ground at X, the light goes out when C1 or C2 is disconnected, but stays on after disconnecting C3. This means the ground is between C2 and C3.

CONTINUITY CHECK

CAUTION: *Be sure power is off in circuit during testing.*

To locate an open circuit, connect one lead of self-powered test light or ohmmeter to each end of circuit. The light will glow if circuit is closed. Switches can be checked in the same way.

"GOOD GROUND" CHECK

Turn on power to circuit. Perform Voltage Check between suspected bad ground and frame. Any voltage means ground is bad.

Turn off power to circuit. Connect one lead of self-powered test light or ohmmeter to wire in question, and the other to known ground. If light glows, circuit ground is ok.

SWITCH CIRCUIT CHECK

In an inoperative circuit with a switch in series with the load, jumper the terminals of the switch to power the load. If jumping the terminals powers the circuit, the switch is bad.

This test also finds an open in part of a circuit.

The above test procedure can be applied to any of the components of the chassis electrical system by substituting the component that is not working for the light bulb. Remember that for any electrical system to work, all connections must be clean and tight.

DO-IT-YOURSELF TOOLS AND EQUIPMENT

Basic Hand Tools

Installing a super-expensive component system where speaker enclosures have to be fabricated will frequently require a number of specialized tools ranging from power bench saws to power routers.

The average installation requires surprisingly few specialized tools. Most of the tools you'll need are those that can be found in the ordinary handyman's collection. The rest can be begged or borrowed from friends or acquaintances. The list includes:

1. A handful of assorted wrenches both sockets and box/opened—you'll need American or metric sizes depending on the origin of the car you're working on.
2. Screwdrivers—both large and small, flat blade and Phillips.
3. Wire stripper or combination wire stripper/crimper.
4. An electric drill—the common ¼″ type is best.
5. An assortment of drill bits.
6. Black electrical tape and masking tape.
7. Pencil, compass, piece of chalk.

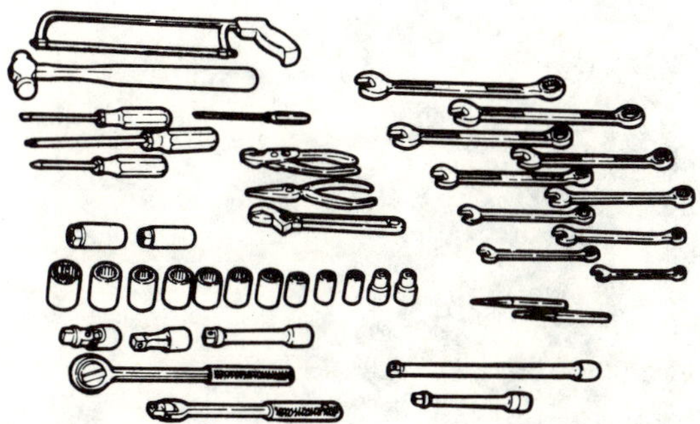

Common hand tools are necessary for most installations

8. Razor blade—the single edge kind is the safest and easiest to use.
9. A round and flat file.
10. A keyhole saw or hole cutting attachment for the electric drill.
11. A selection of male and female spade connectors, and other terminal hardware. Optional equipment includes a soldering gun, solder, flux and a combination volt-ohmmeter. These last items may come in handy for solving specialized problems and for checking continuity, but in general, you won't need to have them on hand before you begin.
12. Pliers—both slip-joint and needle-nosed.
13. If you are installing speakers in the doors of a GM car, you'll need the handy little tool for removing the window cranks so that you can remove the door panels. These can be purchased at most auto parts stores inexpensively.

SERVICE MANUAL

You may want to consider a service manual for your vehicle, to guide you through the temporary removal or disassembly of unfamiliar parts of your car or truck. Radio, speaker or antenna installation may require any of the above for proper installation.

SOLDERING GUN

Soldering is a quick, efficient method of joining metals permanently. Everyone who has the occasion to make electrical repairs should know how to solder. Electrical connections that are soldered are far less likely to come apart and will conduct electricity far better than connections that are only "pig-tailed" together.

NOTE: *Some late-model, US built passenger cars, such as GM, use sections of solid-core aluminum wire in the body loom. About the only caution to keep in mind when working with aluminum wire is to splice it properly,* do not solder. *Special splice clips are available.*

After skinning the wires and slipping the special splice clips into position and locking it there with crimping pliers, the splice clip and adjacent ¼ inch of each wire are coated generously with petroleum jelly to retard oxidation. The entire spliced area is then covered with at least two layers of insulating tape.

The most popular (and preferred) method of soldering is with an electric soldering gun. Soldering irons are available in many sizes and wattage ratings. Irons with high wattage ratings deliver higher temperatures and recover lost heat faster. A small soldering iron rated for no more than 50 watts is recommended for home use, especially on electrical projects where excess heat can damage the components being soldered.

There are three ingredients necessary for successful soldering—proper flux, good solder and sufficient heat.

A service manual for your vehicle will help with removal or disassembly of unfamiliar components

Flux

A soldering flux is necessary to clean the metal of tarnish, prepare it for soldering and to enable the solder to spread into tiny crevices. When soldering electrical work, always use a resin flux or resin core solder, which is non-corrosive and will not attract moisture once the job is finished. Other types of flux (acid-core) will leave a residue that will attract moisture, causing the wires to corrode.

Good Solder

Tin is a unique metal with a low melting point. In a molten state, it dissolves and alloys easily with many metals. Solder is made by mixing tin (which is very expensive) with lead (which is very expensive). The most common proportions are 40/60, 50/50 and 60/40, the percentage of tin always being listed first.

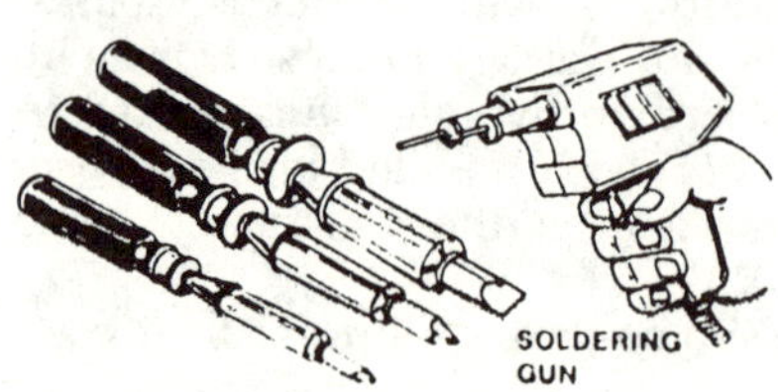

There are several types of soldering irons and guns

Low-priced solders often contain less tin, making them very difficult for a beginner to use because more heat is required to melt the solder. A common solder is 40/60 which is well suited for all-around general use, but 60/40 melts easier, has more tin for a better joint and is preferred for electrical work.

Sufficient Heat

Successful soldering requires that the metals to be joined be heated to a temperature that will melt the solder, usually somewhere around 360–460°F., depending on the tin content of the solder. Contrary to popular belief, the purpose of the soldering iron is not to melt the solder itself, but to heat the parts being soldered to a temperature high enough to melt solder when it is touched to the work. Melting flux-cored solder on the soldering iron will usually destroy the effectiveness of the flux.

How to Solder

1. Soldering tips are made of copper for good heat conductance, but must be "tinned" regularly for quick transference of heat to the project and to prevent the solder from sticking to the iron. To "tin" the iron, simply heat it and touch flux-cored solder to the tip; the solder will flow over the tip. Wipe the excess off with a rag.

2. After some use, the tip may become pitted. If so, simply dress the tip smooth with a smooth file and "tin" the tip again.

3. An old saying holds that "metals well-cleaned are half soldered." Flux-cored solder will remove oxides, but rust, bits of insulation and oil or grease must be removed with a wire brush or emery cloth.

4. For maximum strength in soldered parts, the joint must start off clean and tight. Weak joints will result in gaps too wide for the solder to bridge.

5. If a separate soldering flux is used, it should be brushed or swabbed on only those areas that are to be soldered. Most solders contain a core of flux and separate fluxing is unnecessary.

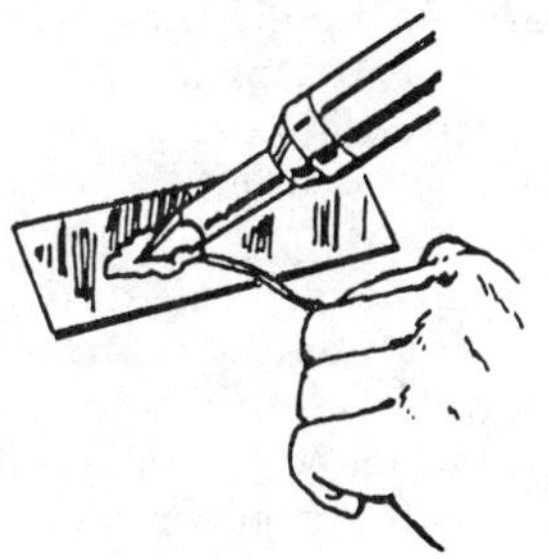

Tinning the soldering iron

Wipe the excess from the iron while hot

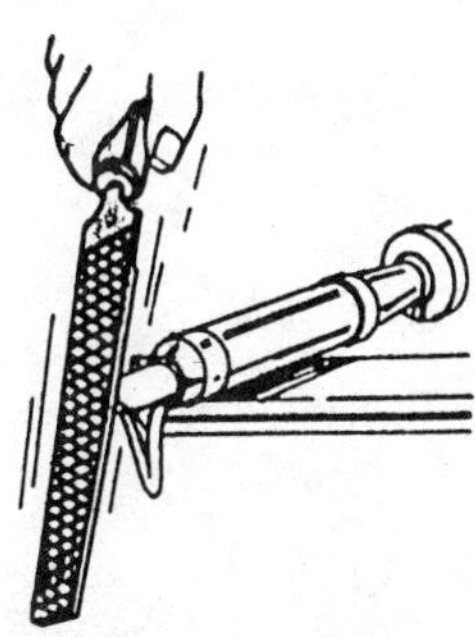

Dress the tip with a smooth file

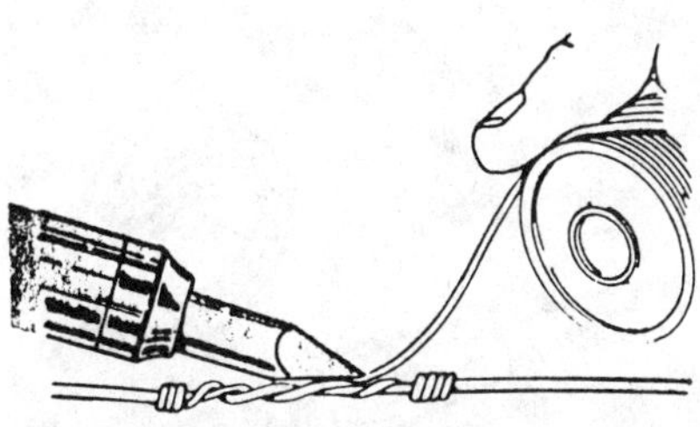

The correct method of soldering. Let the heat transferred to the work melt the solder

6. Hold the work to be soldered firmly. It is best to solder on a wooden board, because a metal vise will only rob the piece to be soldered of heat and make it difficult to melt solder. Hold the soldering tip with the broadest face against the work to be soldered. Apply solder under the tip close to the work as shown. Apply enough solder to give a heavy film between the iron and piece being soldered, moving slowly and making sure the solder melts properly. Keep the work level or the solder will run to the lowest part, and favor the thicker parts, because these require more heat to melt the solder. If the soldering tip overheats (the solder coating on the face of the tip burns up), it should be retinned.

7. Once the soldering is completed, let the soldered joint stand until cool.

Test Equipment

TEST LIGHTS

A test light is nothing more than a light bulb connected to a lead and a probe or two leads. Test lights are normally used to determine whether or not a particular wire, circuit or component is "hot," that is, whether or not current is flowing through it.

To use a test light to check for the presence of current, simply attach the ground wire on the light to a good metal ground. Then touch the probe end of the test light to the end of the power supply wire that has been disconnected from the component using the power (light bulb, horn, gauge, etc.). If the component has been receiving current, the test light will go on. If the test light does not go on, then the problem is farther back in the circuit.

VOLT/OHMMETERS

A voltmeter is used to measure the difference in electrical "pressure" between two points in a circuit. Just as water pressure is measured in pounds per square inch, electrical pressure is measured in volts. When a voltmeter's two probes are placed on two "live" portions of an electrical circuit with different electrical pressures, current will flow through the voltmeter and produce a reading which indicates the difference in electrical pressure between the two parts of the circuit.

An ohmmeter differs from a voltmeter in that it incorporates its own source of power so that a standard voltage is always present. An ohmmeter is connected in the same way as a voltmeter, but since it is self-powered, all the power in the circuit to be measured should be off.

Remember that a voltmeter is measuring volts or electrical pressure, while an ohmmeter is measuring ohms, or circuit resistance. Volt/ohmmeters are only useful if you have some knowledge of electricity and of course have the factory specifications for whatever you are testing. It does you no good to know that a certain circuit has twelve volts unless you know what the factory specification for that circuit is. They are not used very often but are handy in certain situations.

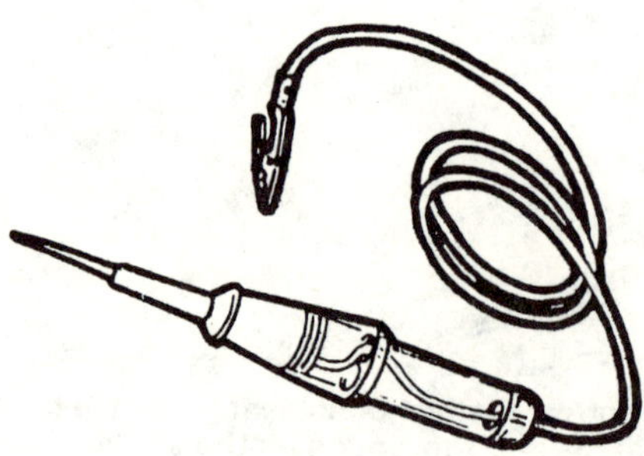

A simple test light

WIRING DIAGRAMS

As cars have become more complex, and available with more and longer options lists, wiring diagrams have grown in size also. It has become virtually impossible to provide a readable reproduction in a reasonable number of pages. Because of this, most vehicle manufacturers provide wiring diagrams as a separate publication or for individual vehicle lines.

Automotive electrical wiring can be divided into two categories: primary wiring and secondary wiring. Wiring that is used for lighting, instruments, and accessories is primary wiring. Wiring that is used for the ignition system is secondary wiring, even though the ignition system can be broken down into primary and secondary circuits.

It is common practice to present primary-wiring information in three separate forms: 1) pictorial views, 2) diagrams, and 3) schematic views. Let's discuss each view:

Pictorial—A technical illustration using line drawings to show the vehicle in outline form is called a pictorial view. The drawing is overlaid with heavy lines that show the routing of the main segments of vehicle wiring. While there are hundreds of feet of wire used per vehicle, only two or three segments are shown on the pictorial view because many wires are gathered together and wrapped with insulating tape to form a loom (or harness). The looms attach to each other and to the main fuse block at junction points by means of quick-disconnects (terminal blocks with male and female multiple connectors). Each junction point is shown on the pictorial view along with the quick-disconnects, and each is identified by letter or number for easy reference. If you want to know where the main looms run on a given vehicle, consult the pictorial view.

Diagrams—If you took the wrapping off each main loom and spread the exposed wires individually on a flat surface, you would have a wiring diagram in physical form. The manner in which the wires are arranged in the diagram has little or no resemblance to the way the same wires are arranged on the vehicle. The diagram shows such things as wire color coding, wire size in gauge, switches, fuses, quick-disconnects, splices, lamps, motors, etc. The quick-disconnects are shown in "open book" form to show what wire terminal plugs into what terminal socket. Some main quick-disconnects incorporate 35 or more individual sockets, all of which can be identified by number or letter with reference to the electrical circuit each socket services. Individual wires are identified by number and/or letter on the wiring diagram. With the diagram it is possible to determine the size and color of the wire(s) that are used on given circuits, plus the location and reference identification of the quick-disconnects immediately involved.

The classic ground symbol (⏚) is used on the wiring diagram (also on the schematic) to indicate completion of each individual circuit through the vehicle's body, engine, or frame. By use of this type of ground return the need for separate return wires is eliminated for a substantial savings of manufacturing money and greatly reduced wiring complexity.

Schematic—What happens inside an electric switch or motor is shown in a view that resembles a wiring diagram; that is, both the wiring diagram and the schematic view are "flat-surfaced" drawings. The schematic, however, does illustrate the parts and components in the outline, with size and relationship as they actually are on the vehicle. The schematic is probably the least used type of wiring information presentation because most switches, motors, etc. are not repaired in the field.

Typically there are three looms used per vehicle: 1) body, 2) instrument, and 3) engine compartment and three ways to present technical information relative to each loom: 1) pictorial view, 2) wiring diagram, and 3) schematic view. Don't fail to recognize the importance of the junction points of each loom (quick-disconnects) because they are very convenient points that are used in troubleshooting.

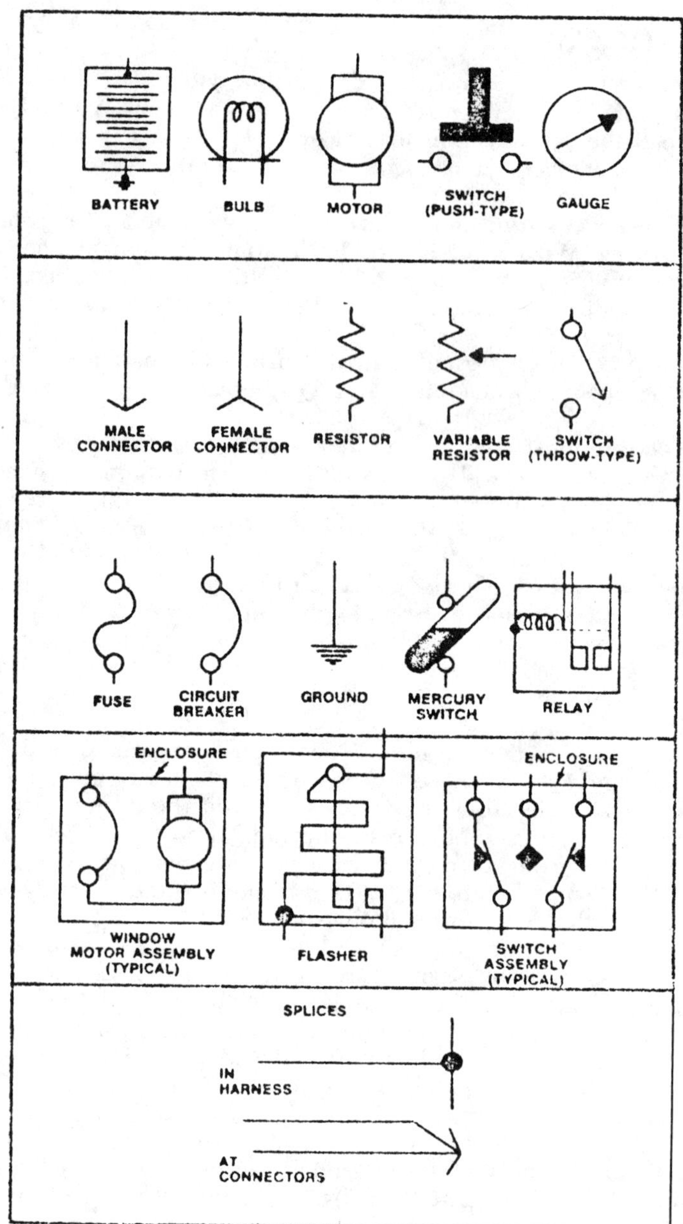

Commonly used wiring diagram symbols

Circuit Boards

Circuit boards are used in place of conventional wires for certain applications such as instrument clusters. Think of a circuit board as consisting of ribbons of conductive metal that are carefully applied to a non-conductive board, maybe ⅛ inch thick. No protective cover (insulation) is applied to the conductive ribbons. Be very careful, therefore, when poking around a circuit board with metal tools, such as a screwdriver. On some specific applications of circuit boards, namely GM's Electronic Lamp Monitoring System, do not troubleshoot for shorts by temporarily substituting a circuit breaker for a fuse without first disconnecting the involved circuit boards. Failure to disconnect the boards will result in permanent damage.

2
Auto Sound

DRIVING WITH GOOD SOUND

Music has gone along with motion ever since man first learned to sing or hum. What's changed today is that the music we move along to isn't restricted to what we can hum, sing or whistle. Instead, we can hear polished performances of anything we like, from Renaissance to Rock, wherever and whenever we choose—right in our cars. Acoustically, that's quite a feat.

America was the first nation to put itself on wheels. It was inevitable—we were the first nation with both the distances to make it necessary and the affluence to make it possible. The auto industry, in fact, contributed to that affluence: it was Henry Ford, for example, who introduced the assembly line and who first gave factory workers the famed "Five Dollar Day."

We spend more time in the car than others, both because of our long distances and because of traffic—and because our love of individuality has led us to emphasize the car and its mobility for the individual over the mass mobility of public transit.

So, when Soviet premier Nikita Khrushchev visited the U.S. 20 years or so ago, what startled him was not how many cars we had, but that so many of those cars carried just one person. Americans don't just ride—they ride alone. We've built our country and our living patterns around the individual mobility the automobile gives us.

Those factors, plus Americans' deep love for music of all kinds, have led us to rely on electronics in the car to keep us company. Turn a knob and push a button, and you travel with road information, news, sports, occasional comedy and drama and, above all, music.

We have had radio in our cars for more than 50 years (Chevrolet offered it as an option back in 1926), and tape in our cars for nearly 20. There was even an attempt, back in the Fifties, to put phonographs in cars (Chrysler Corporation's "Highway Hi-Fi"). Obviously, the need for music and for electronic company runs deep.

Over the years since 1926, the quality and convenience of this sound equipment has increased continuously. The earliest car radios were more for roadside picnics than for listening on the road—turn on the motor, and static from the ignition drowned them out. Even tuning early radios was an art, involving several interacting knobs to turn.

Today a finger-touch brings us a favorite station, while another makes our radios scan through the airwaves, searching for a station that will please us. If none does, we just slip in a tape, for music we have chosen personally.

The quality of the sound has increased continually, too: from AM to FM, from FM to FM stereo; from tape with more hiss than highs to full-fidelity tape with noise that's virtually inaudible on the road. Car sound today can almost equal home stereo. Indeed, the best car stereo systems sound even better than many systems found in homes!

Just as in home high fidelity, specialist dealers have sprung up who concentrate on the problems and potentials of car stereo. Just as in home stereo, the general quality of the equipment available and the widespread knowledge about its installation, allow you to get good sound from a wide variety of sources.

Having that wide choice, though, simply substitutes one problem for another. You can get good sound in your car—that problem has been solved. The problem now is *how* to get it: what to buy, where to buy it, how to install it and how to meet all those requirements within your budget.

WHAT IS "GOOD SOUND"?

What you hear from a good sound system depends on the music you're listening to. The traditional description is that good sound systems recreate the illusion of listening from the best seat in the house at a "live" performance—but with todays music that definition doesn't always apply.

It does apply to classical, jazz or folk music, which are performed on "acoustic" (non-amplified) instruments. But with rock or other music performed on electronic instruments, records often create their own "reality", using studio techniques that can't be applied in a live concert—rock performances, in fact, often strive in vain to match the sound of records. Here, though, a good sound system should be able to approximate at least the sound levels (especially in the bass) that you'd hear at a "live" performance.

A good sound system will let you hear everything in a recording or broadcast, with as little unwanted change as possible (though it should also let you change the sound a bit to reflect your own tastes). But you can't tell what's on the recording until you hear it properly. So before shopping for sound—whether it be for car or home—you need to form a clear idea of what specific problems and virtues you should listen for. If you've never been able to put your finger on why some stereo systems sound much better than others, this section will help you identify the sonic factors involved.

A good sound system is an open window on the music, one that calls no attention to itself but lets the music draw you in. Just how open that window is depends mainly on four specific factors—distortion, volume, noise and frequency response.

Distortion

Distortion is the worst sin, because it modifies the music by adding sounds that shouldn't be there. Light distortion puts a slight veil over the music; heavy distortion buries it in fuzz.

If you want to know what distortion sounds like, take the poorest sound system you have (a small pocket portable radio will do) and gradually turn up the sound until it's as loud as you can stand, then turn it down again. You'll note that as the volume rises, the sound quality grows harsher—shrill, fuzzy and more jagged sounding. That's distortion.

If you have a good sound system, repeat the test, using a clean-sounding tape or record. On a good system, you won't hear distortion until the sound becomes extremely loud—but you'll still hear it, if you turn the volume up enough. (Turn the sound down again as soon as you start to hear distortion, though—extremely high volume can damage your speakers and your ears.)

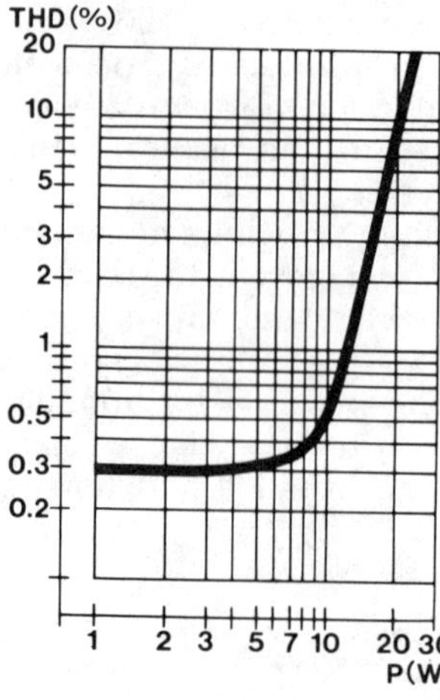

When you turn up the volume, harsh distortion rises—slowly at moderate volumes, rapidly at the sound system's limits

Some music (principally rock) actually uses distortion for musical effct—a "fuzz box", for example, is designed to add distortion to the signal. So the degree of distortion is easier to judge when listening to acoustical rather than electronic instruments. But even if you prefer music that uses distortion for artistic effect, you want a system which adds no audible distortion of its own. The effect an artist intends when he switches in a fuzz box is largely lost if everything sounds fuzzed already.

Distortion comes in many forms. Harmonic distortion (sometimes abbreviated "THD", for "Total Harmonic Distortion") adds spurious frequencies which are multiples (harmonics) of the frequencies that form the music. Because natural sounds already include such overtones, some authorities feel that harmonic distortion is less objectionable than other types. But it's the easiest type to measure, and hence the one you'll find most often in test reports or manufacturers' specification sheets.

Intermodulation distortion (IM, for short) is caused when the system adds and subtracts tones in the music to create still other tones that don't belong there. Because these spurious frequencies ("distortion products") are not harmonics of musical tones, IM is generally considered one of the most objectionable forms of distortion.

A third, more controversial type, is Transient Intermodulation Distortion (TIM). This occurs, according to some authorities, when a note starts faster than the amplifier can handle it. The amplifier distorts for an instant, like someone stumbling for an instant when startled into running; then it settles down until the next fast "transient" tone. One controversy about TIM is over how it should be measured; there are several tests. But there's also some controversy over whether its effects are audible at all—a sure indication that those effects must be quite subtle.

Knowing one form of distortion from another is of great value to the engineer, who can use that knowledge to help cure the problem. As a buyer, though, you needn't know what kind of distortion is present—only how much you'll hear. If you want to know, you'll find that THD, at least, is frequently stated in amplifier power ratings, but is listed much less frequently for FM/AM tuners, rarley for tape players, and almost never for speakers. Other forms of distortion are rarely listed for car stereo at all.

So you'll have to judge for yourself how much a system distorts—which isn't too hard once you've heard both very clean and very distorted sound. Take a clean-sounding tape of familiar music with you when you shop, so you can compare how different systems sound on the same music—at least in stores that can demonstrate the equipment you're interested in. Pass up any system which adds audible distortion to the tape at low volume levels. Search for the system which adds the least distortion at the loudest listening levels you're likely to use. What you hear in your car won't be exactly what you hear in the showroom—but if one system distorts more than another in the showroom, it will do so in your car, as well.

Volume

You want to be able to play music as loud as you like. But that's only half the story. Since every system begins to distort when it plays too loud, the other half is to make sure the system you want will still sound clean when it's playing as loud as you like it.

How loud you want it depends on several things: your ears, your preferences in music, the amount of road noise that must be overcome in your car, and how much the system distorts (the cleaner the sound, the louder and longer you'll be able to enjoy it).

Remember, though, that for safety's sake, you should never play a car stereo so loud that you can't hear car horns and other warnings from outside. You should be especially sure never to drive when listening to music through headphones—that's always unsafe and illegal in some states.

The maximum volume you can get from a system depends on several factors: the electronics (especially the amplifier power), the speakers, the material you're playing, and even the car itself. So it's best to judge a system as a whole if you can get the chance. If you can't, remember that the amplifier power and the speakers make the biggest difference, so that speakers which sound adequately loud in one system will probably sound that way in another system with the same amount or more of amplifier power. Be careful; there are several ways of rating amplifier power, which are discussed later.

Frequency Response

The sounds we hear cover a wide range of frequencies, from very low to very high. How low or high depends upon our ears, but the average range covered by good, young ears is about 20 to 20,000 Hz (vibration cycles per second), and a good sound system should cover all those frequencies.

If all you want is to hear the notes, you can get by with a much narrower frequency response. Most musical notes fall into a much smaller range, from about 100 to 5,000 Hz, which is why even inexpensive portable radios let you hear the tune.

But the range of musical sounds goes up much higher, because musical instruments generate overtones that are multiples (harmonics, again) of their fundamental frequencies. Those overtones are what give different instruments their different characters, the reason why a trumpet and a violin playing the same note sound completely different. (They're also the reason why you can "hear" bass notes on small sound systems that don't go down as far as the notes do: what you're actually hearing is the notes' harmonics.)

So frequency response should be as wide as possible. A good minimum is 50–15,000 Hz (which is all that FM stations transmit), and 20–20,000 Hz is a reasonable maximum. (Wider response than that may add subtly to the clarity of sound within the 20–20,000 range, but may also open the door to other problems).

Frequency response must be wide, and also be even. Within the frequency range that the system is rated to handle, all frequencies should be handled equally well. If an amplifier, delivers five watt of power for a one-volt signal at one frequency, it should deliver the same five watts for the same one volt at any other frequency.

Relative Loudness of Common Sounds Measured in Standard dB SPL

The chart below shows typical sound levels in dB for everyday noises. The softest sound that can be detected by humans is called the threshold of hearing and is labeled 0 dB. Note the range between very soft music and loud classical (95-32 = 63 dB) or loud rock n' roll (115-32 = 83 dB)

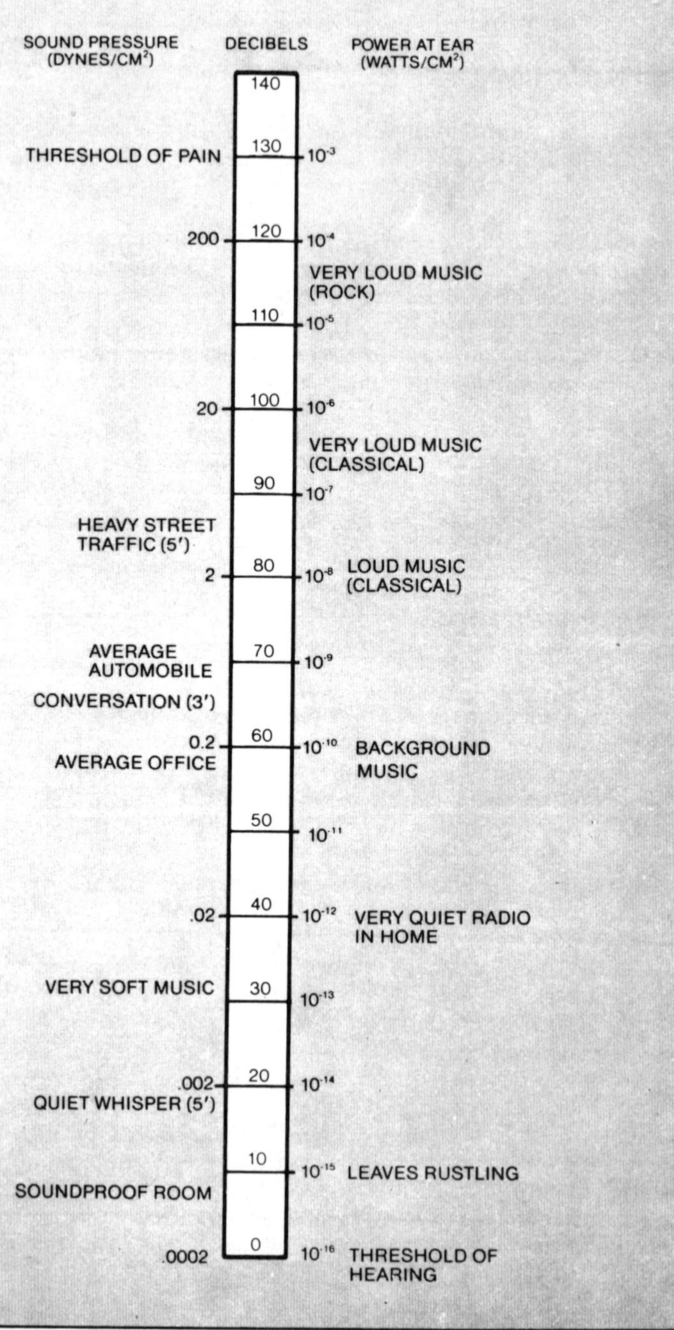

Loudness of common sounds. Note that you can play a radio at home at sound levels which would be drowned out in the car (Courtesy Audiomobile)

Frequency Response Curve

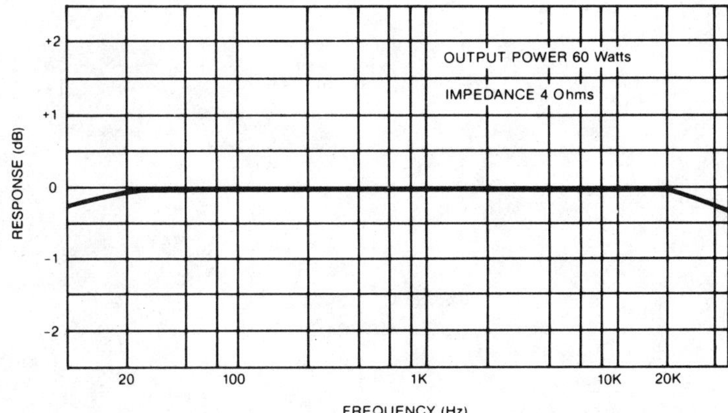

Frequency curve for a car amplifier. Note flat response through the audible frequency range, with 'rolloff' above and below (Courtesy Precision Power)

Otherwise, some tones will be slighted and some over-emphasized, and the music won't sound quite as it should.

In practice, nothing's perfect. Amplifiers, which are about the least imperfect parts of the car stereo, will have perfectly "flat" frequency response (so-called from the shape of their frequency-response curves), but that response will "roll off" at the high and low ends—below 20 and above 20,000 Hz., if the amplifier is a good one. An amplifier will usually have broader frequency response at low power output levels than at full rated power, too.

FM tuner circuits usually have response that's about as flat as that of amplifiers, but over a narrower range (FM broadcasts only cover the range from 50 to 15,000 Hz.). Tape decks typically have a few response irregularities. Speakers are rarely "flat"—an honest curve for even the best speakers will show peaks and dips in an otherwise flat curve, while one for a bad speaker would be extremely irregular.

No matter how flat your system, the sound you hear in your car will never be completely flat, since it's shaped by the car's own acoustics. However, the flatter your system is, the closer to more natural your sound will be.

How do you recognize uneven frequency response? There are several ways. If the music sounds shrill, that usually means there's too much high-frequency response; if it sounds soft and lacking in detail, then high-frequency response is probably insufficient. If voices sound far away, there's probably a dip in the midrange; if they seem to leap out at you, or sound "honky" (as though they were singing or speaking into a box or megaphone), then the mid-range probably is excessively boosted. If the bass booms out at you, or seems to harp relentlessly on one note with all music, there's probably a peak in the bass. If you don't hear low notes at all, there's too little bass.

Many good car stereo systems today are equipped with an "equalizer" (a set of five or more tone controls covering different portions of the frequency range). You can train your ear to recognize the effect of the controls or different frequency ranges. Just play with all the equalizer's controls, one at a time, and listen to what each control does. You'll soon learn what boosts and dips in each part of the frequency range do to the sound.

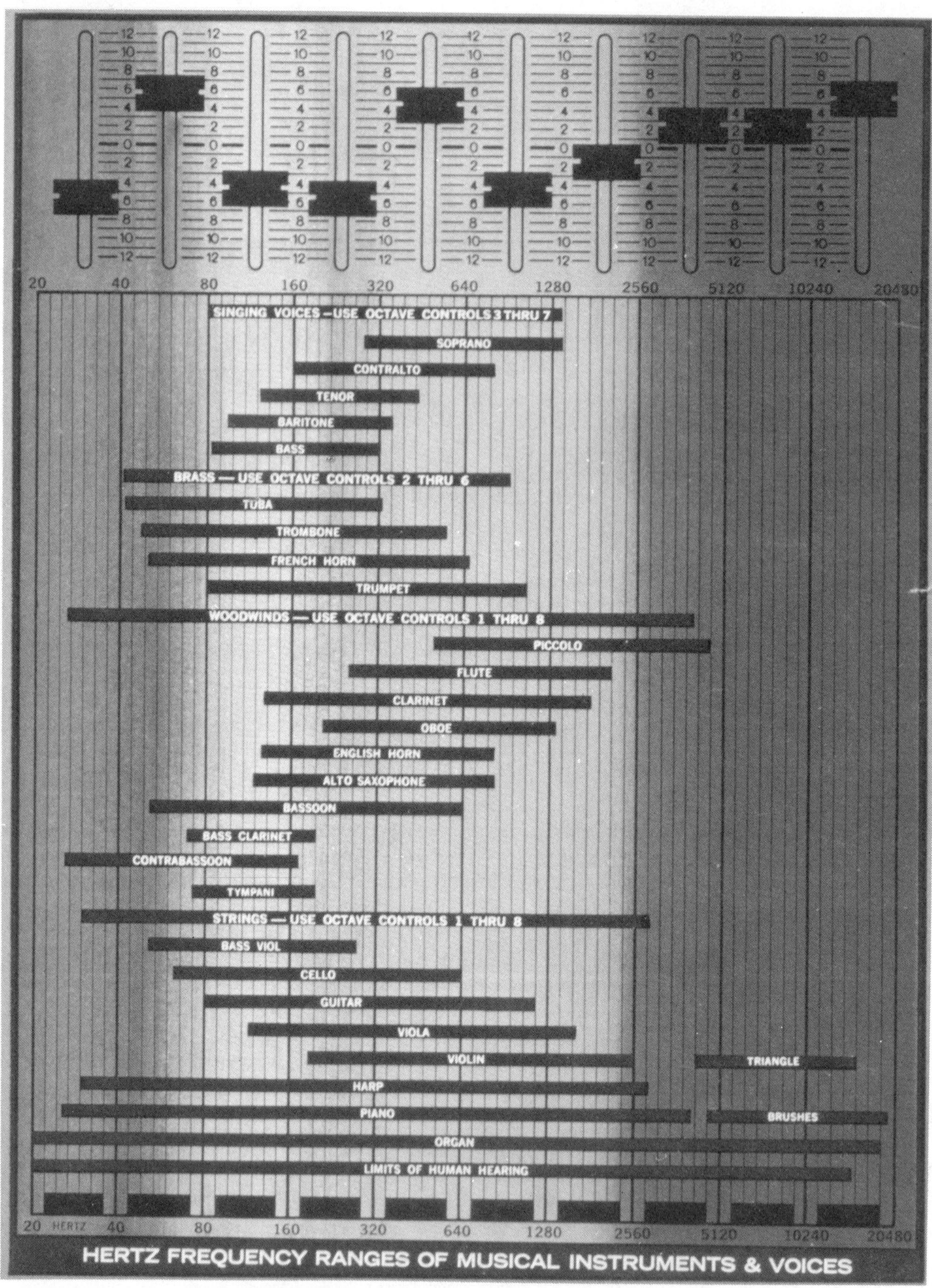

Reproducing all the sounds in music requires a wide frequency range (Courtesy Soundcraftsman)

Noise

Like distortion, noise is an unwanted addition to the music. Unlike distortion, noise doesn't change with the nature and level of the signal, just with the level of your volume control.

There are some circumstances under which noise is inevitable: if the station is broadcasting worn and noisy records, if your tapes are noisy, and sometimes if you're listening to a faraway station that's hard to pick up. But better tuner circuits, better tapes and recordings, plus Dolby and other noise reduction systems have greatly reduced the problem.

In the car, there can often be additional noises (especially when listening to radio) picked up from the car's ignition system. Good car sound equipment has circuits to suppress this noise, but additional, external suppressors are sometimes needed.

When checking out a sound system, listen to some FM and AM stations, especially the weakest or furthest ones you're likely to try listening to. On tape, listen for noise in the quiet passages (loud passages mask the noise, so you won't hear it), and compare it with the noise you hear when listening to the same tape at home. (Your tape will probably have some noise of its own; listen for any noise added by the car-sound system.) If the system is installed in a car, try making all these tests with the engine running, to make sure the system doesn't pick up ignition noise.

The better the quality of the sound you get, the longer you'll be able to listen to it pleasurably. Even imperfections of which you aren't always conscious can tire your ears, a phenomenon known as "listener fatigue". And since you may spend, at times, more concentrated hours listening to your car stero than you get the

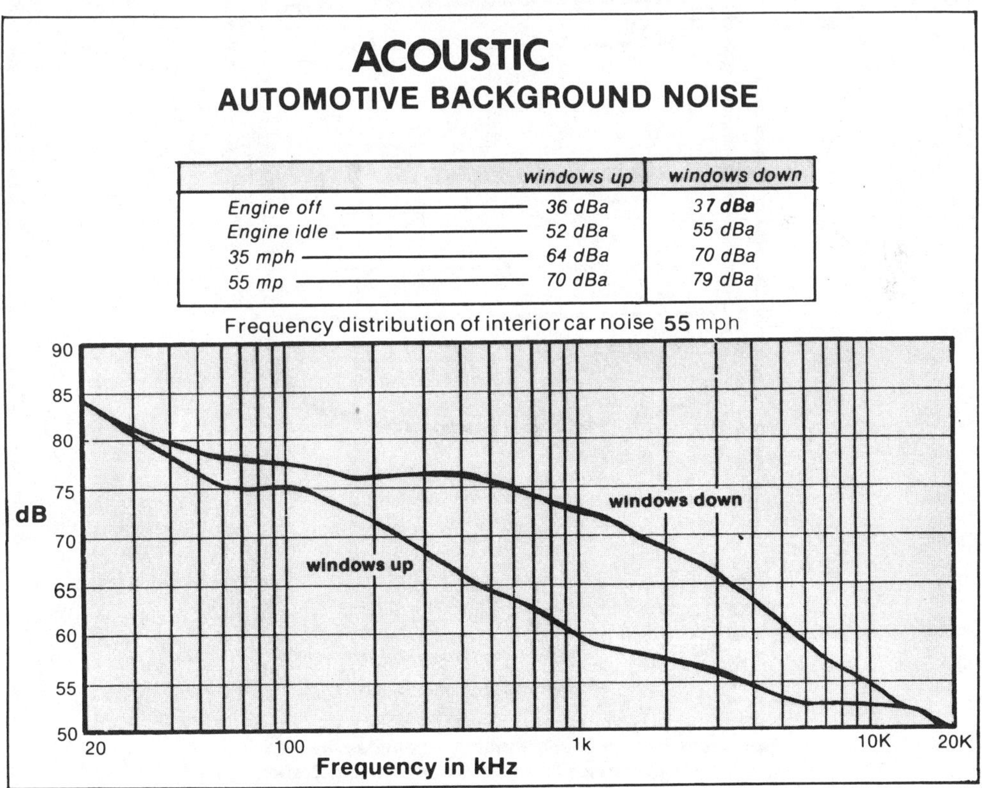

Road noise mainly interferes with bass sounds (Courtesy Audiomobile)

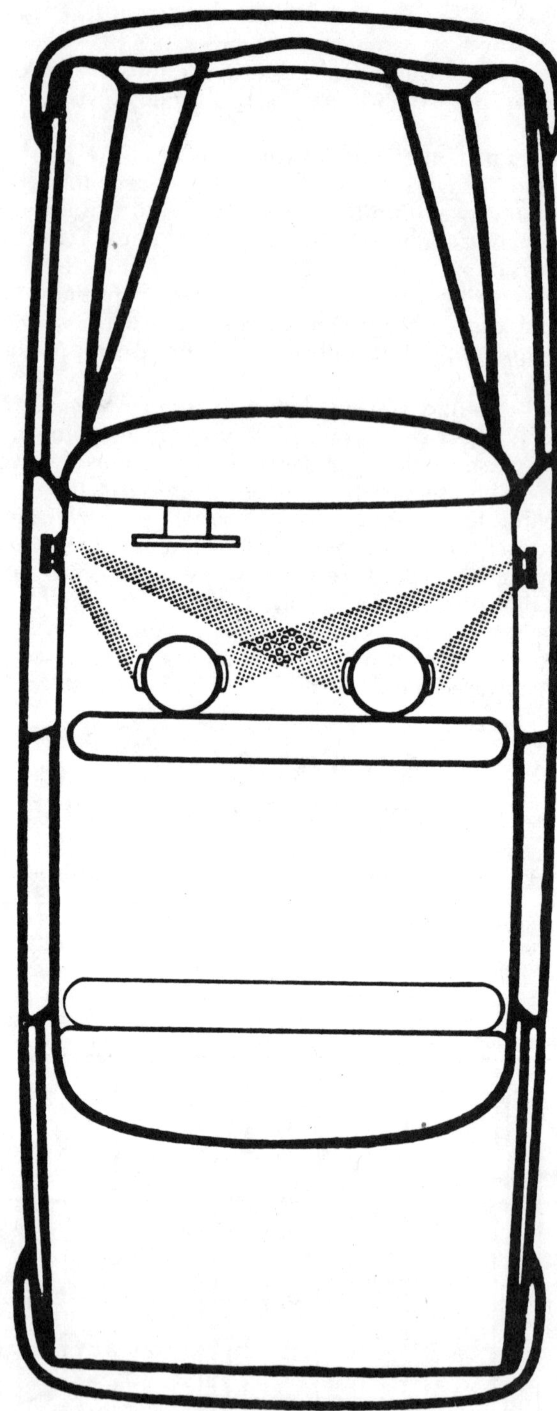

(Speakers flanking listener—from Bose)
Speakers in the door, flanking the listeners, give a sound perspective similar to headphones (Courtesy Delco-Bose)

chance to spend listening at home, avoiding that fatigue is quite important. It's even a safety factor, since listening fatigue could add to road fatigue, and impair your driving.

PROBLEMS OF CAR SOUND

Concert halls are designed for music, with large spaces, careful mixtures of hard and soft materials, and surfaces carefully placed and angled to control sound reflections. Cars, of course, are nothing like that. With the possible exception of the Delco-GM/Bose Music System optional on some 1983 and later GM models.

With rare exceptions, acoustics are seldom considered in car design. Car interiors are relatively small, and the mixture of their hard and soft surfaces are chosen with little regard for sound. A good deal of attention is paid to minimizing sound reflection rather than controlling it, but that's in response to another problem of the car: high levels of wind, road and motor noise.

All of these problems (except high noise) occur at home, too. But they don't occur to the same degree, at home, and you can control them to some extent by careful placement of your speakers, and sometimes by rearrangement of the furniture. The car's "furniture" is bolted down, and you can never quite put speakers where you want them. Most of these same problems also apply to vans, trailers, campers, boats and airplanes, too.

But if cars pose problems as listening room, they're still not sonic disaster areas, Good sound can be achieved in any car; and even great sound isn't impossible, though it may be expensive.

Sometimes, the car's disadvantages have their compensations. for example, while the speakers used in most car installations are too small to give good low frequency response in home environments, they may give good bass in the car because you're never far enough from them to hear the bass drop off. (Acousticians call this the "near-field" effect.) And while it's difficult in many cars to get "natural" sound perspective, with the sound arrayed across a "stage" in front, almost any car can give you the more spacious effect of headphone stereo listening, without your wearing headphones.

Not all the autosound problems are acoustical. Car-stereo equipment, must also be extra compact, to fit into dashboard radio slots. It must be able to run on the car's 12-volt DC power rather than the home's 120-volt AC.

Then there are environmental problems to be dealt with. The temperature inside your home probably ranges from a minimum of 40° or 50°F. up to a maximum of 85°F. or so. The temperature inside your car can vary from well below 0°F. in the

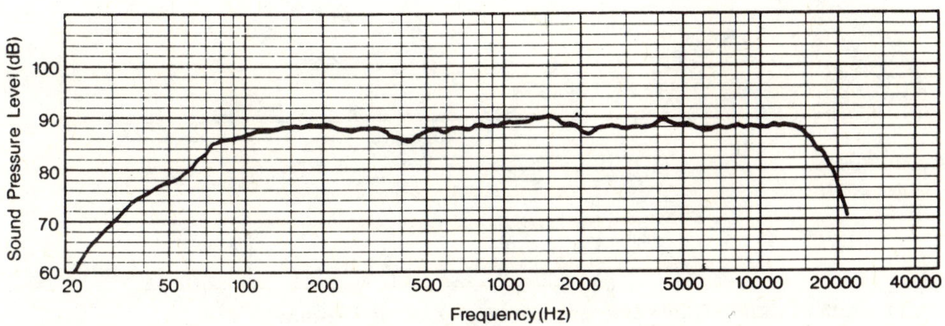

Good speaker curves are reasonably flat, especially when measured in the laboratory

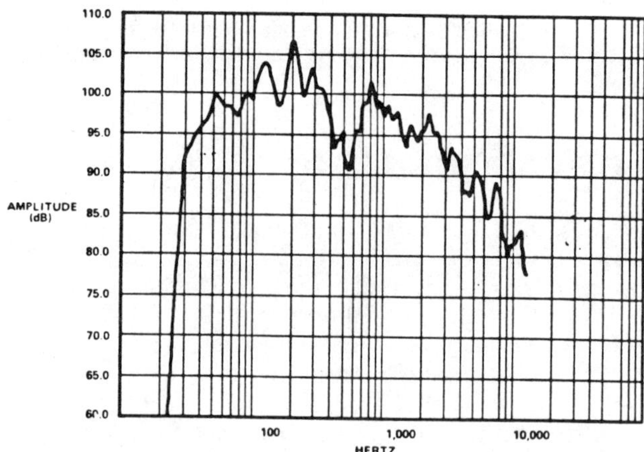

Less expensive speakers, measured in the car, are rather more irregular

winter to oven-like temperatures well above 100°F when parked in the summer sun.

Cars move, too, which can produce further problems. Tape decks can change speed when the car vibrates or hits a bump, causing speed irregularities known as wow and flutter. Vibration can even shake loose the mounting bolts or electrical connections.

As the car moves, FM and AM reception conditions change, too, making the tuner's task still harder. The tuner has to cope with signals that weaken as the car moves out of town, with signals which may become too strong as the car drives past the station's transmitter, and with signals that grow alternately strong and weak as the car moves past large buildings.

Car stereo equipment also has to cope with a potent interference generator—the engine—just a few feet away. Ignition interference radiates both into the electrical system powering the stereo and into the air where sound-system components (especially the tuner) can pick it up.

Car stereo manufacturers and installers know these problems, and have developed solutions to virtually all of them. Those solutions will be covered in more detail in later chapters.

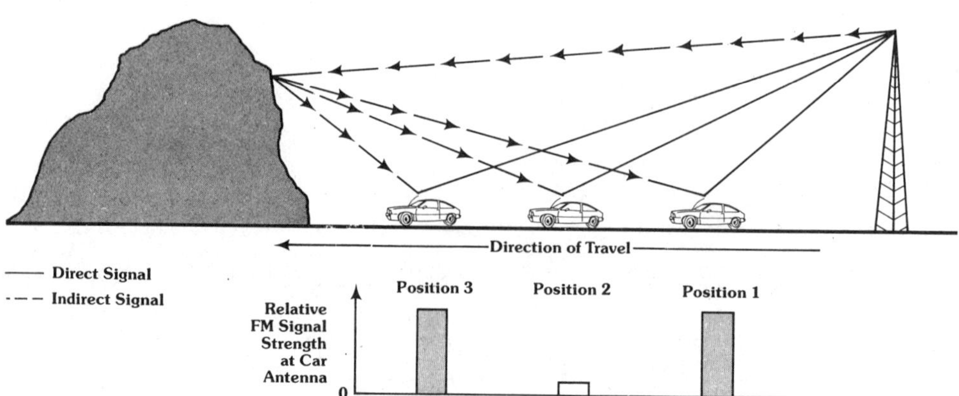

The strength of radio signals changes constantly as the car moves

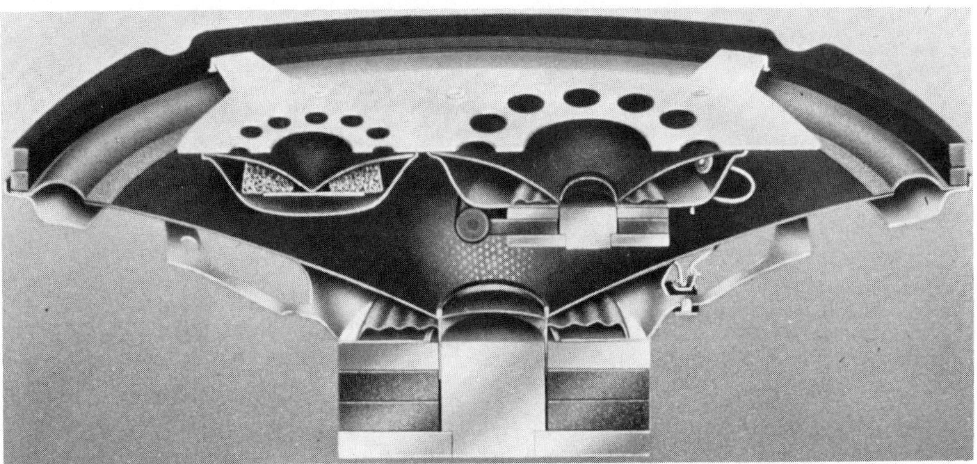

Cutaway view of a loudspeaker—actually, three speakers in one, as a high-frequency tweeter (upper left) and a mid-frequency speaker (upper right) nestle within the large, low-frequency woofer (Courtesy Jensen)

Woofer/Midrange

1 Cone diaphragm
2 surround
3 basket
4 spider
5 front plate
6 back plate
7 pole piece
8 ceramic magnet
9 dust cap
10 magnetic gap
11 voice coil

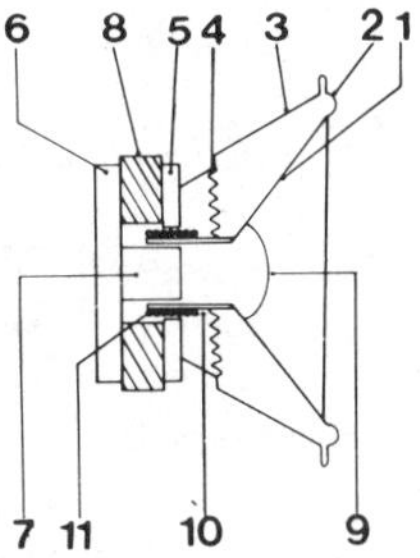

6 8 5 4 3 2 1

7 11 10 9

Tweeter

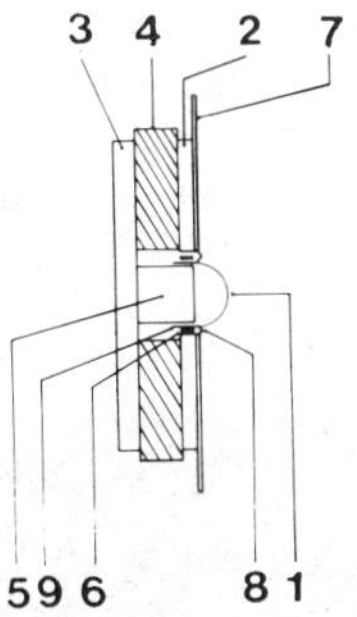

3 4 2 7

5 9 6 8 1

1 dome diaphragm
2 front plate
3 back plate
4 ceramic magnet
5 pole piece
6 voice coil
7 mounting plate
8 lead out wires
9 magnetic gap

Loudspeaker parts

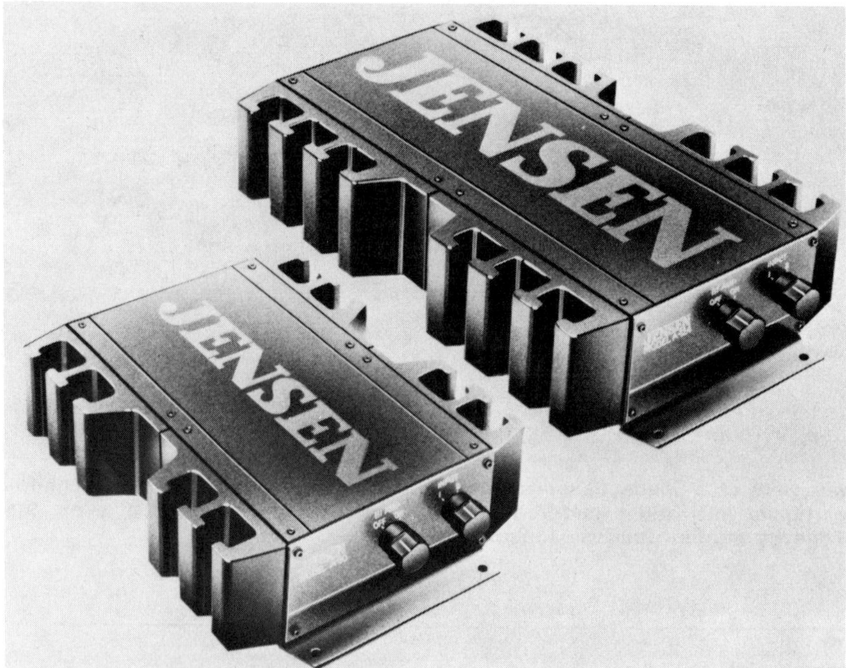

A typical car amplifier. The fins are for cooling (Courtesy Jensen)

TYPES OF EQUIPMENT

What you want is sound. What you buy, though, is equipment.

That equipment can take a number of forms. But the functions it must perform are very much the same for any system, whether it's for home or car use.

The sound comes from speakers. Speakers for home systems generally come in wood or wood-like boxes ("enclosures"), designed to enhance their sound. Mobile speakers generally must use cavities in the car body as enclosures, although some hang-on speakers use a small enclosure.

The speakers are driven by an amplifier, which may either be a separate component or be built into some other component (usually the tuner) of the system. The amplifier generally gets its signal from either a tape deck or an FM/AM tuner. (Car systems usually have both, and switch automatically between tuner and tape as cassettes are inserted or removed.) The tuner, in turn, gets signals from an antenna. Those are the basics, but various extras (such as "equalizers," which provide separate tone controls in each of five to nine frequency bands) can also be added.

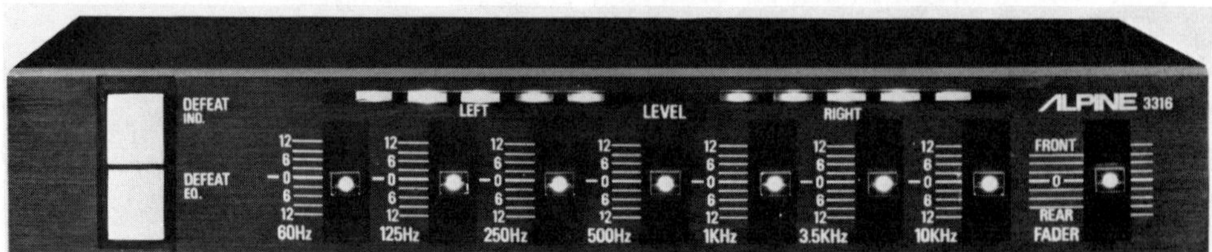

Equalizers can help flatten a sound system's frequency response, or shape it to your tastes

An external antenna is necessary for good radio reception (Courtesy Harada)

The speakers usually stand alone (though some have amplifiers built into them). The antenna always stands alone. Aside from that, though, these functions have been combined in almost every conceivable way. Most systems, though, fall into one of five major categories:

ALL-IN-ONE SYSTEMS

The tape deck, tuner and amplifier—everything but the speakers and antenna—are combined in a single unit, usually designed to fit the radio slot in a dashboard. Low-cost systems usually take this form.

A typical, all-in-one system, complete except for loudspeakers (Courtesy Audiovox)

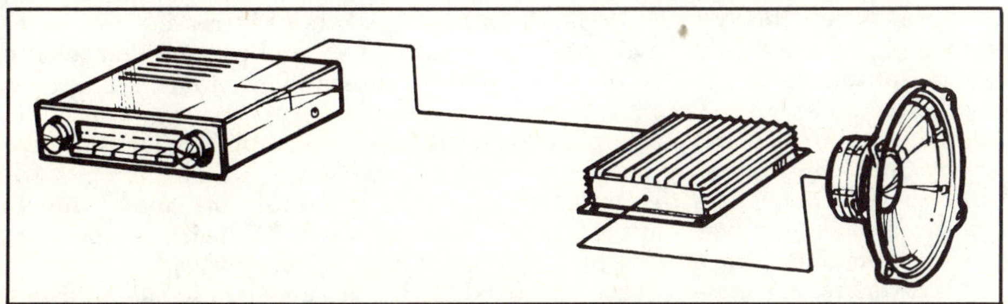

Separate amplifiers, used in more elaborate systems, can be larger and more powerful (Courtesy Audiomobile System)

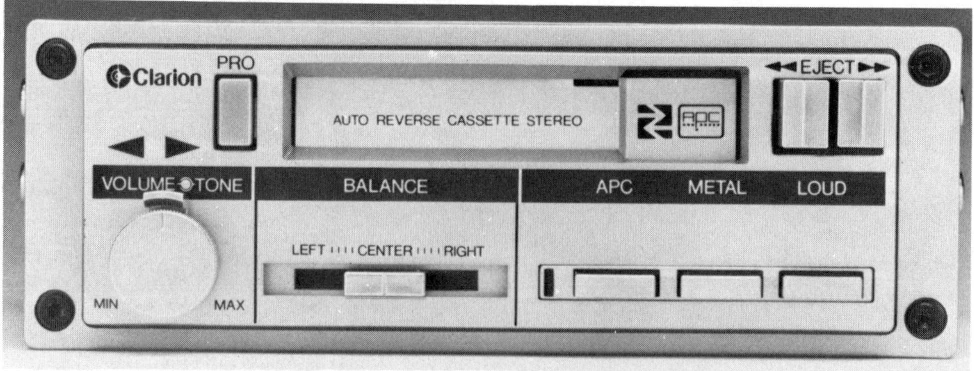

Under-dash units are usually tape players, like this one, or combination tape/FM units, on the presumption that you already have AM in your dash (Courtesy Clarion)

COMBO SYSTEMS WITH SEPARATE AMPLIFIERS

As amplifiers grow more powerful, they grow too big to be part of in an all-in-one package that can fit into the dashboard. Take the amplifier out of the package, and you can make it as big as you please, and place it beneath the dash, under a seat, in the trunk or elsewhere. This frees up a bit more space in the main unit for the tuner and tape deck sections, or allows the main unit to be made a little smaller to fit today's smaller cars.

IN-DASH PLUS UNDER-DASH

Tape deck and tuner needn't be in the same box at all. If your car already has an in-dash radio, you can add a tape deck that mounts beneath the dash. If the radio receives only AM or monophonic FM broadcasts, you can get an under-dash deck with an FM stereo tuner built in. Such under-dash units usually have more powerful amplifiers than those built into in-dash radios, which improves the sound.

UNDER-DASH ALONE

If all you want is tape or tape and FM, an under-dash tape unit can serve by itself.

INDIVIDUAL COMPONENTS

In some car systems, each function is built as a separate component, as is more often done in home systems. Such systems don't fit into dashboards at all, but are sometimes mounted under the dash. More often, though, they find themselves in the backs of vans, or the back seats of limousines.

This by no means exhausts the possibilities, of course. Hybrids abound. All-in-one systems, for example, are frequently augmented by booster amplifiers, which connect between the systems amplifier and its speakers to increase power output. And many all-in-one units have both built-in amplifiers and preamplifier-level outputs permitting their eventual conversion to Combination systems, with separate amplifiers.

Some systems also are "bi-amplified", using separate amplifiers for the low-frequency and high-frequency speakers (woofers and tweeters). The circuits which divide the frequencies for this may be built into the in-dash, or "head" unit, built into an amplifier, or built into a separate box of its own. Equalizers, too may be separate components or may be built into amplifiers or boosters.

This diversity only exists because it's needed. There's a system to suit your needs, no matter what those needs are. The problem is finding out just what those needs are, and which system type fulfills them.

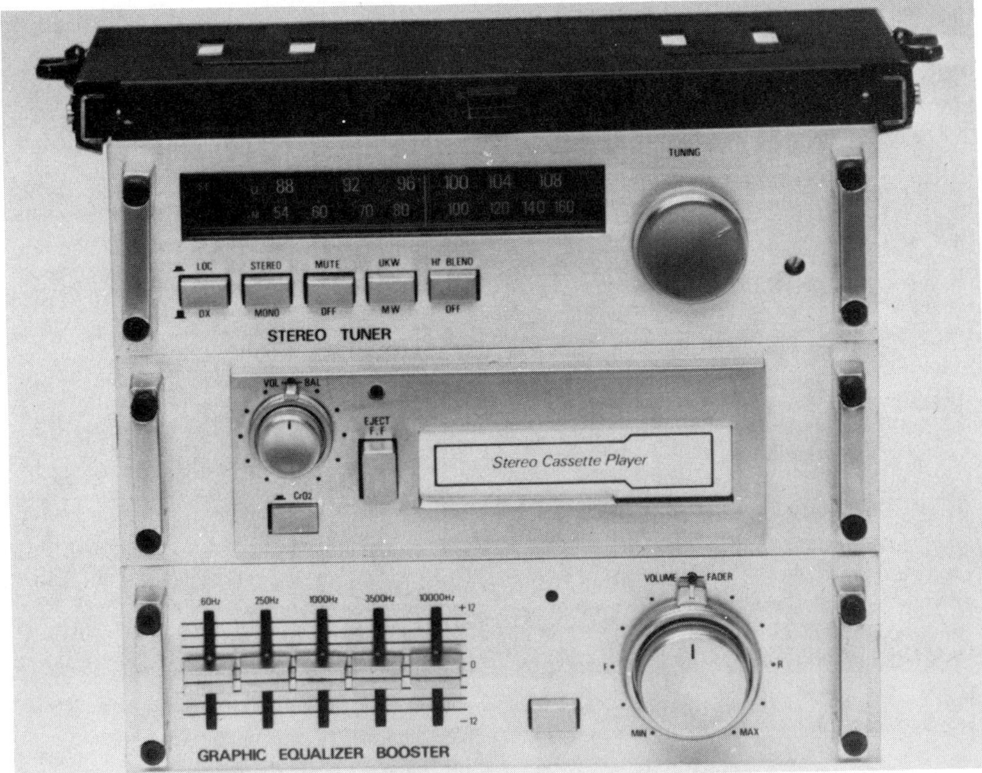

Separate tuners, amplifiers and tape decks make systems which resemble home component systems

The In-Dash System

There are probably more cars with all-in-one, in-dash systems than any other type. They're among the least expensive systems, for one thing: An in-dash unit with FM and AM radio reception plus tape can be purchased for around $100 (though more deluxe models are available at prices up to a few hundred dollars). It's simple to install, which means that you won't pay much for installation, or that you'll save even more by doing it yourself. (This also makes such systems popular for factory installation on new cars—another reason the type is popular.) Low cost is not the only reason for this type of system, though; some under-dash units are comparably priced. In-dash units also have some inherent advantages over under-dash systems.

Most cars have radio slots built into their dashboards. An in-dash unit looks built-in, which makes it far more attractive than something hung beneath the dash. And it's far less likely to bang passenger's knees.

Another advantage is convenience. If your dash is reasonably well designed, the radio slot will be easy to see and reach for both driver and passenger. That's especially important for the driver, who shouldn't have to take his eyes from the road for more than a fraction of a second to find the sound system controls, and who should never have to bend or twist out of normal driving position to reach them.

A third advantage is actually an inconvenience—for prospective thieves. An under-dash system can be removed from a car in seconds, even without tools; an in-dash one takes tools and a bit more time. That makes in-dash systems a bit less attractive to the casual thief.

Most cars have convenient dashboard positions prepared for in-dash car sound units (Courtesy Sparkomatic)

If you want a simple, no-frills system, you'll find many to choose from amid equipment of this type. But if you want something fancier these systems are available with high-performance radio sections, good tape decks, and quite a few convenience features. The only thing they can't offer is high amplifier power—and not everyone needs that.

In-Dash plus Separate Amplifier

Powerful amplifiers are comparatively large and need some ventilation room around them. The spaces car-manufacturers leave for radios and stereos are small and cramped, though—and getting smaller.

Take the amplifier out of that space, however, and you can make it as large and powerful as you like. You also wind up with more room in the main system housing for better tape or tuner sections.

Separates also let the manufacturer and dealer offer you a wider choice. A dealer who carries four amplifierless "front-end" units with different features and four amplifiers of different power ratings can offer a choice of 16 different combinations while carrying only eight items in stock.

It's easiest if all eight units come from one manufacturer, because their connections and electrical requirements are known to match. But amplifiers and front-ends from different companies can be mixed and matched, almost at will, if you don't mind a more elaborate (and expensive) system.

Just how expensive? If you like, the sky can be the limit—custom systems can cost upwards of $12,000 but these are mostly found in expensive sports cars. But if your ceiling is a little lower, front-end units without amplifiers are available from about $200 up, while amplifiers run from about $100 up. (These prices do not include installation costs, since those vary greatly.)

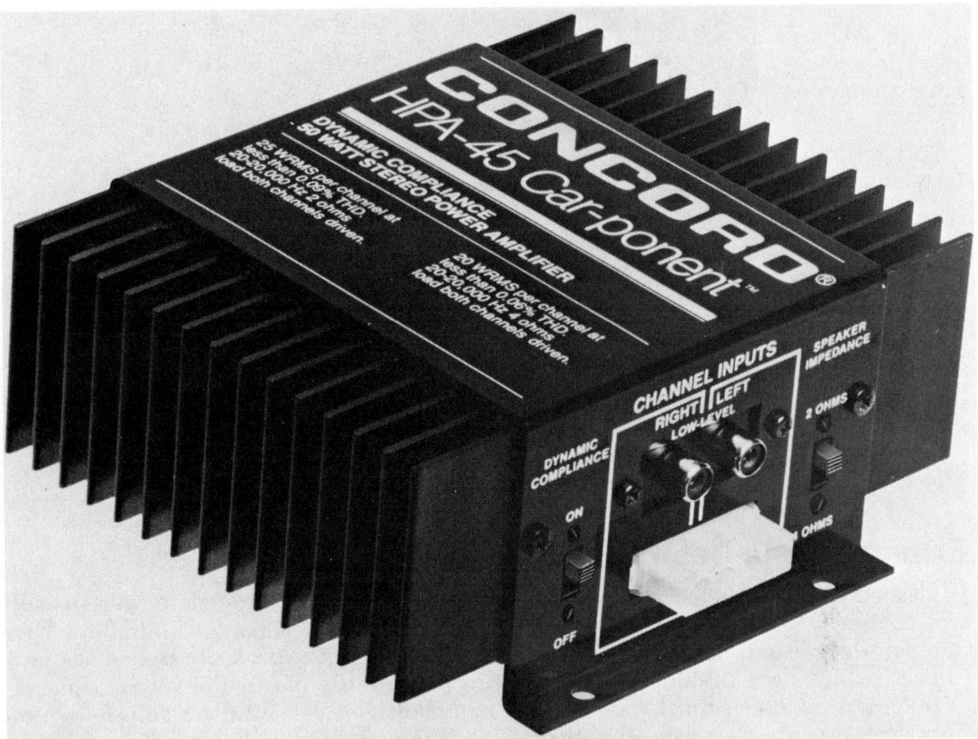

This amplifier has inputs for preamp-level and for speaker-level signals (Courtesy Concord)

You can get as much amplifier power as you want. There are amplifiers that deliver at least 150 watts per channel. And if that's not enough for you, you can use several amplifiers.

Higher power is not the only reason to use multiple amps. Some systems use high-power amplifiers for the rear speakers (which can generally take it better) and low-power ones for the front. Others use separate amplifiers to handle the low bass frequencies, a technique which can yield better bass and cleaner, lower-distortion sound.

Part of the price difference between two-piece and one-piece systems is due simply to the extra cost of making two circuit packages instead of one; if you can get the same features and performance from one of the more deluxe, one-piece units as from one of the less deluxe two-piecers, the one-piece unit will definitely be the better buy. But when you buy a two-piece system, you generally get more power, more features, and more performance. That's a better reason for its higher price.

Installation is more complicated with a two-piece system, and so will cost more, too (or take you more time and effort, if you're doing it yourself). On the other hand, two-piece systems take more time to remove: thieves are less likely to get the entire system, unless both pieces are under the dash or the thieves know they'll have plenty of time to operate safely.

One type of installation actually gets easier with these systems: if you want to add equalizers, spatial expanders, noise-reduction units, or the like, you can just plug them in between the front-end unit and the amplifier.

Booster amplifiers, such as this one, can add extra power to low-powered in-dash units

Expandable In-Dash

In-dash units have "speaker-level" outputs, which deliver enough power (usually two to ten watts) to drive loudspeakers. Systems with separate amplifiers have "preamp-level" outputs, with no power of their own, to speak of, and so use amplifiers (which have preamp-level inputs) to provide the power the speakers need.

But there is also a third, newer type with both speaker- and preamp-level outputs. You can use these systems two ways. If your budget is limited now, but you want to add more power later, you can install the system and use just its built-in amplifier at first. Then, when your budget permits, you can plug in a higher-powered amp and switch your speakers over to that.

The other way to use such a system is to use its built-in amplifier to drive small, limited-range speakers in the front of the far, and the separate amplifier to drive larger, full-range systems in the back. (Limited-range speakers require less power than those which deliver the full range of frequencies because the bass notes require more power than the rest.)

If you want to expand the power of a one-piece system that has only speaker-level outputs, there is still a way: you can connect a "booster amp" between that output and the speakers. Booster amps have speaker-level inputs, instead of the preamp-level inputs of ordinary amplifiers.

Don't expect this to sound quite as good as a true power amplifier used with a system designed for it. Booster amps themselves offer only limited power. And speaker-level signals are usually noisier and more distorted than preamp-level ones; booster amps boost that noise and distortion, too, then add a little of their own. Since amplifiers with preamp-level inputs are amplifying signals that are cleaner to begin with, they're bound to produce cleaner results.

Just as there are in-dash units with both types of output, there are amplifiers with both types of input, so you can use them as both power amplifiers and as boosters. If you want to expand a one-piece system now and replace that system later, amps like these are perfect.

In-Dash, Under-Dash

Systems with the radio tuner in the dash and the tape deck below are not very common. They're inexpensive, but the main reason people buy them is because they serve a few, specialized needs.

For instance, if your car came with a radio, it may be easier or less expensive to mount a tape player below the dash than to remove the old radio and replace it with a one-piece system.

It also makes more sense for some people's driving and listening habits. If you usually drive in an area where there are many good AM and FM stations, you may find tape unnecessary there—even something of a nuisance, if you're trying to juggle tapes in traffic. On trips, where you don't know where to find the stations playing your kind of music, tapes are more often worth the trouble. If so, you can mount an under-dash tape player on a slide-in mount and only slide it in for trips, leaving player and tapes in the house when they're not needed.

In multiple-car families, an under-dash tape player on a slide-out mount can readily be transferred from one car to another. This prevents arguments over who gets the car with the tape player, though arguments about the player itself may still arise.

Slide mounts normally come in two-piece sets, one of which mounts to the dashboard while the other attaches to the stereo. All connections for power and speakers are made automatically when the two halves are slid together. (If you're mounting a one-piece system with a slide-mount, you'll still have to connect and disconnect the radio antenna separately.) Since many people do use these mounts to transfer one tape player between vehicles, some manufacturers also offer the dashboard half of the mount separately, at lower cost.

A note on security. Slide-mounted units can be as safe or unsafe as their owners make them. There is no system safer from theft than one on a quick-detach slide mount that has been detached and put in a safe place. There is no system less safe than one which has been left where any thief can reach in and detach it. That doesn't mean you need always take your stereo with you when you park. You can hide it under your front seat, to make it look as if the stereo's been removed. Or you can put it in the trunk, (preferably before you get to your parking spot, so those who know you've stashed it don't know where the car is, and vice versa).

Component Systems

In home stereo, the best and most expensive systems are made up of many individual components: a turntable, preamplifier, amplifier, tuner, tape deck and speakers, to name only the basic ones. Some of the most expensive car-stereo systems are made this way, too—but not many of them.

In the home, separates have many advantages: More control panels means space for more controls. More boxes means room for more elaborate circuitry. Separate power supplies for each unit minimize interactions between components. And by "cherry-picking" from the lines of several manufacturers, you can see to it that each component in your system is the very best of its kind for your use that you can afford.

In the car, these advantages are a bit less clear-cut. Having controls spread over several panels can be inconvenient when you're trying to play stereo and drive—they may be easier to find this way, but some are bound to be harder to reach. You may not always get more controls on all those panels, either—many of the most useful convenience controls, such as push-button tuning, are found far less frequently on separates than on one-piece or two-piece in-dash systems.

The circuitry in separates may be better, and may outperform that found in less elaborate systems. But it isn't always, so don't take this on faith. If specifications, test reports, or other concrete factors lead you to believe that separate components will perform better, fine; and so much the better if that difference can be demonstrated.

You also have less freedom in selecting individual components for the car than you do when buyng them for the home. While many companies make amplifiers and preamps (a few make nothing else), few companies make tuners or tape decks designed to be used in such systems. Components of different makes usually require different plugs, and may also have different signal levels, making installation harder. And since components from different companies are likely to be slightly different sizes, a neat installation will generally require a custom cabinet, which raises the cost further. (Racks are available at moderate prices for most single-make component systems.)

There are places, though, where components make sense: in the back of a van or limousine, for example, they'd be no inconvenience to the driver and would be relatively invisible to thieves. And owners of limousines or elaborately-fitted vans are unlikely to quibble over the extra cost.

Knowing the general configuration of the system you'll be buying is just the first, and easiest step. Now it's time to consider what you need from all the circuits of that system: the tuner, tape deck, amplifiers and (though they're not exactly "circuits") speakers.

RADIO FEATURES AND CONTROLS

There's no longer much question over whether to get a car-sound system that can tune in AM, FM or both. You'll find both in almost all car-stereo equipment. Inexpensive car radios may have AM only; a few component tuners and some underdash tape/tuner combinations may have only FM. But these are exceptions although each has its advantages.

FM offers higher sound fidelity—it has less static, less fuzzy distortion, and covers a wider range of sound frequencies from deep bass to high musical overtones. Almost all FM stations broadcast in stereo and FM signals don't fade out as quickly under bridges and similar obstructions.

AM, on the other hand, can carry longer distances, which means you can keep listening to the same program for hours of driving (especially in winter and at night). It's also less sensitive to signal reflections from hills and buildings, which makes it far more listenable in some locations. And AM stereo is on the way, though FM still has a major head start.

Most important of all, perhaps, is that with both AM and FM, you're equipped to hear all possible programs. With only one band, you're always missing something.

Problems of Mobile Reception

Contrary to a good home hi-fi system, which may have very few controls and switches, the better the car-stereo tuner, the more controls it is likely to have.

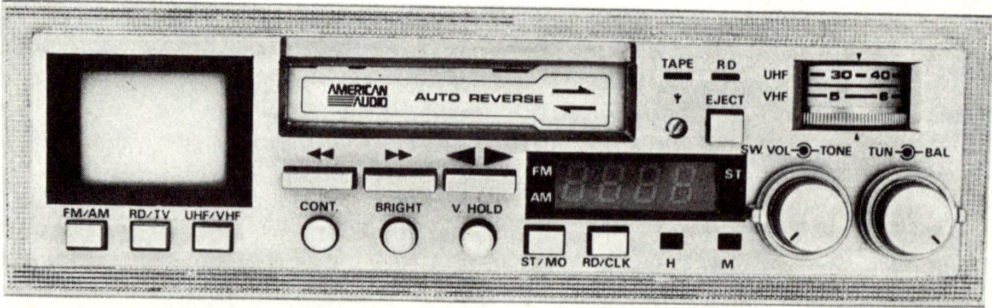

American Audio's $1500 ET-9000TV model incorporates virtually every feature available. The unit is designed for safe driving, since when installed properly, the TV is disabled when the ignition key is ON

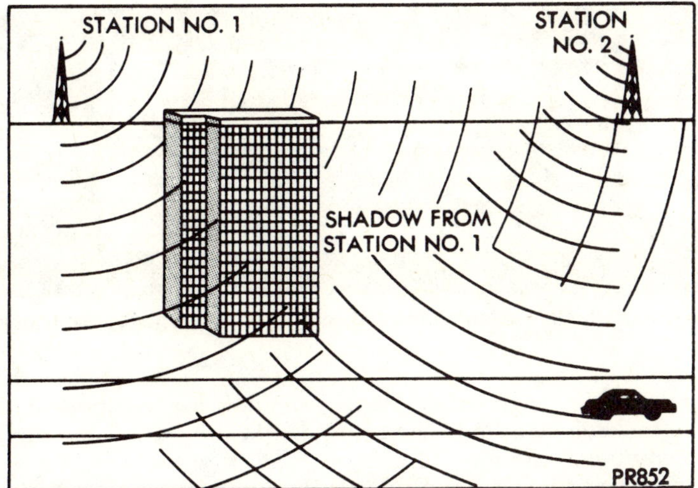

Because the car moves, radio reception conditions can change drastically during the course of a single program—a problem not found in home listening

That's because a car radio suffers from four problems not found in home listening: it's always moving; its antenna can't be turned toward the station; the driver has little free time or attention to spare for tuning or adjusting controls, and the car's ignition generates interference.

The problem of motion is actually two problems in one. The obvious part is changing distance: in an hour's driving, you can move more than fifty miles farther from or nearer to the station you're listening to, with signal strength changing as you go. Additionally, the station signal can be relatively weak or strong, and subject to rapid fluctuation in signal strength. As cars go past hills and valleys, up hill and down, through streets crowded with buildings, under bridges and through tunnels, signal conditions change each second. Listening conditions must stay stable through these changes, though. The better the system, the better it will keep those problems from affecting what you hear.

When you're driving, you frequently can't even spare much attention to tuning in the stations you want. Today's car stereo systems help you with that job. These tuning conveniences that activate automatic circuits have proved so popular, in fact, that they've even been added to home stereo equipment, especially as the demand for them in car stereo has lowered their price to the point where they can be added to home or mobile tuners inexpensively.

Interference is a constant problem, so most car radios and stereo systems have some built-in interference suppression. Installers (either do-it-yourself or professional) usually add external suppressors, too, in cars which pose special problems. But you will also find switches on some units which can add an extra touch of suppression where required.

Digital Displays

The biggest—or at least, most visible—change in car stereo systems in the past few years has been in their radio tuner sections. In conventional, or "analog" radios, the station frequencies you tuned in were shown by a pointer moving along a numbered dial. In new ones, they're more and more likely to be shown by a digital display which doesn't move but whose numbers change. When the radio is off, the display may even double as a digital clock.

Digital dials (1) are gradually replacing the old, knob-and-dial type (2) (Courtesy Audiovox)

In most such models, that visible change signifies a revolution in the way the tuner works—a technology called "frequency synthesis"—but some digital dials are attached to conventional circuits.

The radio receiver's tuner section has two basic functions. The first is to extract a single, precise signal from the jumble of signals in the air, while ignoring all the others, so that you only hear one station at a time. The second is to strip ("demodulate") the sound information from that radio signal and send it to the amplifier section, which in turn feeds the speakers, producing sound.

Analog radios can be tuned continuously, to any frequency on the dial. That means they can not only tune to frequencies where stations are supposed to be (such as 99.7 MHz FM), but frequencies where stations won't be found (such as 99.73).

Frequency-synthesis or "digital" tuners, though, can only tune in steps, which are usually limited to those frequencies where stations might occur. Such a tuner might jump from 99.7 to 99.9 if made for use in the U.S.A. (or from 99.7 to 99.8, if it's made for use in some other countries as well), but it can never tune in any frequencies between. Radios with frequency-synthesis tuning almost invariably have digital "dials", whose numbers change stepwise as the tuner jumps from frequency to frequency.

Digital dials also show up on some analog tuners, though. To the designer, digital displays have two advantages over analog dials: they convey information more precisely and clearly in a minimum of space (and space is at a premium in car-stereos with many controls); and they give the system a more modern, up-to-date look.

Whether they're an advantage to you or not depends somewhat on how you think of stations when you're tuning them. If you think of a station as "somewhere about two-fifths up the dial", for instance, you'll find analog dials somewhat clearer. If you think of it as "94.3," though, you'll find digital dials easier to use. In any case, you'll soon have little choice. Digital synthesis tuning is working its way down from the very highest priced sets and soon will be the only type of tuning available. In part, it's because of economics. Digital tuners are all-electronic systems, which now cost less to build.

Synthesis tuning also has some practical advantages. One is reliability. Digital systems are less likely to drift out of tune as analog systems do. When they do fail, they tend to fail unmistakeably, which may be annoying but at least ensures you'll get them fixed.

Another, and perhaps the most important asset, is ease of tuning. If the tuner only stops at frequencies where stations can be, then you needn't fiddle with it to get the tuning perfect. You're either right on target or so far off that you can't help noticing; and when you are off, you have only to tune over a notch or two to be right on again. In the car that's a safety factor, too.

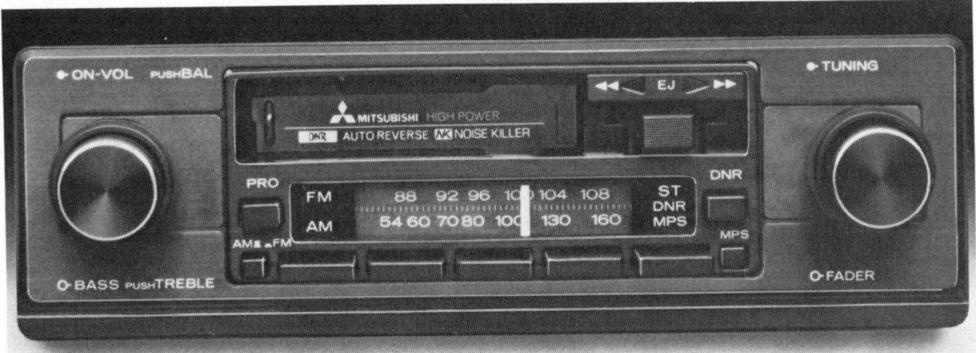

Push-button tuning lets you tune in a favorite station with a single push. In the car, that's a safety feature (Courtesy Mitsubishi)

Tuning Aids and Controls

ELECTRONIC TUNING

Digital tuners also adapt readily to various, semi-automated tuning conveniences. Push-button tuning is a good example. Most car stereos, today, let you pre-set anywhere from five to fifteen of your favorite stations, and tune each with a button-push.

Analog tuners had that at least as far back as the Thirties. But it was always a clumsy and expensive, mechanical system which had to physically tune the radio to preset spots on the dial. With digital systems, it's all-electronic, simply a matter of storing each station frequency in a computer-like memory. That makes the system less expensive and more reliable (analog push-button systems used to need frequent readjustment). It also allows the use of small, feather-touch buttons, which are both easier to use and easier to fit into cramped control panels. Because of that, some designers have been able to increase the number of buttons; where five buttons is the norm, many new designs have six, and a few even have ten.

Electronic tuning also makes it easy to increase the number of stations each button brings in. Most such tuners have separate sets of preset-station memories for AM and FM, so that a set can be pre-tuned for ten stations, five on each band, with just five buttons. One company has even brought out a model whose five buttons can memorize five AM and ten FM stations, for a total of fifteen.

AUTOMATIC SEARCH

Push-button tuning is fine for travel in your local area, where you know which stations are your favorites and what frequencies they broadcast at. But what do you do when you're travelling, and the stations are all strange to you? Or when you're bored with the stations you normally listen to and want something fresh?

One answer, of course, is to fiddle with the manual tuning control until you find a station you like. But on many modern sets, that's not the only answer. Instead, you can use automatic station-finding features like "Search," "Seek," and "Scan."

In "Seek" mode, a radio will tune its way up the band, stopping at the first strong signal it finds. If you like that station, fine. If not, just tap the button and the radio will seek out the next station for you. When it hits the top of the band, it generally starts over from the bottom. "Search" is generally synonymous with "Seek", though occasionally it is used in place of "Scan".

"Scan" is even more highly automated than "Seek". In this mode, the radio plays each station it finds for a few seconds, then—if you haven't touched a control to stop it—moves on up to the next station on the band. In areas with many stations,

"Seek" usually tunes to the next station up the dial, and stops. "Scan" plays each station it finds then, after a few seconds, moves on to try another station till you stop it (Courtesy Kenwood)

a complete circuit of the dial can take about two minutes; in more remote areas, it's all over in half a minute or so. Either way, you only have to touch the controls twice—once to start the scan, and once to stop it.

These systems are generally designed to sense only strong stations, which ensures that any station they find will still be clearly heard when you've moved a few miles down the road. If they don't find anything you like, you can scan the dial manually to uncover stations they missed.

Seek and scan have some interesting variations, too. A few sets seek a new station automatically if the station you've tuned in fades away. That's useful if you just want continuous music, or if your preference runs to whatever kind of music is most popular in the area you're driving through; but if your tastes run toward something rarer, such as jazz, classical or folk music, it's not much help. One or two sets can be programmed to switch to specific, pre-selected stations as each old one fades away. That can be especially nice if you know which stations you'll want to hear along your route.

A few sets add a further variation on the theme, keeping a tape on standby to play automatically when a station fades out. That ensures that whatever fades in will be something you like, even if it isn't radio.

A very few, premium-priced sets can even be programmed to switch stations automatically at pre-set times. That ensures you'll never miss a favorite show while driving—especially as these sets even turn themselves on if you don't.

MUTING

Not all tuner controls are tuning aids. Some aid listening in other ways. Muting, for example, eliminates the annoying roar you'd otherwise hear when tuning between stations on the FM band. In car stereo, muting works only on FM, but unless you do all your tuning by pushbutton or with seek and scan controls, you'll find it makes your listening far more pleasant (which makes it surprising how many sets still lack this feature). If the specification sheet doesn't mention muting you can check for it in seconds when you try the radio—just tune to a frequency where there are no stations in your area and listen for the roar or the muted silence.

If you hear the roar, check whether there is no muting or whether it's just been turned off. Since the muting control also cuts out weak signals, some sets let you shut off the muting for those times when you want to hear a weak signal, no matter how bad it sounds, just to hear that program. Other sets have no such switch, on the principle that stations weak enough to be muted are usually so marginal that they'll fade in and out annoyingly as you drive.

The muting switch cuts noise between FM stations; the stereo/mono switch helps clean up some noisy FM stereo signals (Courtesy Kraco)

STEREO/MONO SWITCH

Another aid in dealing with weak signals is a Stereo/Mono switch. Both weak signals and multipath interference (the signal reflections that cause "ghosts" on television) cause more problems in stereo FM listening than in monophonic listening. Frequently, switching to mono will clean up such signals. Since one normally only needs the mono switch on weak signals, it is often combined with the muting switch: for strong signals, both stereo and muting will be on, but both can be switched off for weak ones.

Most FM radios switch automatically between mono and stereo, which might make a manual switch seem superfluous. But most switch only when signal strength falls below a certain level, not when other factors, such as multipath, make stereo listening intolerable. It's even more annoying when you're riding at just the right distance to make the radio pop back and forth between good mono and bad stereo sound. By switching manually to mono, you can solve these problems.

Smarter automatic switching circuits are appearing, though. An increasingly common version (given different names by every manufacturer who offers it) fades gradually from stereo to mono as the signal weakens, and fades back to stereo as it improves. Such circuits can clear up minor signal problems with only minor reductions in stereo effect, rather than switching all the way to mono when problems occur. And because the shift is gradual, there's none of that annoying "picket-fence" alternation between stereo and mono.

In many cases, these automatic blending circuits are combined with circuits that gradually reduce high-frequency response as signals weaken, since noise and distortion are most prominent in the high frequencies.

LOCAL/DISTANCE SWITCH

The third common signal-improving tuner control is the Local/Distant (Lo/Dx) switch. It's hard to build a tuner that can cope equally well with weak, distant signals and strong, local ones. A tuner designed for maximum sensitivity to weak signals may overload on strong ones; a tuner with good overload resistance may lack the sensitivity to pick up distant stations. The Lo/Dx switch more commonly applies to FM, but will normally affect AM reception as well.

By adding a switch that changes the tuner's sensitivity, though, you get a tuner that can handle both extremes. At one time, you were likely to find such switches primarily in expensive car-sound systems. Now, they're becoming available in lower-priced models, while some top models now have circuits which automatically switch from local to distant sensitivity. Not having to switch modes when switching be-

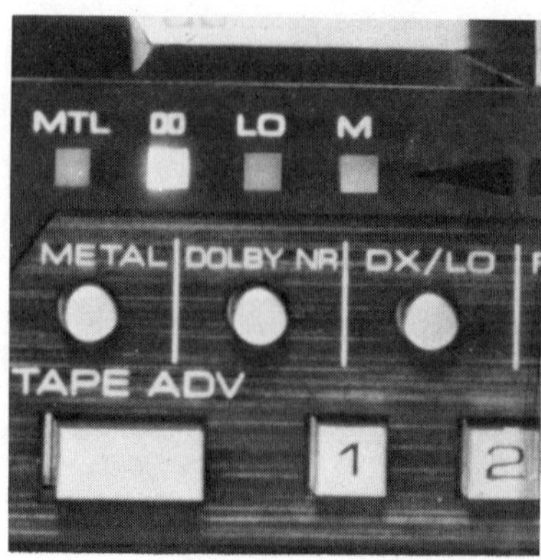

The Local/Distant switch optimizes the tuner for strong or weak signals

tween far and nearby stations can be a blessing, but not being able to do so when you have to is a pain. If the stereo you're considering doesn't have a Local/Distant switch, check carefully into the reasons for its absence—cost-cutting, or elimination of the need.

On many sets with Scan or Seek, the Lo/Dx switch also adjusts the sensitivity of the auto-tuning system. On "Lo," the tuner will only stop itself at very strong signals, assuring you the clearest possible reception; on "Dx", it will stop at somewhat weaker ones as well, giving you more stations to choose from.

NOISE REDUCTION

Some stereos have separate buttons to eliminate noise and other interference from FM and, more rarely, AM. Other noise reduction systems, such as DNR and Dolby, are applicable to both radio and tape. DNR (which will be covered in more detail later) suppresses noise with any signal source—FM, tape, or even AM. Dolby works only when decoding signals which have been Dolby-encoded at their source. That includes most cassette recordings, but only a few FM stations; so while the Dolby switch will always work on tape, it often does not affect sound on FM at all. Where the Dolby circuit is used for both FM and tape, it should only be used with those stations broadcasting Dolby-encoded sound.

AUTO SOUND FEATURES AND AUDIO SPECIFICATIONS

The features, facilities and performance specifications of autosound systems affect everything you will hear from the system.

Sound Controls

At a minimum, every system will have a volume or a loudness control. There's a difference between them: a volume control just makes the sound louder or softer, while a loudness control adds extra bass (and sometimes a touch of treble) when the sound is turned down. This compensates for the ear's lower bass and treble sensitivity at low sound levels. Without it, the sound could seem thin and lifeless at low volume levels. Some car stereos have loudness switches, so you can use this compensation or not, as you wish.

When cars had one speaker in the middle of the dash, a volume or loudness control could handle all sound level problems. But with stereo, where there are speakers on both sides of the car, there should be a balance control too. When you're driving by yourself, you'll get the best stereo effect with the balance set

Low frequencies become harder to hear as the sound level decreases; so many models have "Loudness" switches which boost bass when the sound is turned down (Courtesy Jensen)

towards the passenger side of the car, so that the near and far speakers will sound equally loud to you. With passengers in the car, you'll want to set the balance back more towards the middle, so you'll both hear equal sound levels. You can also use the balance control to compensate for unbalanced tapes, or if the people on one side of the car are slightly hard of hearing.

Most cars, today, have speakers in both front and rear, which also require balancing. The control for this is usually called a "fader." If your system does not already have a fader, you can add one as an accessory. There are two types: one is designed to go between a preamp-level output and two amplifier inputs; the other is intended to go between an amplifier and two pair of speakers. Be sure you get the right type for your system.

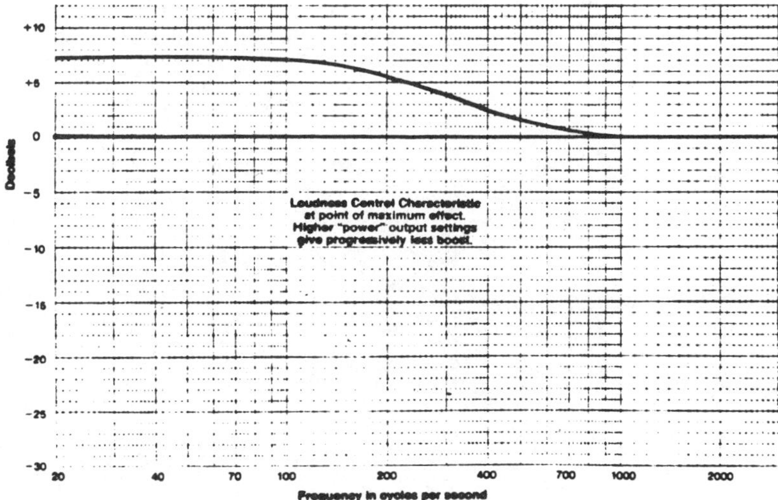

Loudness curve

The balance control adjusts the relative loudness of the left and right channels, to compensate for off-center listening positions (Courtesy Aiwa)

TONE CONTROLS AND EQUALIZERS

All but the least expensive systems generally let you control tone as well as volume. Tone controls let you compensate for frequency imbalances in tapes and broadcasts, turn down the highs when the tape or radio reception is noisy or distorted, and let you adjust the sound to your tastes.

A single control labelled "tone" usually just cuts the highs as you turn it down. This helps get rid of noise and distortion. It also gives the illusion of increased bass since, if less of the sound is treble then bass makes up more of what's left.

Separate bass and treble controls can either cut or boost either end of the frequency range. That gives you much more flexibility in shaping the sound the way you want it.

Some systems have three tone controls, usually in a separate control box. The third control is for the mid-range. That doesn't so much give you more control as make it more convenient. The mid-range control adjusts "presence", making soloists seem to stand out from the musical mix when it's turned up, and blend back into it when the control is turned down. On a two-control system, though, you can boost the presence by turning down the bass and treble, then raising the volume a bit to compensate.

Three-control systems are sometimes called "equalizers", but that term is usually reserved for systems with five, seven or even ten tonal controls, each covering a separate frequency band. Equalizers, too, are usually separate boxes (often combined with boosters or amplifiers), but some in-dash units have five-band equalizers built in.

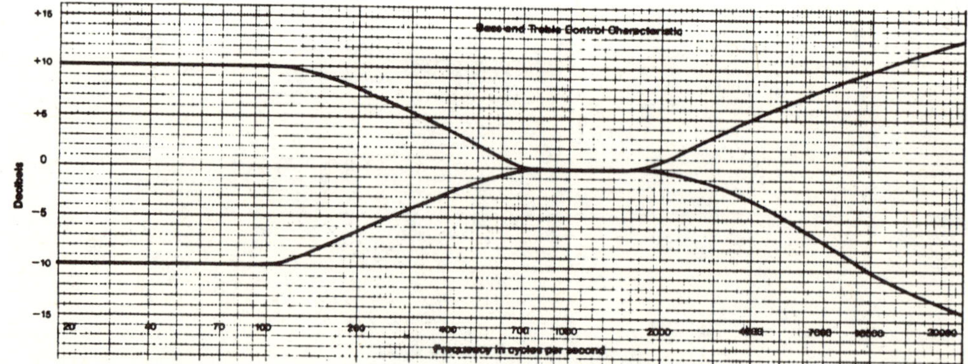

Bass and treble controls can boost or cut high and low frequencies up to the amounts shown, to partially overcome sonic problems, or to create a more pleasing frequency balance

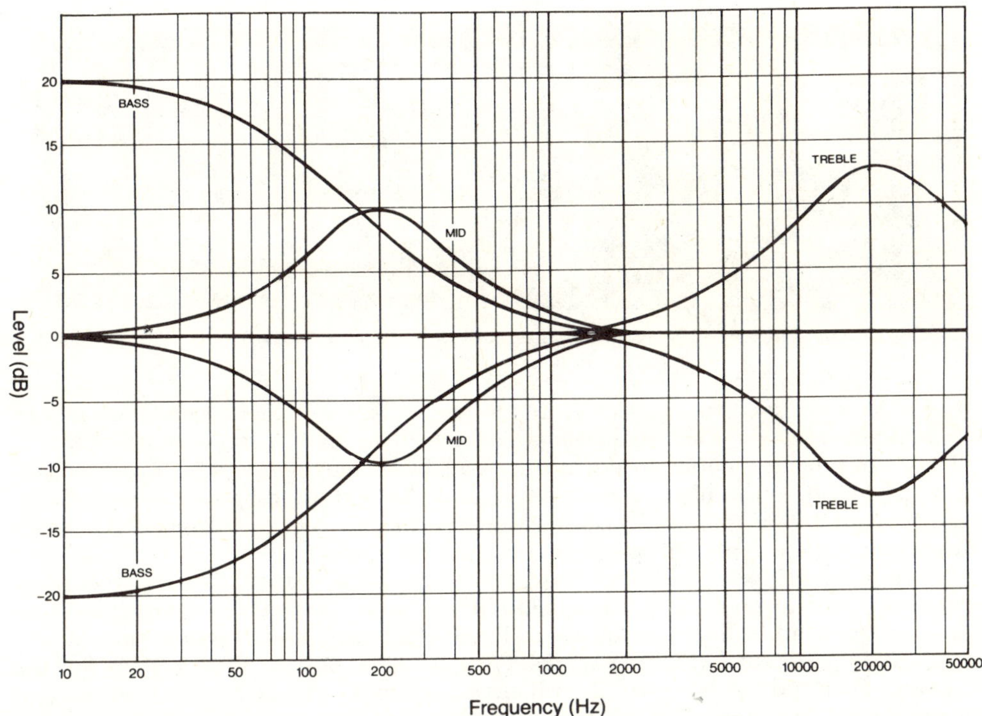

Some systems have a third tone control, to emphasize or de-emphasize midrange tones

Most equalizers are "graphic" types—that is, they have sliding controls whose positions effectively graph the frequency curve the equalizer is imposing on the sound. That creates a problem for the equipment designer, though: the longer the slide, the more precisely you can control the sound—but the shorter the slide, the smaller the equalizer can be, and the easier it is to fit it into a car.

Some designers choose compactness over controllability and just use short sliders—that's always the case when the equalizer is built into the in-dash unit. Other designers have chosen other solutions. A few use very long sliders, on equalizers designed to slide out of sight when you're not adjusting them. Some slant their sliders to fit longer ones diagonally into shorter panels. A very few use knobs in-

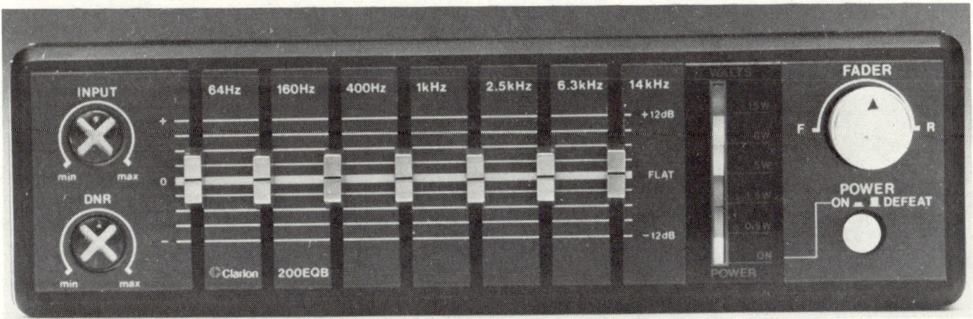

Multi-band equalizers like this can compensate more accurately for a wider range of sonic problems (Courtesy Clarion)

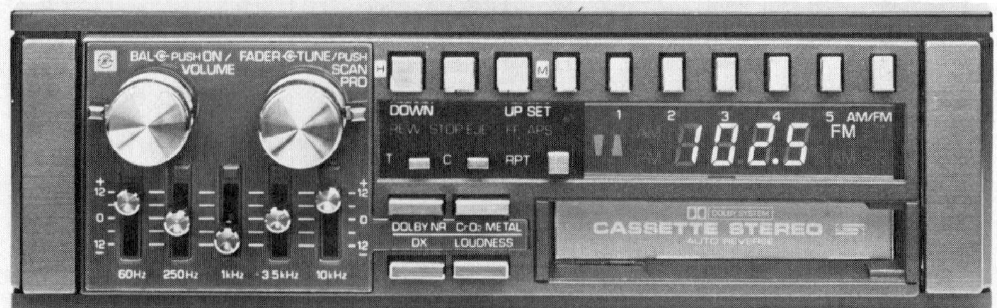

Some in-dash systems even have equalizers built in (Courtesy Fujitsu)

stead of sliders, since this gives effectively longer travel in less space: a knob with a 1-inch diameter gives about the same control precision as a three-inch slider.

How many bands should an equalizer have? That depends on what you want an equalizer for. If you want to use your equalizer like a super tone control, adjusting each tape or station to sound just the way you like it, then a five-band equalizer (the most common type) will probably be right for you.

If you want to use it to compensate for your car's and speakers' acoustical ups and downs, then you'll need more bands than that; about nine or ten is a good minimum, and up to thirty could be useful. In that case, you'd get best results by using test equipment (which some installers have) to set up your system for flat response, then hiding the controls so that your careful settings wouldn't be undone by passengers or others. The more bands, the more precisely you can control the sound, but the more you have to fuss around to do it.

Some equalizers, the "paragraphic" type, claim more control bands than they have controls—and with some justice. In graphic equalizers, the bands are fixed: one slider might, for instance, cover the two octaves above and below 250 Hz., or a range from 125 to 500 Hz. In paragraphic types, the bands can be moved, so that one slider could be used for the range centering on 250 Hz, or 200 Hz or 375 Hz, depending on where you set a switch.

Incidentally, there's no law stating that equalizer bands must be evenly spaced. Some home equalizers have several, closely-spaced bands in the bass (where equalizers can best help acoustics), a broad band in the midrange, and a single, narrow band in the high treble. This approach could be used in the car as well.

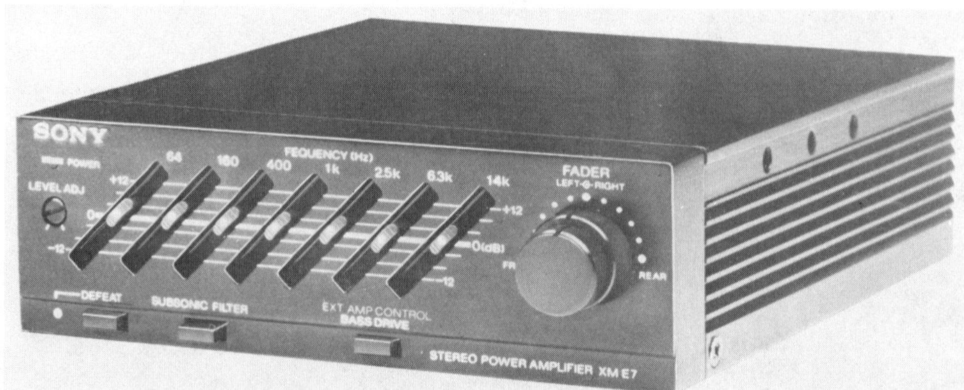

Equalizer controls with long travel give you finer control, but take up more room. Angling them helps keep the equalizer panel compact (Courtesy Sony)

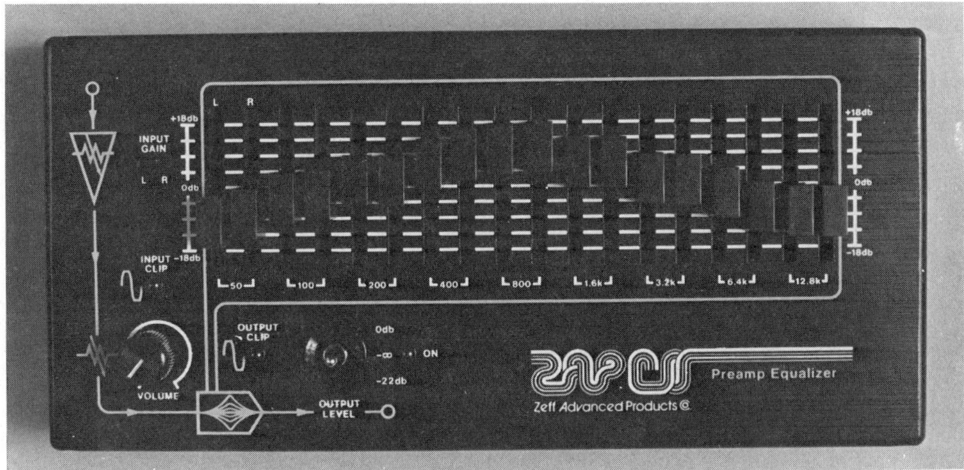

Complex equalizers, such as this one with separate left and right controls for each of its nine frequency bands, are best set to compensate for specific sonic problems, then left alone (Courtesy Zapco)

In addition to these variable controls, some systems have stepped tone adjustments, too. These are switches which boost bass or treble frequencies by fixed amounts, sometimes accompanied by switches which select the frequency at which the boost will take place.

Some equalizers slide out of sight after you've set them, so you won't accidentally change your settings (Courtesy Jensen)

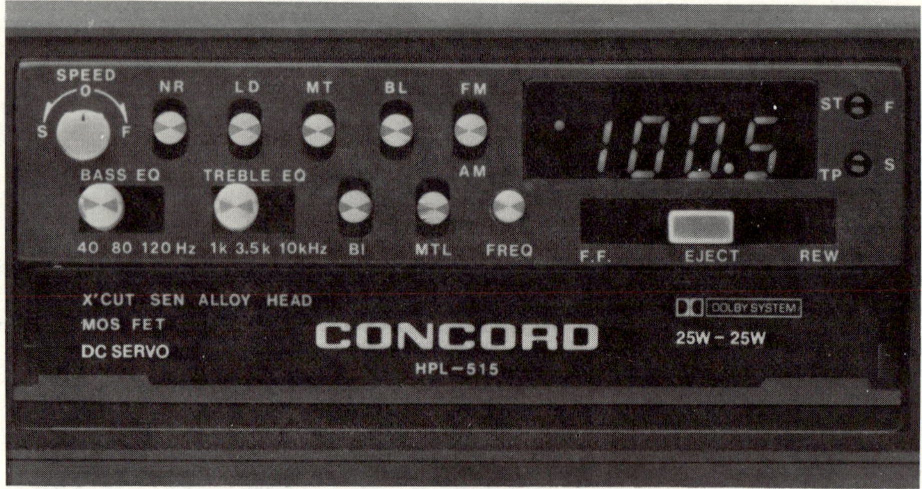

The "Bass EQ" and "Treble EQ" switches on this deck select which frequencies will be affected by the bass and treble controls (Courtesy Concord)

OTHER CONTROLS

Another common general sound control is a stereo/mono switch. Most car stereo systems automatically switch to a monophonic mode when receiving monophonic AM or FM broadcasts or radio signals too weak to be picked up well in stereo. And monophonic tapes also play monophonically, because both channels of the stereo playback head "read" the double-width, monophonic track.

Nonetheless, there are times when it pays to switch to mono manually. This usually occurs when multipath or other reception problems make a stereo broadcast hard to hear clearly while the signal is still strong enough to keep the tuner from switching to a blend or mono mode. It can also happen when people on both sides of the car are trying to hear all parts of a tape with unusually bad side-to-side recorded balance or unusually pronounced stereo separation.

All the above controls are common in home systems. One common home control you'll rarely find in a car, though, is a selector switch. In home systems, this switch is needed to choose one of several, separate signal sources (tuner, phono, tape deck, etc.) for listening. In the car, with only two sources (radio and tape) in the same unit, selection is usually automatic: turn on the system and the tuner plays; push in a tape, and you hear that instead; pull out the tape, and you hear radio again. This automation helps the driver concentrate on driving.

There are some variations, however. Since some listeners prefer not to hear a blast of radio each time they pull a tape out, some systems have "tuner-off" switches so that silence will follow withdrawal of the tape. A very few systems will automatically turn on if you insert a tape without first turning on the power switch, and turn off (without a peep from the tuner) when you remove the tape.

About the only place you will see selector switches is on separate-component systems, where all the signal sources are separate. And even here, smart designers have found ways to make source selection automatic.

Audio Specifications

The specification that gets the most attention from car-stereo buyers is power output, a specification which applies to amplifiers alone. But in order to understand what it really means, one must first understand three other specifications.

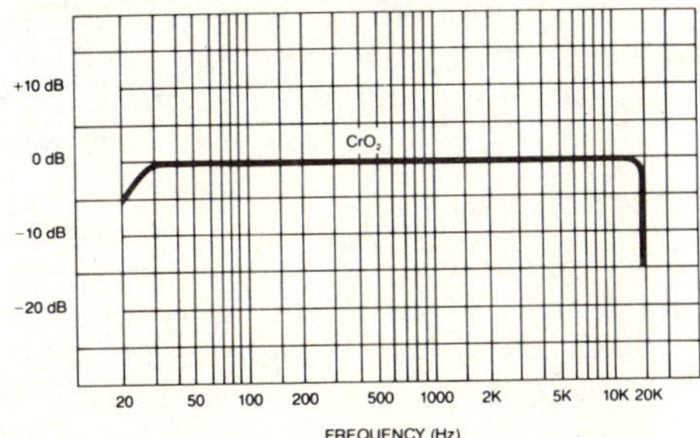

Good amplifiers have flat response (a); but curves like (b) are more typical (Courtesy Grundig)

These three, which basically determine sound quality, are frequency response, noise (or signal-to-noise ratio) and distortion. And unlike power, all of them apply to every part of a system's electronics—tape, tuner and amplifier sections.

FREQUENCY RESPONSE

Frequency response should define both the range of sound frequencies or tones a system can handle and how well it handles them. Ideally, the system would handle all sound frequencies (from 20 to 20,000 Hz) equally well, in which case its response could be stated as "20-20,000 Hz, ± 0 dB"—that is, there would be no variations in its response at any frequency between those points. A graph of that response would be a straight line.

With the exception of a few amplifiers, though, you're unlikely to find such a specification on car stereo equipment. A more realistic figure, especially for moderately-priced equipment, might be "40-11,000 Hz, +0/−4 dB", which would look like curve b in the figure.

The same curve could also be described as "40-10,500 Hz, ± 2 dB". Since the smaller the dB variation, the flatter the response, that figure tends to look a little better. It's a slightly less candid way to give the specification, though. The dB variation figures for frequency response should refer to variations above and below the response at some middle frequency (usually 1000 Hz), and are required to be so under EIA specifications for FM tuners and tape players). And while frequency response curves for loudspeakers can look a bit uneven, those for amplifiers, tuners and the better tape decks are generally straight lines that slope off at the top and bottom ends.

Frequency response curves tell you more than figures. You can derive several honest sets of figures from the same curve, depending on whether you choose to emphasize the size or flatness of the frequency response. The previous curve, for example, could be specified, with equal justice, as "flat from 100 to 8,000 Hz, ± 0 dB," or "30-11,000 Hz, +0/−6 dB".

You may also find a reference to frequency response for tone controls, such as "+/− 10 dB at 100 and 10kHz". Here, the larger the number the better, because what's being specified is the control's ability to vary the response.

NOISE

In most applications, it's not the absolute amount of noise that matters, but the amount relative to the sound level, which is why it's usually stated as the ratio between signal and noise, in dB. The higher this ratio, the better; noise is quite apparent when it's only 30 dB lower than the signal, relatively innocuous at −50 or 60 dB, and virtually inaudible at −80 dB.

Noise figures may be "weighted" or "unweighted." The ear is more sensitive to some noise frequencies than others, so many manufacturers count the most obnoxious frequencies more heavily and give less weight to the ones the ear is less sensitive to, according to a standard weighting curve (usually the "A" curve, though others are sometimes used). Weighted figures usually look a few dB better than unweighted ones because electronic circuits tend to be noisiest at frequencies which are relatively inaudible; but since weighted figures correspond more closely to what we hear, they're actually the more significant, even if more flattering, of the two.

DISTORTION

The signal that comes out of an amplifier, tuner or tape player should exactly match the signal that went into it. In practice, however, it never quite does. Every component in the system changes or "distorts" the sound a little; but the good ones do it so little that the difference is inaudible.

Distortion is measured as a percentage of the signal; the lower the percentage, the better the sound. In practice, anything under 1% is good, and anything under 0.1% is very good indeed.

There are many types of distortion. The one most commonly measured is "harmonic distortion," caused when sound equipment adds extra frequencies which are multiples (harmonics) of the frequencies which belong in the sound. This is usually called "total harmonic distortion," or "THD", to indicate that all harmonic frequencies are included in the measurement. THD is usually implied when specification sheets don't mention which kind of distortion they're specifying.

One may occasionally find specifications for "intermodulation distortion," or "IM." This is produced when sound equipment adds extra frequencies which are the sum or difference of frequencies belonging in the signal. For all practical purposes, acceptable limits for IM are just about the same as those for THD.

AMPLIFIER POWER OUTPUT

Power output is not only the most often mentioned specification in car stereo, it's also one of the most misunderstood. A system rated as "10 watts" might actually deliver as much power as another rated at 20 watts—or only as much as yet a third one that's rated at a mere 7 watts or so. To tell the difference, you have to read beyond the mere mention of watts, and see what the specifications are really trying to tell you.

The difference between these ratings has to do with distortion. Most amplifier circuits have fairly low distortion up to a certain power level; above that, you can get more power, but only with increased distortion, which increases at an accelerating rate as you push the amplifier harder.

For example, an amplifier might deliver anywhere up to 7 watts per channel at less than 1% distortion, deliver 10 watts at 5%, 15 watts at 10%, and 20 watts at 80%—after which, any attempt to squeeze more power from the amplifier squeezes out only more distortion, instead. The manufacturer can use any of these figures as his power rating, according to whether he preferred to stress high power or clean sound. All these ratings would be legal, and all are often used (though the 20-watt spec here would usually be called "maximum power").

There's a long tradition in the car-sound field, dating back to AM car radio days, of measuring power at the 10% distortion level. Since at one time, everybody did it that way (and since buyers in those days didn't understand about distortion), such power ratings were usually given only in watts, with no mention of distortion level. To this day, when a power rating makes no mention of distortion, it's usually safe to assume that it was measured at a distortion level of 10%.

Other companies rate their amplifier power at distortion levels of 1% or less. These companies almost invariably say so. Some companies list power both at 10% and at 1% or less, so you can compare their specifications with anybody else's, regardless of which system they use.

Distortion isn't the only factor to take into account, though. Frequency response and amplifier power are related, too. At the top and bottom of the frequency range, amplifier power drops off. And as the amplifier is driven to higher power levels, its frequency response diminishes. This is unfortunate, as high power is most often needed at low frequencies, where many amplifiers can't deliver it. So, to help you tell which amplifiers can deliver it down there, some makers also tell you what frequency range that power rating covers.

The EIA car-stereo rating standard states that the rating should not only specify the power, frequency range and distortion level, but also specify its power per channel (not the sum of all channels), and to what speaker impedance it applies. Since most car-stereo speakers have 4-ohm impedances, and since most amplifiers deliver more power at 4 ohms than at higher impedance, that figure is almost invariably four ohms. Thus, a typical EIA-standard specification would read something like:

10 watts per channel into 4 ohms, 30 to 18,000 Hz., at 0.7% THD

More elaborate versions of the specification might also state that the power was "minimum continuous average power, both channels driven." This means that: (1) the rated power is the minimum the amplifier will deliver under the specified conditions; (2) that it's continuously available, not just in short spurts, and (3) that it's available from both channels at once—not just from one at a time. You'll rarely see things stated this elaborately, though.

UNDERSTANDING TUNER PERFORMANCE

Dealers in home stereo equipment usually have specification sheets for the components they sell, to give you some idea of how well those components perform. Car stereo manufacturers and dealers have begun to do that, too, but those sheets aren't as widely available, and don't list performance in as much detail.

Ideally, those specifications would tell you everything you need to know about performance. In reality, specifications don't tell you everything. But they do give you a lot more comparative information than you could assemble from brief listening experience—especially if that experience is in a showroom, not out on the road. And, what the specifications tell you can be useful, if you know how to interpret them.

There were no agreed-upon measurement or specification standards until the Electronic Industries Association (EIA) published such standards in 1981.

That there was a need for such standards was apparent long before that—so much that, in 1979, a group of major manufacturers formed an Ad Hoc Committee to establish them. Those standards, themselves based on EIA home audio standards, formed the basis of the EIA's current standards for car stereo. You'll generally find that specifications which state that they're listed according to either Ad Hoc or EIA standards are among the most informative. Specifications covered by this standard will be marked with an asterisk (*) in the discussions that follow.

Tuner specifications may be listed many different ways, but most fall into three categories: sensitivity, other reception properties (selectivity, interference rejection, and capture ratio), and audio specifications (such as frequency response, noise and distortion). Experts differ on the relative importance of individual specifications; in April, 1982, Stereo Review magazine asked fourteen experts involved in FM tuner manufacture, testing or broadcasting, how they rated the importance of various FM tuner specifications for car and home use. Here's how they ranked them overall:

- AM suppression
- Sensitivity
- Capture Ratio
- Selectivity
- RF intermodulation distortion (see spurious-response rejection).

Radio manufacturers develop and test products in special labs like this, encased in metal screening to keep out stray radio signals (Courtesy Sparkomatic)

Sensitivity

A sensitivity specification tells you how strong a radio signal the tuner needs in order to achieve a given level of performance. Of all FM tuner specifications, it's the one most often listed, even though it's not necessarily the most important FM specification. Sensitivity is most important when you want to pick up weak or distant stations.

There are several different ways to measure sensitivity, depending on what level of performance is specified. A typical FM tuner's performance varies with the signal level coming from the antenna. That level may be given in two different units: microvolts (μV) and dBf (decibels referred to a power level of one femtowatt"). A femtowatt is 0.000000000000001 watt. Both units as well as microvolt and dBf equivalents are discussed later in this section. (Don't expect to find such detailed diagrams often on car-stereo spec sheets; they're given here for illustration purposes.)

At very low radio (RF) signal levels (here, about one microvolt), the tuner has very little audio output (solid line) and its noise (dashed line) is almost as strong as its audio output. You might be able to detect such a weak signal, but you certainly wouldn't want to listen to it.

But as the station's signal strength increases, the tuner's output rises and its noise falls. It takes much less signal strength to reach maximum output than to reach minimum noise, however. In this example, the maximum audio output occurs at about 2.5 microvolts (19.2 dBf), so that figure is defined as the tuner's "limiting sensitivity."

It takes 100 microvolts (71.2 dBf) of signal, though, to bring the noise down to its rated minimum of −70 dB. Above 100 microvolts further increases in signal strength make no difference in tuner performance . . . until the signal becomes so

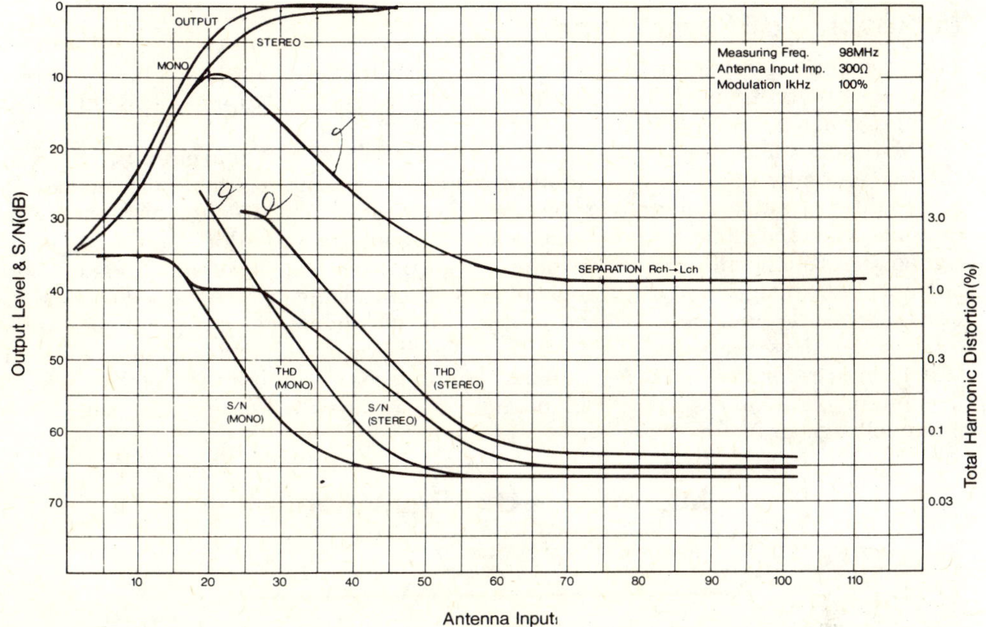

Tuner performance curve. Note how, as radio signal gets stronger, the tuner's audio output rises and noise decreases, and how noise decreases more rapidly in mono than in stereo (Courtesy Nakamichi)

strong that it overloads the tuner and performance starts deteriorating. (Such overload should rarely happen, with good tuners.)

"Usable sensitivity*", which is the sensitivity specification most often cited for car-stereo tuners, is measured at the point where the tuner's noise has fallen 30 dB below its audio signal output. For this receiver, that requires an RF signal input of about 2.5 microvolts (19.2 dBf). It's pure coincidence, though, that this is the same as the limiting sensitivity; if the slope of the noise curve had been different (as it is on many tuners), the two figures would have been different.

You might listen to a 2.5-μV signal if you really had to hear that program. But otherwise, you'd pass it by, for a 30-dB signal-to-noise ratio is still far too noisy for comfortable listening. (The higher the signal-to-noise ratio, the lower the noise.)

When the FM signal strength increases to about 6 μV (26.7 dBf) the noise decreases even further, to -50 dB. That's not as quiet as this tuner can get, but it's quiet enough for comfortable listening. Many specification sheets therefore state this "50-dB quieting sensitivity*" figure, too. More of them should: it's actually one of the two most revealing measures of tuner sensitivity.

The other most revealing one is the 50-dB quieting sensitivity for stereo signals. Since most listening is done in stereo when signal conditions permit, this figure tells most about the tuner's sensitivity under normal listening conditions. And since reception is always noisier in stereo, it's a more rigorous test, too. For home tuners, the stereo figure is usually about 20 dBf worse than the mono one.

With any sensitivity measurement based on signal strength, higher sensitivity is expressed in lower figures. In other words, the more sensitive tuner can get by with a lower signal input.

Microvolts, dBf and Ohms

The preceding information about sensitivity measurements applies equally to home tuner sensitivity figures. The only difference between the two, in fact, is the meaning of the signal strength in microvolts.

FM tuners for home use generally have "300-ohm" antenna circuits; those for the car generally use 75-ohm antenna circuits. For an input signal of given power, a 300-ohm antenna will deliver twice the voltage that a 75-ohm one will. That doesn't make the 300-ohm antenna twice as good, though. Both antennas, if designed the same, will deliver the same signal power. But power depends on both current and voltage; and the ratio between them changes with impedance: a 75-ohm antenna delivers only half the voltage, but it delivers twice the current, so the total power stays the same. That can fool you if you try comparing microvolt sensitivity figures for home and car tuners. A mobile tuner with a usable sensitivity of five microvolts, for example, will be only as sensitive a home tuner with a 10-microvolt figure.

Microvolt to dBf Equivalents

Microvolts (75-ohm)	Microvolts (300-ohm)	dBf
0.50	1.00	5.20
0.55	1.10	6.03
0.60	1.20	6.78
0.65	1.30	7.48
0.70	1.40	8.12
0.75	1.50	8.72
0.80	1.60	9.28
0.85	1.70	9.81
0.90	1.80	10.31
0.95	1.90	10.78
1.00	2.00	11.22
1.05	2.10	11.64
1.10	2.20	12.05
1.15	2.30	12.43
1.20	2.40	12.80
1.25	2.50	13.16
1.30	2.60	13.50
1.35	2.70	13.83
1.40	2.80	14.14
1.45	2.90	14.45
1.50	3.00	14.74
1.75	3.50	16.08
2.00	4.00	17.24
2.25	4.50	18.26
2.50	5.00	19.18
2.75	5.50	20.01
3.00	6.00	20.76
3.25	6.50	21.46
3.50	7.00	22.10
3.75	7.50	22.70
4.00	8.00	23.26
4.25	8.50	23.79
4.50	9.00	24.28
4.75	9.50	24.75
5.00	10.00	25.20
5.00	10.00	25.20
5.50	11.00	26.03
6.00	12.00	26.78
6.50	13.00	27.48

Microvolt to dBf Equivalents

Microvolts (75-ohm)	Microvolts (300-ohm)	dBf
7.00	14.00	28.12
7.50	15.00	28.72
8.00	16.00	29.28
8.50	17.00	29.81
9.00	18.00	30.31
9.50	19.00	30.78
10.00	20.00	31.22
10.50	21.00	31.64
11.00	22.00	32.05
11.50	23.00	32.43
12.00	24.00	32.80
12.50	25.00	33.16
13.00	26.00	33.50
13.50	27.00	33.83
14.00	28.00	34.14
14.50	29.00	34.45
15.00	30.00	34.74
15.50	31.00	35.03
16.00	32.00	35.30
16.50	33.00	35.57
17.00	34.00	35.83
17.50	35.00	36.08
18.00	36.00	36.33
18.50	37.00	36.56
19.00	38.00	36.80
19.50	39.00	37.02
20.00	40.00	37.24
20.50	41.00	37.46
21.00	42.00	37.66
21.50	43.00	37.87
22.00	44.00	38.07
22.50	45.00	38.26
23.00	46.00	38.46
23.50	47.00	38.64
24.00	48.00	38.82
24.50	49.00	39.00
25.00	50.00	39.18

Comparison of signal levels in (left to right) microvolts across 75 ohms (car radios), microvolts across 300 ohms (home radios) and dbf (both)

If you measure signal power instead of signal voltage your ratings will be the same for 75-ohm or 300-ohm circuits, which shows that the two sensitivities are the same—in this case, 25.2 dBf, according to the standard unit used for FM signal power measurements.

Measuring power instead of voltage puts all tuner types on an equal footing. But dBf measurements have more significance than that. Because they're logarithmic (as all decibel or "dB" figures are), they emphasize the real meaning of differences in sensitivity. A difference in tuner sensitivity of 3 dBf always means one tuner is twice as sensitive as the other, whether the figures we're comparing are 8.8 and 11.8 or 33 and 36 dBf. But a sensitivity difference of 0.5 μV, while quite significant when we're comparing 1.5 and 2.0 μV (14.7 and 17.2 dBf), is of almost no significance when comparing 35 with 35.5 μV (42.09 and 42.22 dBf).

Muting and Stereo/Mono

While the preceding graph shows what the various sensitivity ratings mean, it also shows how two of the features mentioned later work: Muting and the Stereo/Mono switch.

Note, first, the muting curve. Performance with signals weaker than 11 μV (21.7 dBf) only holds true if the Muting switch is off. When the switch is on, muting starts rapidly cutting off the audio output (signal and noise alike) as radio signal levels drop below that level. "Usable sensitivity" and "limiting sensitivity" no longer apply: by the time the RF signal has fallen to that level, the tuner's output is cut off. The muting circuit's main job is to make sure you don't hear a blast of noise where there's no signal. But in practice, it makes sure you don't hear weak signals, either.

Signals weak enough to fall below the muting point are too weak to be heard well in stereo. So, when the Muting is switched off to let you hear such stations, the stereo circuits are switched off as well, as indicated by the "Mono" arrow on the diagram. This is also the point where this particular radio's automatic stereo circuits switch between mono and stereo.

Other Reception Specifications

Many car-stereo manufacturers give sensitivity ratings, though usually just "usable" sensitivity. Only a few manufacturers cover other areas of tuner performance in their specifications. Selectivity and capture ratio aren't the ones experts rank as most important, but they are the ones most often given in car-stereo spec sheets.

SELECTIVITY

This is a measure of how well the tuner can pick out the one station you want, rejecting all those on nearby frequencies.

The FCC tries to arrange station frequencies and locations so that, for most listeners, there will be few if any stations on adjacent channels (such as 98.3 and 98.5) and as few as possible on alternate channels (such as 98.3 and 98.7), to minimize interference between them. So "adjacent-channel selectivity" measures a tuner's ability to reject FM signals 200 kHz (one FM channel) away from the frequency it's tuned to, and "alternate-channel selectivity*" measures its rejection of signals 400 kHz (two channels) away.

Since alternate-channel interference is the more likely of the two (and since alternate-channel selectivity figures are always higher), most tuner manufacturers give this figure for selectivity. A few give the adjacent-channel figure, too. And one or two may give only the adjacent-channel one.

An alternate-channel selectivity of "60 dB" means that a signal 400 kHz from the desired station would have to be 60 dB stronger than that station to create substantial interference. The higher the figure, the better, but adjacent-channel figures will always be lower than the alternate-channel ones.

CAPTURE RATIO

One of FM's advantages over AM is that you rarely hear two FM stations simultaneously, even when you're in an area where the signals from two stations on the same frequency overlap. That's because FM tuners can "capture" the stronger signal and ignore the weaker one.

Capture also helps FM tuners ignore "multipath" signal reflections (which cause distortion in FM). Those reflections are also additional, weaker signals on the same frequency. (If a reflection is stronger than the main signal, which can happen, the tuner will capture that reflection and ignore the direct signal and the other reflections; but that's just about as good.)

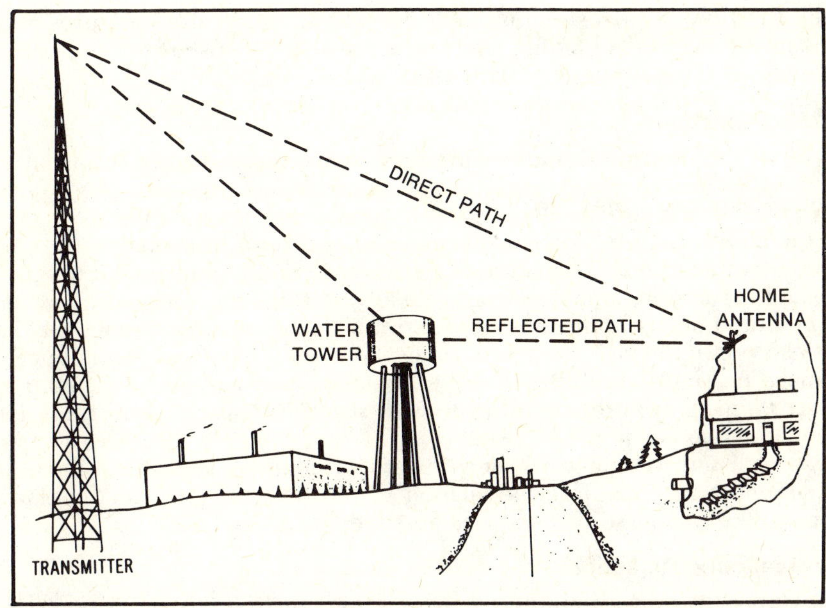

Multipath interference occurs when a receiver picks up both a direct signal and one or more reflections of it. In TV, this creates "ghosts"; in FM, distortion (Courtesy EIA)

"Capture ratio*" measures how well the tuner does this. It states what ratio between the stronger and weaker signals (in decibels, or "dB") will permit the tuner to suppress the weaker one by 30 dB. As with signal-to-noise ratio, 30 dB is not enough to make the suppressed signal inaudible, but enough to let you clearly make out the stronger one. So the lower this number, the better.

CIVILIZED REJECTIONS

Occasionally, car-stereo makers specify (in dB) the tuner's ability to reject various types of undesirable signal or interference. These rejection (also known as "suppression" or "response ratio") figures are most important to the city listener. The higher these figures, the better. In case you wonder just what they mean, here's a brief summary:

*AM Rejection

Multipath reflections can make the strength of an FM signal fluctuate the way an AM signal's strength normally does. AM rejection measures the tuner's ability to ignore such fluctuations, so it's probably most important as an indirect indication of

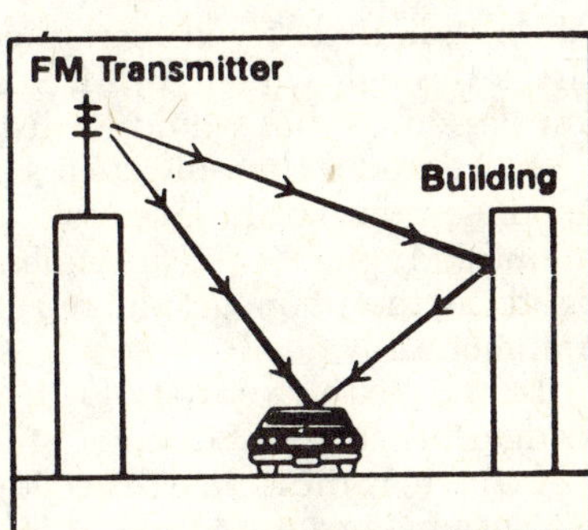

Capture ratio is the minimum ratio between 2 signal strengths on the same frequency that allows the tuner to suppress the weaker by 30 db so both signals will be heard at once

how well the tuner will resist multipath distortion. But it also measures resistance to slight mistuning, signal fading and flutter caused, for instance, by a passing airplanes.

*Multipath Rejection

A direct (but seldom stated) indication of resistance to multipath distortion.

*Spurious-Response Rejection

This is the ability to reject signals on frequencies distant from that of the station to which the radio is tuned. Two of these (image rejection and i.f. rejection) are sometimes listed separately, and are covered below. A third is strong-signal overload.

When your tuner is bombarded with strong signals, strange things can happen: stations can pop up at several points along the dial, or you may get strange signals which make no sense at all. These are spurious responses—and the better a tuner can reject them, the better it will cope with strong signals, such as those found in metropolitan areas.

Instead of listing resistance to such overload, some specification sheets list the overload's effect, as "r.f. intermodulation distortion" or "cross-modulation". This number should, of course be as low as possible.

*Image-Response Rejection

This measures the tuner's ability to reject signals in the aircraft band. It matters mostly to those who live or drive near airports.

*IF-Response Rejection

This measures the tuner's ability to reject signals at 10.7 MHz, the frequency of its internal "intermediate-frequency" oscillator.

Other Specifications

Many specifications (such as stereo separation* or crosstalk, distortion, signal-to-noise and frequency response*) apply to every part of a stereo system, not just the tuner. Those will be covered in later sections. The few remaining specifications which apply specifically to FM are almost never found in descriptions of car-stereo equipment.

The main thing to remember is that it's not always true that the higher the number the better the performance. That is true for the various interference rejection specifications, for selectivity, signal-to-noise ratios, and for stereo separation. But with sensitivity, capture ratio and distortion, the lower the number, the better.

CASSETTES AND OTHER FORMATS

With radio, what you hear is controlled by the policies of the radio stations in the areas through which you drive. So there's always been a demand for some mobile music source that would let listeners control what they hear.

For decades the only such source was the phonograph. Chrysler tried a specially-engineered record player for automobile use in the Fifties, but the special records required brought the experiment to a quick end. Tape wasn't as vulnerable to bumpy roads as the phonograph, but asking drivers to thread it through the machine was impractical.

In the Sixties, easy-to-load tape formats were developed—first the 4-track cartridge format (now defunct, though broadcast stations still use one of its descendents), then the 8-track cartridge (still around, but fading), and finally the cassette (today's major tape format), although systems using similar, but smaller "microcassettes" are beginning to appear. And in a few years we may have record players in our dashboards once again, using new, digital recordings of super fidelity.

Tape today offers not only musical choice but higher fidelity than FM radio, far higher fidelity than AM. It was tape and these virtues that sparked the car-stereo boom.

Since tape is so popular and so important, manufacturers have devoted a great deal of effort to making it not only as good, but as convenient as possible. That gives you a wide range of tape features from which to choose.

CASSETTE'S COMPETITORS

With several recording formats now available and others in the works, which should you choose? The cassette is the most popular; but there's more to consider than popularity alone. Each has virtues and vices of its own.

Eight-Track

The 8-track cartridge system was originally developed for the car and was for years, the most popular tape format for automotive listening in the U.S. That popularity was largely due to its rapid adoption by Detroit for factory-installed car stereos. (The rest of the world didn't get into car stereo till cassette was well along in its development; so cassette has always outsold 8-track in most countries outside of the U.S.)

Eight-track cartridges use tape one-quarter inch wide, in endless loops that can recirculate continuously to keep the music running as long as you like. The tape moves at 3¾ inches per second, a speed high enough for reasonable fidelity. The music is recorded on the tape in four pairs of tracks. Each time the tape completes one round and gets back to its beginning, the tape head moves down about $^{1}/_{16}$ inch to read the next pair of tracks. After it's played the last pair, the head moves

Loading an 8-track cartridge. As on many cassette units, the dial swings back to admit the tape (Courtesy Sparkomatic)

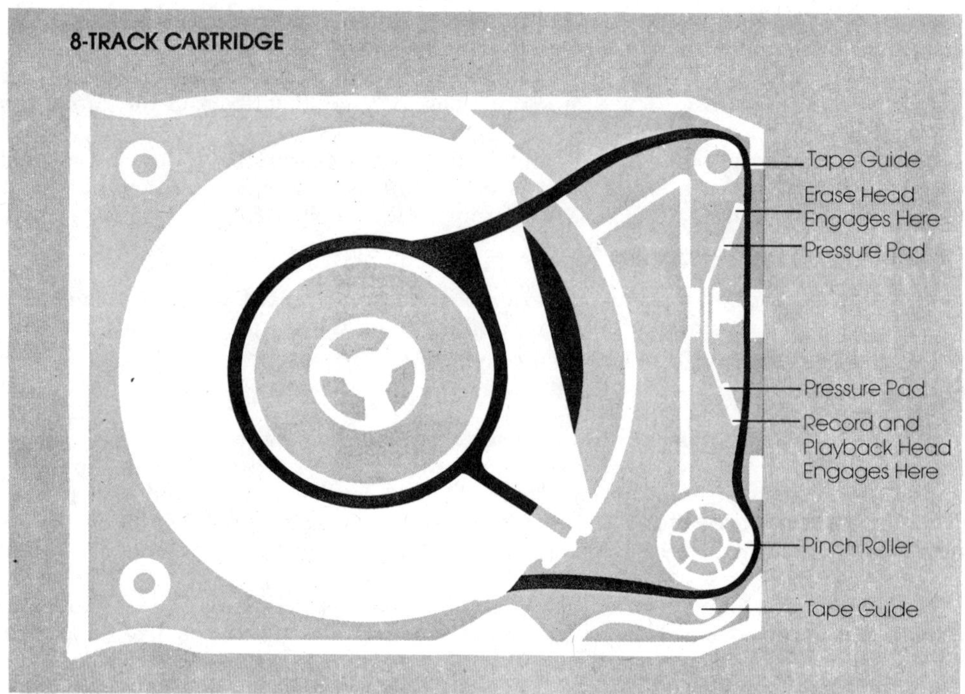

Inside the 8-track cartridge, tape moves in a continuous loop

back to the first pair of tracks and plays them again, continuing till you pull out the cartridge. The music isn't quite non-stop—there are three brief interruptions at track-switching times.

The 8-track system has some other disadvantages, too. You can't rewind a tape to its beginning, though you can usually shift back to the first track and can often fast-forward to the head of the tape. Not all 8-track players have fast-forward, and it's not very fast on those that do. The cartridges are also bulky, and all that track-switching can throw the heads out of alignment. And far less attention has been paid to improving the sound of 8-track than has been paid to improving cassette.

As a result, though 8-track is still popular in many areas of the country, its pop-

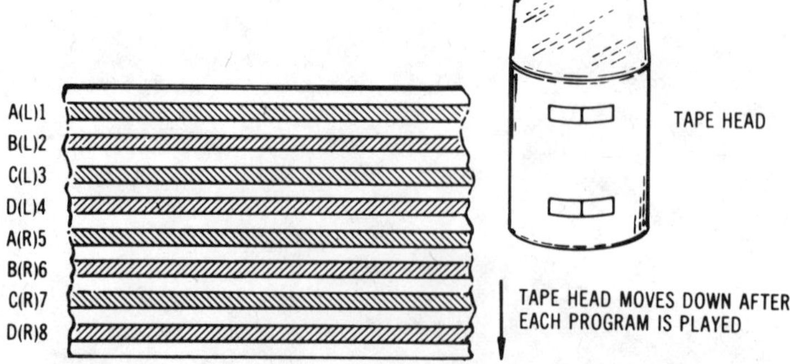

Only two of the eight tracks are played at once; the tape head moves down each time the complete loop of tape is played, to play the next pair of tracks. After four pairs, it moves back to the top again (Courtesy EIA)

ularity is on the wane. Most manufacturers now offer many more cassette than 8-track players, and many have dropped the 8-track format altogether.

This also means that fewer and fewer recordings are commercially available on 8-track, limiting your choice of material. And though home 8-track players are still in service (letting you use the same tapes at home that you play in the car), home recorders for 8-track tape have virtually disappeared from the market.

You might consider 8-track if you already own a large number of tapes in this format. Even then, however, you're probably better off in the long run buying a cassette unit for your car and a recording cassette deck for your home, then copying all your 8-track tapes onto cassette.

The Cassette

Today, cassettes are everywhere: we walk along the streets listening through headphones to pocket-sized cassette players; we carry portable systems to play stereo cassettes on picnics; and, we have cassette decks in our car-stereo systems.

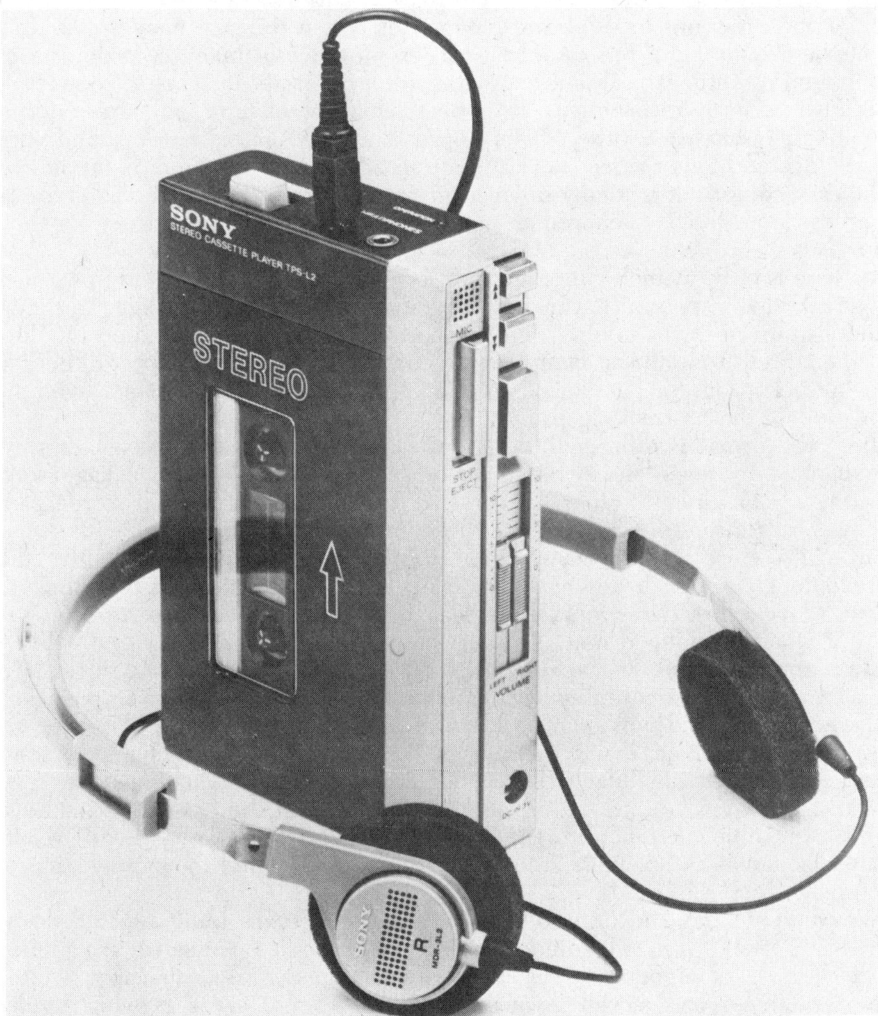

Large and small portables let us play cassettes anywhere, not just at home or on the car (Courtesy Sony)

A typical combination FM/AM/cassette unit for the car (Courtesy Fujitsu)

To make tapes for them all, we have high-fidelity cassette decks from which to record radio programs or duplicate records for use in the car. Easy home taping is one of the keystones of the cassette's success; for, while many recordings are also available on cassette tape, home taping is still a necessity for most listeners.

Because cassette recording is so popular, makers of tape and tape equipment compete to outdo each other. This popularity pays off in better sound, greater convenience and lower price, not to mention a far wider choice of equipment.

The cassette format is totally different from the 8-track cartridge. The tape is not an endless loop, but is anchored at each end to hubs which are turned by the tape deck.

The tape is only $^1/_7$ inch wide, and moves at $1\frac{7}{8}$ inches per second (ips), one half the 8-track tape's speed. That means less tape and a smaller package. In theory, it should also mean lower fidelity; but with competition concentrated on this format, it has benefited from almost every tape recording advance in the past fifteen years, while 8-track progress has stagnated. So the cassette actually offers even better sound, today, than 8-track does.

The track format is different, too. In 8-track, the two tracks of each stereo pair are separated by three other tracks, for better "separation"—less leakage between one stereo track and the other. In cassette, the two tracks of each stereo pair are side by side, running in the opposite direction from the other pair.

Pairing the stereo tracks this way may cut down stereo separation slightly (though improvements in tape heads have made up for most if not all of this loss), but it ensures that most of the "crosstalk" or leakage, is between the two stereo channels, where it won't be noticed much, rather than between tracks carrying totally unrelated program material.

It also ensures compatibility with monophonic, portable cassette recorders. A mono recorder's head will span both stereo tracks. So when you play your stereo tapes on such a player, it will pick up all the sound from both channels; the only difference in what you hear will be the blending of both channels through one speaker. And when you play your monophonic tapes in the car, both channels will get the same information from the wider, mono track; so you'll hear everything clearly through both speakers, though without the channel-to-channel differences which make it stereo.

Two conveniences and one potential inconvenience are built into the design of the cassette itself. One convenience is more compact size. Cassettes are about one-fourth the size of eight-track cartridges, which means you can carry about four times as many—even more, if your car has nooks and crannies which will hold cassettes but not the larger cartridges.

The other convenience, and the potential inconvenience, stem from the fact that

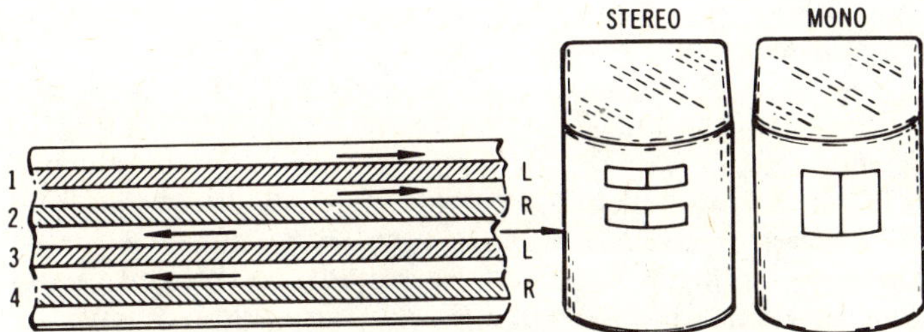

In cassette, tape moves from one hub to another; when it's all played, either the tape is flipped over or the deck reverses direction to play the other side

cassette tapes are not endless loops like 8-track cartridge tapes; the tape plays through from one side to the other, then must be played back in the opposite direction if you want to hear its other side.

The convenience in that is better tape handling. Freed from the endless-loop format, cassette tapes can be rapidly wound, forward or back, so you can quickly get to the part you want to hear; and since the tape is anchored at both ends, finding the beginning is easy.

The potential inconvenience is having to remove the tape and flip it over to hear the other side, instead of having continuous music, as with 8-track. But shortly after the first cassette decks for the car came out, models with auto-reverse, which automatically played both sides of the tape, made their appearance. And today, many such models are available at prices well below $200.

At the moment, the case for the cassette is a compelling one—but at least two competitors are in the wings.

The Microcassette

As the name implies, a microcassette is much like a regular cassette, only smaller. The tape layout is basically the same, with the tape winding from one hub to an-

Players for tiny microcassette tapes such as this, are coming soon (Courtesy Matsushita)

other. The tape size and track layout are the same, too. But the tape moves at only half the speed of ordinary cassette tape, $^{15}/_{16}$ ips. Halving the speed lets the microcassette get the same playing time from half as much tape, which can then fit into a far smaller cassette—about one-fourth the size of regular cassettes.

Halving the speed also cuts the fidelity, of course. So it wasn't practical to use microcassettes for music until such developments as metal tapes and improved noise reduction systems became available. Since regular cassettes take advantage of the same advances, they'll still have the edge in sound quality. But microcassettes are so much smaller that they're expected to make big inroads in the portable stereo market, and at least some inroads in the car-sound market, too.

Small size cuts two ways, of course. Because micro tapes are so small, you can carry a lot more of them conveniently. But that small size also limits the amount of information that can be printed on the label, and makes those labels harder to read (especially in a moving car). Those tapes are about as small as can be conveniently handled, too—future micro tapes may be longer, but they'll probably get no smaller.

Because micro tape is new, there will be but a limited choice of both tapes and equipment for the next few years.

The new, digital Compact Discs were deliberately made small enough to fit dashboard players of the future

The Compact Disc

A new sound medium, the compact digital disc, is on its way. Because it's digital, it will have far greater fidelity than any earlier home music medium. And because it's compact (the discs are only 4.7 inches in diameter) you'll probably be able to play it in your car, as well. That, in fact, is one of the reasons this size was chosen. And these discs and players are far less vulnerable to vibration than regular phonograph discs are, because a laser, not a needle in a groove, "reads" the discs, locked onto the spiralling signal path by automatic servo-mechanisms.

There are some problems to be solved, of course. The main one is expense: it will probably be at least the middle to late 1980's before the cost of digital players comes down anywhere near as low as the cost of cassette players. Another is that, for the first few years of digital, there will be relatively few titles available on such discs—and you won't be able to make up for it by recording your own.

The last, least problem is a paradox: the digital disc may actually have too much fidelity for the car. Its "dynamic range", from the quietest sound it can reproduce without noise to the loudest it can reproduce without distortion, will be so great that it won't be possible to hear it all while driving. If you set the volume high enough to hear the quiet passages, the loud ones will blast you away—and if you set the loud ones to a level you can stand, the quiet ones may be buried in road noise. That's actually a trivial problem, for it's easy to fit an automotive digital player with a compressor circuit to reduce dynamic range to listenable levels.

Why have a digital disc player in the car at all, if you can't take full advantage of its fidelity? Because it will let you get double use from your digital discs, playing them both at home and on the road, without the nuisance of having to make separate, taped copies for the car.

The tape deck and tuner can be removed and taken to a remote unit in the home

Features and Specifications

Since cassette (and possibly microcassette) are likely to be the dominant music media for car use over the next few years, let's start with the features that relate to them. Eight-track features will be covered at the chapter's end. (At this early date, digital-disc features can only be surmised.)

CASSETTE FEATURES

Moving and Handling Tape

The major features in any tape deck are the ones concerned with moving the tape: the controls for Play, Stop, Fast-Forward, Rewind, Reverse, and so on.

Actually, there are no Play or Stop controls on most mobile tape decks. You just push in the tape and it starts playing and shuts the tuner off; you stop play with the Eject control (whereupon the tuner comes back on, except in occasional models whose tuner sections can be shut off separately).

In the context of the car, that's logical: you wouldn't normally push the tape in unless you wanted to hear it, and it isn't wise to stop the tape and leave it in place. If you forgot the tape was there and parked in the hot sun, the heat might warp the cassette so badly that you'd never get it out again.

There are a few exceptions to this. Some in-car decks have had Play, Stop and Pause controls because they could not only play but also record tapes. Such decks have never sold well in the U.S., however, and are now almost impossible to find.

Not all decks play the tape as soon as it's pushed in. At least one company offers a feature called "cassette standby", which actually, only loads the tape half way: the cassette shell is in position, but the tape head (which senses the magnetically recorded impulses on the tape) and the pinch roller (which presses the tape against the rotating "capstan" that moves the tape in playback are not. They move into position only when the station you're tuned to fades away, so you'll continue to hear the music you want.

Fast Forward and Rewind have their exceptions, too. Some, very low-priced decks have only fast-forward or rewind, but not both. On other inexpensive decks, these controls may not lock in place, so that you have to hold them till the tape gets where you want it. Locking fast-forward and rewind controls are worth a little extra cost, though. Having to hold a fast-wind control down and mentally calculate how far to wind is only a minor nuisance at home, but it can distract a driver's attention just a bit too much on the road.

One other variant to look for: not all decks with locking fast-wind do the same things when they reach the tape's ends. Auto-reversing decks usually start playing the tape's other side. Decks without that feature usually shut their motors off when the tape is fast-forwarded to its end; they may do the same when it's rewound to its beginning, but they may also be designed to start playing the tape for you, at that point.

Automatic Features

All the basic functions—play, fast-wind, and even eject—have been automated in various ways to make them more convenient.

Take auto-eject, for example. Having to eject the tape to stop playing it ensures that you won't leave it in place when you switch back to radio; in fact, most systems switch automatically to the tuner when you eject the tape. But it doesn't ensure that you won't forget it's tape you're listening to and leave the tape in place when you turn the power off. That's why more and more systems automatically protect the tape by ejecting it whenever the power is shut off, whether by the system's switch or the ignition key; some also eject the tape when it's finished playing.

This not only keeps the tape from warping in place, but also prevents the prob-

Cassettes left in a car under the summer sun can warp (upper two cassettes), causing tape to jam or, worse, the cassette to jam inside the player. Compare undistorted tape at bottom

Fast-forward and rewind controls (commonly marked with double arrows, as here) let you skip over unwanted portions of the tape (Courtesy Clarion)

lem of "flat spots" forming on the rubber pinch roller. That roller presses the tape against the rotating "capstan" which moves the tape during playback. If the roller isn't absolutely round, the tape's speed fluctuates, making it sound wavery (a problem known as "wow and flutter"). Leaving the tape in place with the system off can affect the tape adversely, too.

Auto-loading is found on many systems with auto-eject. This is a difference you're more likely to feel than see—instead of making you push the tape into place, the deck gently whisks it from your hands when it's half-way in, and gently loads it into position for you. It feels luxurious, but its main advantage is its controlled loading pressure. You might push the tape in too far, and disturb the alignment of the head or other components in the deck; the auto-loader won't.

Auto-reverse brings cassette decks the one major convenience of the eight-track system: continuous music. When one side of the tape has ended, the tape reverses direction and begins to play the other side. Without that, you'd have to eject the tape (though some decks do that for you), flip it over, and press it in again.

Most systems with auto-reverse have manual-reverse buttons so you can switch to the other side of the tape without playing it all the way through. Most also continue playing the tape back and forth continuously until you stop it; few, if any car stereos give you the option of playing the tape through one full cycle, then stopping it for you.

While auto-reverse has been finding its way into ever less expensive models, you may be surprised to find it missing from some high-priced, high-performance decks. That's because some manufacturers feel that auto-reverse compromises tape-deck performance; others, though, feel that such compromises aren't audible. Since some stereos with auto-reverse outperform some others without it, you'll have to let your ears decide.

If you want continuous music without sonic compromise, want to save a few dollars, or both, you might consider a model with "auto repeat." When one side of the tape plays through on such a deck, it automatically rewinds itself and plays through once again. Make sure you can shut that feature off, though. Sometimes, you might prefer to flip the tape to the other side rather than hear it yet again.

Search

Winding to the beginning or end of the tape is simple. But how do you wind to a particular place on the tape? In the home, you usually watch a counter to see how far you're winding. That's not too practical in the car, where your eyes should be on the road (though at least one car stereo system does have a counter). Instead, many of today's decks have "music finders" which automatically stop fast-winding the tape at each gap between selections. In Rewind, this takes you right back to the beginning of the current selection—or back to the one before, if you hit the control again. In fast-forward, it takes you to the start of the next tune, and to the one after that if you press it again, much like the "search" controls on some tuners.

You may also find a variation on this which works like a tuner's "scan" control, playing a few seconds's worth of each selection as it finds it. That feature has only started appearing in home decks, so far, but it makes even more sense in the car, so it's likely to be incorporated into car systems soon.

Music sensors (for which almost every manufacturer has his own name and abbreviation) are more useful on pop music tapes than on classical ones. Pop tapes have more and shorter tunes per side. And music sensors (which actually sense the silences between selections) sometimes stop the tape when they sense quiet passages in the music; classical music is full of such passages, while today's pop has comparatively few of them. If you listen to many classical tapes, you should make sure that any system you buy with a music sensor also lets you fast-wind the tape uninterruptedly—as the vast majority do.

Correcting the Tape's Sound

Modern car-stereo decks often have two switches whose function is to improve tape's sound quality. One affects the tape's frequency response, while the other reduces noise.

The first switch, often labelled "Metal/Normal," "EQ" or "120/70", changes the frequency balance of the system to match that recorded on different tape types. Tapes are never recorded with flat frequency response. Instead, they're recorded with boosted highs and diminished lows, then played back with boosts and cuts that restore the natural frequency balance, a process called "equalization."

Tapes made with ferric oxide (which includes most older and most inexpensive tapes, as well as many premium-quality ones) sound best when recorded and played back with a "type I" or "120-microsecond" equalization curve. Since that was the only equalization curve in use for many years, it's called "Normal", the way manual transmissions are sometimes still called "standard" in an era when most cars have automatics.

Newer, higher-fidelity tapes such as metal, chromium-dioxide ("chrome") or "Type II", sound best when played with a different, "70-microsecond" curve. On car-stereo systems, this switch position is usually labelled "Metal" because most car-stereo manufacturers didn't begin to include it until metal tape became a byword for high quality. While metal tapes are the highest-fidelity types currently available, they're also the most expensive; so the tapes you'll probably play most often with the Metal switch position will be chrome or equivalent types. On microcassette systems, though, you'll probably use metal tapes for nearly all your music—micros need metal tape for really high fidelity.

Changing equalization makes only a subtle change in how a tape will sound. So, while it definitely pays to play the tape with the right equalization, you needn't feel your listening will be ruined if you forget to hit the switch when changing to a different tape type, or if you play chrome and metal tapes on a system having only normal equalization.

Incidentally, the term "metal ready" means a lot less in a car stereo system that only plays tapes than in a home deck that also records them. That's because not all recorders can record metal tapes without severe distortion and other problems, or can erase them completely, but virtually any cassette player can play such tapes back. The sound will be a bit off if the equalization is wrong, but any deck or system can play them.

Dolby and Other Noise Reduction Systems

One of the biggest problems in tape recording is noise, especially high-frequency noise ("tape hiss"). In fact, home tape did not become popular as a music medium until Dr. Ray Dolby developed his first home noise reducer. By now, virtually all home cassette decks save the very least expensive ones have Dolby or some other type of noise reduction.

That Dolby system isn't the only type of noise reduction—or even of Dolby noise reduction. In addition to the original, Dolby "B" home system, you may find car stereos with Dolby "C", dbx, DNR or others.

Both of the Dolby systems and dbx are "closed-loop" or "encode/decode" systems—they don't work properly unless you use them both in recording and in playback. DNR, on the other hand, is an "open-loop" system, used in playback only.

The two Dolby systems work mainly on high frequencies, where tape noise is most noticeable. Both also take advantage of the fact that we only notice noise when there are no louder sounds of similar frequency to distract us from them. Tape hiss is present all the time, but we only hear it during quiet passages, or during passages when there are loud low tones but no loud high ones.

The Dolby and "Metal" switches equip a deck for correct-sounding playback of most tapes. The "Metal" setting is used for most premium tapes, such as "chrome" or chromium-dioxide types

In recording, the Dolby systems boost highs when they become too weak to override the noise. In playback, they cut the highs an equal amount. What's boosted in recording is almost all signal, with very little noise; what's cut in playback includes not only the signal but any high-frequency noise that the tape or the equipment have added. The high frequencies in the signal are restored to their normal levels, but the noise is cut back simultaneously, and is now well below its normal level.

While Dolby B cuts high-frequency noise by up to 10 dB, Dolby C cuts it by as much as 20 dB—and adds some noise reduction in the mid-range, as well. Tapes made with Dolby B may sound a bit shrill when played on systems without Dolby, but that can be corrected reasonably well by turning down the treble or tone control, or with the high-frequency controls on an equalizer. The same is true of Dolby C tapes played with Dolby B. If your car's system has poor high-frequency response, you might even prefer to boost the highs a bit by playing Dolby C tapes with Dolby B decoding, or Dolby B tapes with no playback noise reduction. Don't bring Dolby C tapes along, though, if your car's sound system does not have at least some form of Dolby. Played back without it, they sound too shrill for tone controls to correct.

You'll find Dolby B on more car stereos than any other noise reduction system—including every player with Dolby C and some with other noise reducers. That's because Dolby B has become a standard—virtually every home cassette deck, today, can make and play back Dolby B tapes, and almost all prerecorded cassettes sold today are made with Dolby B as well. Some FM stations even broadcast with Dolby B—and the Dolby circuits on some car stereos are designed to work with such broadcasts, too.

The dbx system is similar to Dolby in some ways, but profoundly different in others. Like Dolby, it boosts the weaker signals, to raise them more above the noise; that's called "compression" because it compresses the dynamic range be-

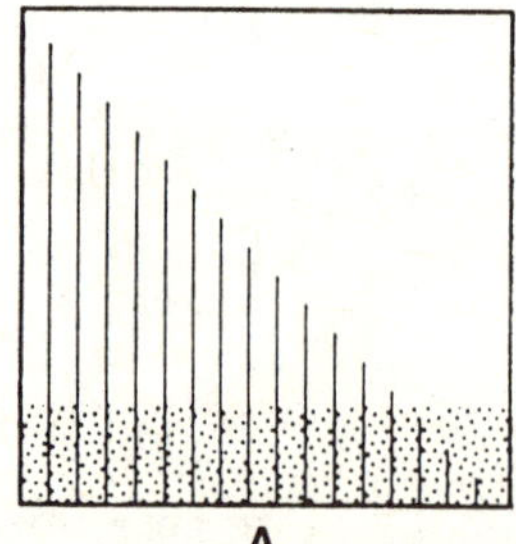
A

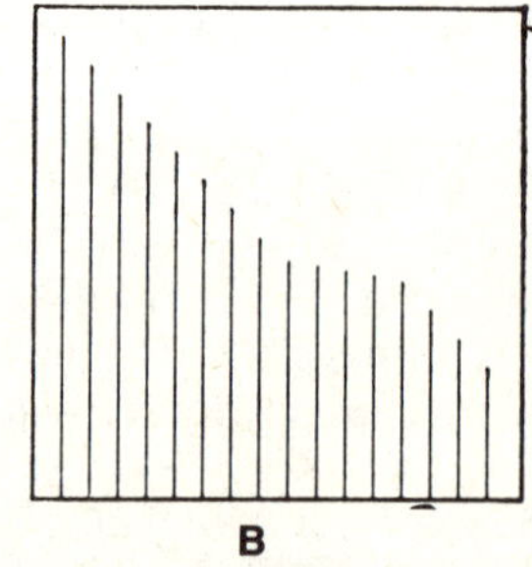
B

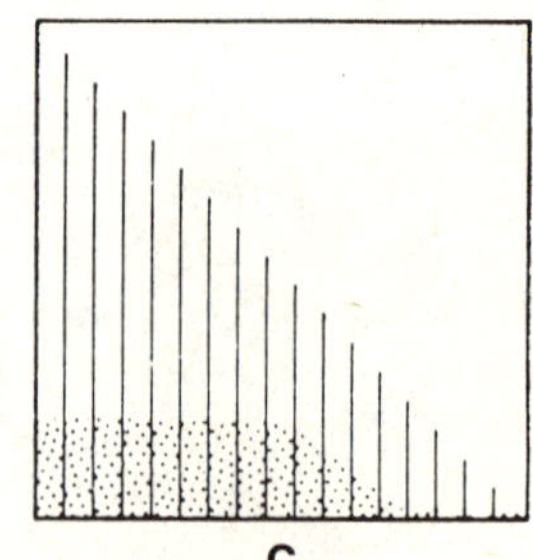
C

How Dolby noise reduction works: In ordinary recording, tape hiss (dots) is louder than the music (lines) at high frequencies (A). Dolby system boosts the highs during recording (B), then cuts them back to normal during playback (C), cutting back high-frequency noise at the same time

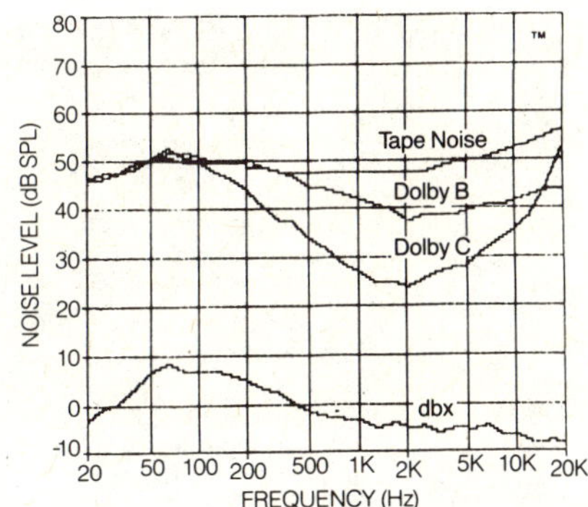

These curves show relative noise levels with (top to bottom) no noise reduction, Dolby B, Dolby C and dbx noise reduction

tween the loudest and softest sounds on the recording. And, like Dolby, it cuts those signals in playback to "expand" the original signal's range back to normal lowering the noise floor.

But dbx compresses and expands all frequencies, not just the highs, and compresses them a good deal more than Dolby does. This has two results, one good and one bad: The good result is that dbx cuts noise at all frequencies, and cuts them even more than Dolby C does. The bad one is that unless dbx tapes are played back through a dbx circuit to re-expand them, they sound too compressed and unnatural.

If you use dbx in your home system, you should consider getting it in your car system, too. Otherwise, you'll have to keep a double set of tapes—dbx tapes for greater dynamic range when listening at home, and Dolby tapes that you can play in your car. Don't be surprised, though, if you run into the problem mentioned in conjunction with digital records in the last chapter: the dynamic range from dbx tapes may be far wider than you can comfortably listen to in a moving car, and sometimes wider than you would find comfortable when the car is sitting quietly.

DNR, like Dolby, works on high frequencies, and takes advantage of the fact that we don't hear high frequency noise when there's enough high-frequency signal to mask it. Other than that, though, the two systems are almost totally different.

DNR (which stands for Dynamic Noise Reduction) analyzes the signal constantly. If there's enough high-frequency musical information to mask the noise, the DNR circuit does nothing except keep on analyzing. If there's not enough, DNR starts filtering out high frequencies, on the justifiable assumption that what's being filtered out is likely to contain more noise than music.

How well DNR works hinges a good deal on how much high frequency infor-

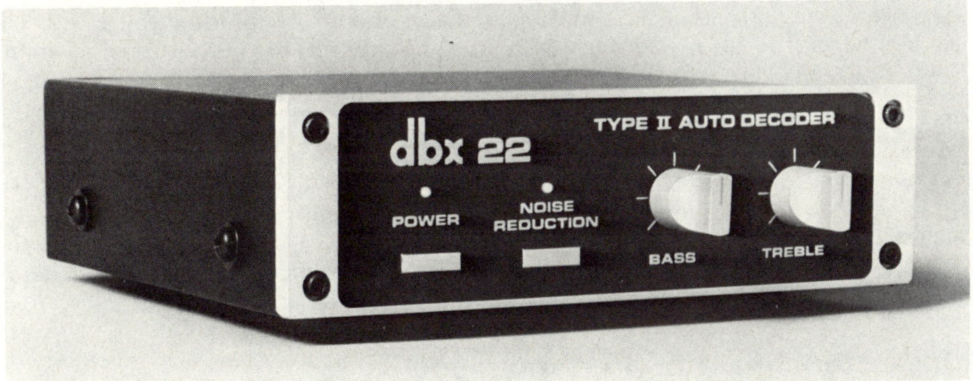

A dbx noise reducer for the car

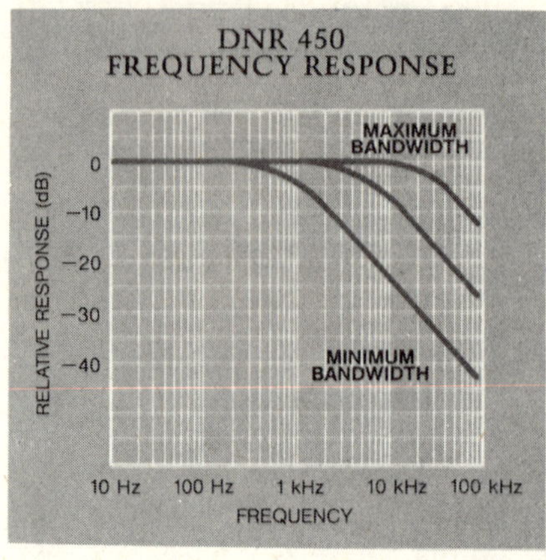

When signal has strong high frequencies, DNR noise reduction lets it all through (right-hand curve). As high frequency level in the signal falls, DNR cuts out more and more of these highs—including more and more of the noise that their absence would reveal (Courtesy National SemiConductor)

mation it considers enough to let pass. If that trigger level is too high, the circuit will start working too soon, and cut out some of the highs you'd like to hear. If it's set too low, the highs won't be affected much, but neither will the noise. Since the "right" level will vary somewhat with the music and the way it was recorded, home DNR units usually let you adjust the trigger point. In the car, where there's not much space for extra controls and not much time or spare attention for drivers, there's usually no such adjustment—just a DNR On/Off switch. So if you're considering a car stereo system with DNR, try it with a few of the kinds of tapes you'll ordinarily listen to and see if it will give you the noise reduction you need without cutting into the highs you want to hear.

EIGHT-TRACK FEATURES

As with cassettes, the main features of 8-track players are those concerned with handling the tape. Pushing the tape in starts the tape deck (and cuts off the tuner). Pulling the cartridge out (there's usually no Eject switch) turns off the tape and switches the tuner back on. You may occasionally find an automatic eject system, too.

Virtually every eight-track deck has automatic track switching—when the first "track" (actually a pair of tracks, for stereo's two channels) is finished the tape head automatically moves down to read the next one. There are usually signal lights to show which track is playing, and there's always a manual switch so you can hurry on to the next track, if you want.

When they reach the end of the last track, most decks will switch back to the first one again. Some can stop there, instead, if you don't want to hear the whole tape over; these decks usually give you the choice of stopping or repeating. On some models, the automatic track switch can be shut off, so you can repeat a single track as long as you wish.

You will never find a rewind control on an eight-track deck. You will sometimes find a "fast-forward" control, but it's usually rather slow, operating the tape at only about twice its normal speed; cassette-deck fast-winding speeds are often as high as 50 or 60 times normal.

Automatic music-finders first appeared on 8-track units, but few 8-track models now have them. Auto-reverse, of course, is neither needed nor possible, and the same is true of automatic rewind and replay. You won't find tape equalization switches or noise reduction on 8-track players, either.

Understanding Tape Performance

You can get some measure of how well a car-stereo unit's tape systems perform by looking at its specifications. Three of these are general specifications, also used to describe other parts of the system (and described in more detail previously: frequency response, signal-to-noise ratio and (sometimes) distortion.

One specification, wow and flutter, applies exclusively to tape. Wow and flutter are two different symptoms of the same disease: speed irregularity. If a tape deck's rotating parts get out of round or develop slippery spots, the tape's speed will change periodically as those parts turn. If those speed fluctuations are slow ones, you hear "wow", named for the "wowowowow" effect it gives to long, sustained tones. If the fluctuations are rapid, you hear "flutter", so called because it makes the tape sound fluttery (and, in extreme cases, so gargly you'd think you were underwater).

Wow and flutter is usually specified as a percentage—the lower the better. There are several ways to measure it, however: weighted and unweighted, average or peak.

At the moment, the most commonly used form is a type of weighted average known as "weighted root mean square" (wrms). Since the ear is more sensitive to some flutter frequencies than others, the most audible such frequencies are given more weight in calculating the figure, while the less audible ones are given less weight. For typical tape decks, the weighted figure will be lower than the unweighted one.

The average (rms) portion of the spec refers to the fact that this represents the average speed variation over several periods of about 10 seconds each. Since this averages out the minimum and maximum flutter measured, rms figures will always be lower than peak (maximum) ones.

Though wrms figures are the current standard, and recognized as such by the EIA Interim Standard on car-stereo specifications, this may change to unweighed peak measurements in the next EIA Standard. If that happens, the numbers given for wow and flutter will go up considerably, though performance will not be changed at all.

SPEAKERS

In the car, as in the home, it's the speakers you hear. All of the sound, whether from tape or tuner, comes through them. And the less you're aware of them, the better they are.

Buying speakers for your car is both easier and harder than buying them for home use. It's easier because there is so little choice: there are fewer types to choose from, and your choice is restricted to those that will fit your car. And it's harder because you rarely get the chance to hear those speakers in use under circumstances which bear any real relationship to how they'll sound in your car. Speakers may not sound the same at home as they do in the store, but there's still more similarity between the average hi-fi store and the average living room than between the hi-fi showroom and your car.

At home, the speakers face you from one end of the room, and everyone sits so far back from them that everyone is at about the same distance from the sound. In the car, the speakers probably can't be placed where they can face you as directly (the ideal place would be mid-windshield), and the space is so small that some people may be three or four times as close to a given speaker as the car's other passengers are.

Simple Acoustics

Some simple, acoustical principles explain why some speaker spots are better than others.

The main factor is that, the higher the frequency, the more directional its sound. You'll hear the best highs when the speaker that's producing them is in plain sight, even if you have to turn your head a bit to see it. If you can't see where the highs are coming from, there's a good chance you won't hear much of them, either. (Speakers on top of the dash are an exception, since the windshield reflects high frequencies quite well. That's only a bit less true of rear-deck speakers.)

Low frequencies are comparatively non-directional, so you can hear lows pretty well no matter where the speaker is placed. If they're coming freely from both the front and the back of the speaker at once, though, you won't hear them at all; since the front of the speaker's pulling while the back is pushing, the two waves will cancel each other when they meet. For this reason, low-frequency speakers should be mounted on baffles (surfaces large enough to lengthen the path between the front and back appreciably) or in enclosures (boxes which either keep the back wave from getting out, or control its passage so that it will reinforce, instead of cancelling the front one).

That's another reason why the difference between the way speakers sound in your car and in other cars or showrooms is greater than the difference between the way a home speaker performs in your home and in the store: Home speakers generally come with their own enclosures, while in most car installations, the speaker is an unpredictable part of the car.

Some audiophiles claim that cars cannot have good bass because the speakers are smaller than those used at home and because the space inside the car is too small for long bass waves to propagate. Nonetheless, good car-sound systems have good bass—better bass than they'd have if they were bigger. The problem with small speakers' bass response is that it falls off rapidly once you get farther than one wavelength from the speaker. You can't get that far away in your car, though: a 40-Hz wave is about 28 feet long, and wavelengths short enough to cause you trouble are well up into the frequency range where the speaker no longer needs to make use of this "near-field" effect. (A 3.5-foot wave, for example, would have a frequency of about 320 Hz.)

Speaker Location

The first thing to consider when you're shopping for speakers is the spaces where they can go, because only the speakers that can fit those spaces will do you any good. There are, however, ways of fitting speakers into spaces where they theoretically should not fit.

THE REAR DECK

The easiest place to put a speaker, in most cars (except hatchbacks), is the rear deck, or parcel shelf, between the rear seat and rear window. Even hatchbacks often use the area next to the removable parcel shelf for speakers. It's the only panel in the car whose back is readily accessible without tearing things apart—just open up the trunk and step in. (With some hatchbacks, it's even easier: the rear deck can be removed to someplace more convenient.)

Rear-deck speakers usually give the best bass, for two reasons: Since the trunk (or trunk area) is the largest cavity in the car, it forms the best available low-frequency enclosure. And since the deck is often fairly large (though less and less so, lately), it can hold a bigger speaker, which can often deliver better bass. Rear speakers are also quite efficient, producing sound levels of 85 dB (about two to three times as loud as road sound) from only one watt of amplifier power; more power would be needed, of course, for louder levels and to handle musical peaks.

For these reasons, rear-deck installations are popular—so much so, in fact, that many cars come with cutouts for speakers in the frame or panel that supports the parcel shelf, and holes cut into that shelf to form a grille. That makes speaker installation even easier.

The rear deck is a good place for speakers, but not a perfect one. Some listeners

Rear-deck speakers are easy to install, in most cars, since both the top and bottom of the deck are easily accessible, and because many cars have holes pre-cut for them in the underpart of the shelf

are put off by music and voices which originate behind them—we're used to facing what we listen to. The direct sound from the speakers and the sound reflected from the rear window can cancel each other at about 700 Hz, causing a dip in response at that frequency.

The sound is never in balance for everyone, either: Turn the rear sound up enough for the front passengers to hear it clearly, and the rear-seat passengers (whose ears are only a few inches from the speakers) will be uncomfortable. Turn it down to comfortable levels for the rear passengers, and the front seat passengers can't hear it.

The same problem, in reverse, occurs if all the speakers are in front. So most good car installations have them in both front and rear, with a "fader" to balance the sound to suit the passengers at both ends of the car. Even if you never carry rear-seat passengers, there's something to be said for rear-deck speakers: they can contribute to the system's bass response, and they can help with the stereo illusion and sense of spaciousness and depth in the car, for reasons which will be discussed.

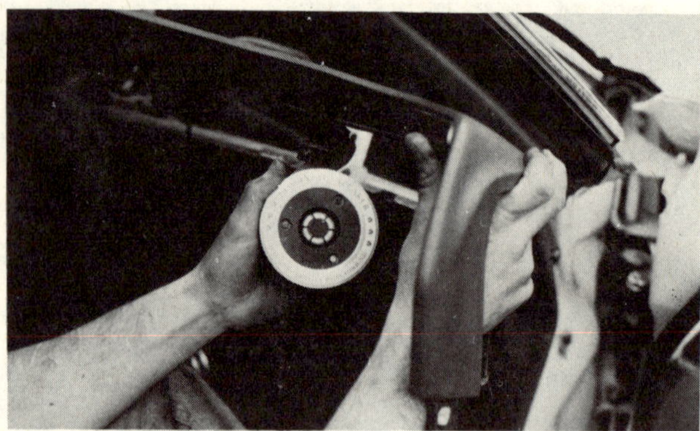

Many dashboards have speaker holes, as well; but getting the speakers into them may take some disassembly

IN THE DASH

In the front, the most common speaker mounting spots are in the dashboard, in the doors or in the kick panels. The advantages and disadvantages of in-dash mounting are precisely the opposite of those which apply to the rear deck. In-dash speakers are usually well positioned for good listening, either directly facing you or bouncing their sound off the windshield (an excellent acoustical reflector) to give the illusion that the sound is originating from the windshield itself. You won't hear much bass, though, because modern dashboards only have space for small speakers (3½ inches is the most common size), and because the dash doesn't really enclose the speaker—the dash's open bottom lets the back and front waves from the speaker meet and cancel each other's low frequencies out. If the speakers are installed from within the dash, getting space to work can be a problem, too.

IN THE DOORS

Not all cars have space in their dashboards for speakers, but nearly all can accommodate some type of speaker in their doors. There are two advantages to this, one of them unquestioned and the other a matter of taste.

The unquestioned advantage is that in-door speakers have better bass than in-dash ones, because the cavities within the doors enclose the speakers so their back waves can't escape to cancel out the front ones. Bass response varies with both the speakers and the doors; it will go lower on a big door like that of a two-door Cadillac, less low on a small one like that of a four-door Fiat.

The other advantage is a matter of perspective. In-dash speakers form a sonic stage in front of you. But since you sit more or less between in-door speakers, they create a sonic image a bit more like that of headphones. The stereo effect of this is often literally fantastic—literally because it is a fantasy, an exaggeration of the sound perspective the recording engineers wanted you to hear. On theoretical grounds, it's indefensible—but listening to it is, even for theoretically-minded people, a good deal of fun.

There are disadvantages, too. One is that, with speakers in the doors, the left-seat passenger is far, far closer to the left speaker than the right one, while the right passenger is far, far closer to the right speaker than the left. This makes it impossible to balance the sound between the speakers so as to give both passengers the best possible stereo, though it can still be pretty good, in most cases. There's no problem when you're driving by yourself, of course—just set the balance control so that the far speaker sounds about as loud as the nearer one to you.

Another problem is that not all doors let you put the speakers where their sound—

Speakers in the door have better base than in-dash ones, and give a headphone-like stereo perspective

especially the high frequencies—has a clear shot at your ear. Speakers must be placed where they won't obstruct the window cranks and door handles, and where you won't bang your knuckles on them when using those cranks and handles. They must also be placed where they won't obstruct the window mechanisms inside the doors, which is hard to judge without opening up the door to see how it's constructed. (Both doors should be opened up for this—sometimes, the doors on each side of the car are built a little differently.) If you're lucky, the spaces where you can put speakers will be the spaces where you'd like to for acoustical reasons; if you're not so lucky, some special types of speaker and mounting will help.

The farther the speaker is from the door's hinge side, the more sturdily it must be mounted, especially if it's a heavy one. Slamming a car door can build up a lot of momentum at the door's latch side—enough to make a speaker fly out of the

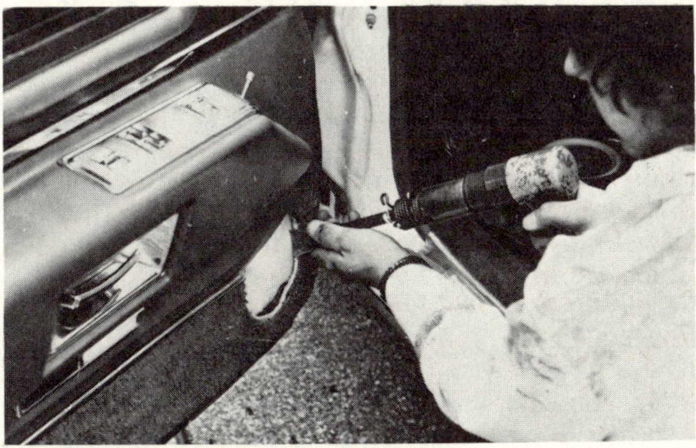

Holes for in-door speakers must be made where the speakers won't interfere with door lock or window mechanisms, preferably as far forward in the door as possible (Courtesy AFS)

door and into your lap, if it's only mounted to a fiberboard trim panel instead of bolted to the steel inner panels of the door.

Door speakers tend to be less efficient than rear-deck speakers. Tests show they require from one to three and one-half watts for the same 85-dB sound level which rear-deck speakers could achieve with one half to one watt.

Door speakers also often tend to have a hump in the middle of their frequency response, which makes them sound a little boomy. This is due as much to the size of the cavity in the door as it is to the speakers themselves. Mounted elsewhere, the same speakers might sound flatter and more accurate. If your system has an equalizer, lowering its midrange control or controls can usually flatten the hump nicely.

Kick panels—the upright panels under the dash—are sometimes used, as an alternative to in-door speakers. This gives the sound a forward perspective, but the highs may not have a clear shot at your ears. The cavities behind kick panels are rarely large enough for good bass; and where there are no cavities, you're cutting holes directly into the fender's inside shell (potential rain leaks and water or gravel damage to the speakers) or into the engine compartment (with possible fire hazards, plus noise problems and potential harm to the speaker again).

OTHER LOCATIONS

There aren't many.

Speakers in the rear doors of four-door cars, or the rear interior trim panels of two-door ones can give rear listeners a more naturally forward-oriented sound, and can minimize the front-rear balance problems by being about equidistant from both front and rear listeners. Speakers at the extreme rear of the doors in a two-door car can have a similar effect.

For cars which have no handy cavities, several solutions are available. Speaker systems in self-contained enclosures can be mounted wherever there is room. Some companies make special enclosures for specific cars with this problem, especially sports cars such as Porsches, Datsun "Z" cars and Corvettes. Some dealers who specialize in custom installations will fabricate their own enclosures for customers' cars. And moderate-sized home systems are sometimes used successfully in vans and large station wagons.

Types of Speakers

Good bass speakers tend to be big, because they have to pump so much air at low frequencies. Good treble speakers tend to be small, because smaller speakers disperse the highs around the car more evenly, and because high frequency speakers must move back and forth more quickly than a large speaker's higher inertia would permit.

Obviously, no speaker can be both at once. So most good speaker systems use at least two speaker "drivers"—a large cone "woofer" for the lower frequencies, and a small cone or dome "tweeter" for the highs. In addition to the "two-way", woofer-tweeter type, there are three-way speakers (with the third drive handling the midrange), and even some four-way and five-way systems. All these systems use "crossover networks," usually built in, to divide the frequencies among the drivers.

A simpler speaker type uses a single driver with a small, hard "whizzer cone" attached to the center of the main cone. This type's high-frequency response is limited, largely by the cone assembly's high mass and inertia. But the small whizzer acts like a tweeter otherwise, so that whatever highs the system does produce are more evenly dispersed than they would be from the main cone alone.

If you want more low bass than your system can provide, you can add a "subwoofer," a speaker designed to handle only the very lowest frequencies. Typically, a subwoofer will mount in the rear shelf, and will require an amplifier of its own to

Separate tweeters and woofers can be placed more flexibly—woofers where there's room behind the panel, tweeters where they'll have a clear path to the ear

A "coaxial" speaker has its woofer and tweeter mounted on a common axis (Courtesy AFS Krisket)

Rigid, supplementary "whizzer" cones improve a speaker's high-frequency response—though not as much as real tweeters (Courtesy JBL)

drive it. It will always require a crossover circuit to feed the lowest frequencies (usually below 100 Hz) only to the subwoofer, leaving only frequencies above that point for the rest of the system.

You could get a bit more bass if you fed those low frequencies to the main system, too. But you'd get only a bit more bass, and considerably more distortion; many car speaker systems above the subwoofer range tend to distort when they're trying to handle very low frequencies. To many listeners, reduced distortion is a bigger advantage of subwoofer use than increased bass is.

Auxiliary tweeters can be added, too, either to get more highs or to put the source of those highs in a better place. Since they surface-mount and don't take up much space, they can be mounted almost anywhere. That lets you put them where the highs have a clear path to your ears, or use them to move the apparent sound source to a more natural position—if you're flanked by door speakers but prefer the sound to come from a "stage" ahead of you.

Matching Speaker and Location

Most car speakers are designed to be "flush-mounted" in holes cut into the car's interior panels. These speakers may have only one "driver" (the speaker itself), or

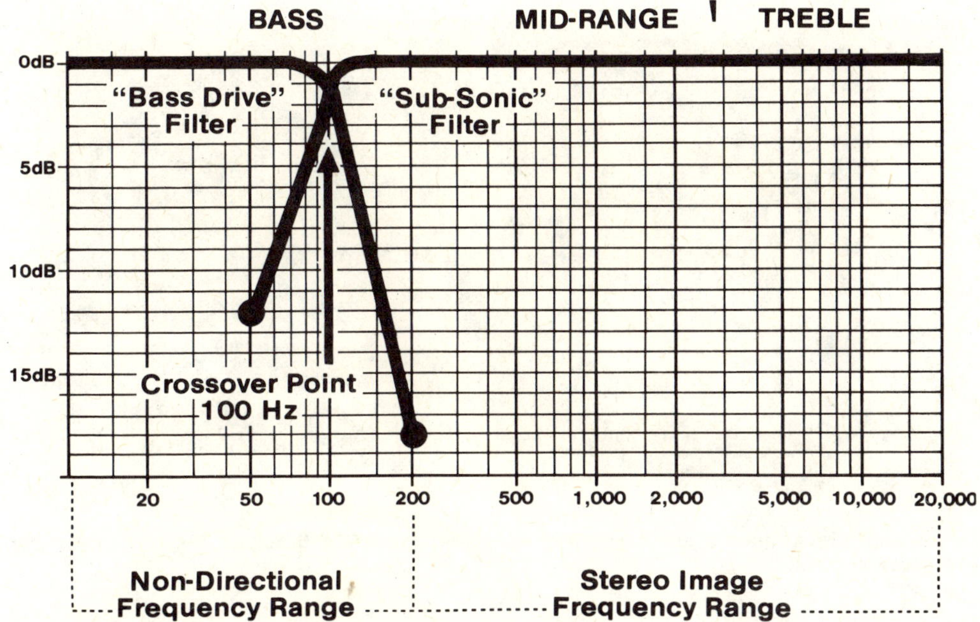

By feeding all the very low frequencies to a subwoofer, you get better bass, plus cleaner sound from the main speakers (Courtesy Sony)

may have two or more such drivers mounted coaxially, to handle different parts of the frequency range.

A second type of multiple-driver flush-mount system mounts each driver separately, sometimes with a hole for each, sometimes with the high-frequency drivers mounted on the surface of the car's panels rather than set into them.

If you can't mount your speakers flush in holes, you can buy some designed for surface mounting, with enclosures of their own. The simplest variety consists of a flush-mount, single-driver or coaxial speaker in a wedge-shaped enclosure which can be oriented to direct high frequencies toward the passengers. Often, the backs of these enclosures can be taken off (sometimes the back is missing altogether, and the box just seats itself against the panel it's mounted on); if you drill a large hole in the car panel behind that open back, you get the bass benefit of whatever cavity lies behind the panel. This is handy if the space behind the panel is obstructed by window mechanisms or the like, or when you want to aim the speaker at an angle to the panel it is mounted on.

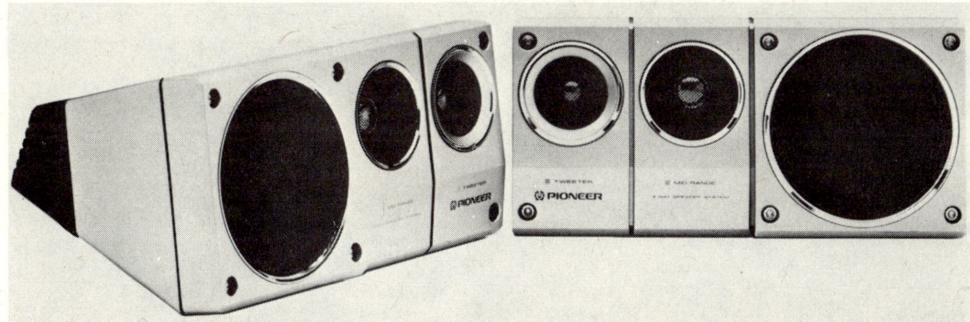

Wedge-shaped speaker enclosures can be aimed at the listener; large ones like these do not depend on space behind the mounting panel for a bass enclosure (Courtesy Pioneer)

Home-type mini-speakers are frequently sold with mounting brackets for use in the car (Courtesy Visonik)

Larger, more elaborate wedge enclosures usually don't have removable backs, because they're large enough to give decent bass if the speakers are properly matched to them. The same is true of the popular "mini-speaker" boxes, often identical to those used in home systems. Mini-box systems usually are mounted on brackets which swivel in at least one direction, for easier aiming.

The last type looks like (and often is) the front plate of a mini-speaker, with all the speaker system components but the box. This type mounts semi-flush, partly extending through a hole cut in the car's interior panel, partly projecting from it (though usually by less than an inch). It comes in very handy where there's limited mounting depth, but where there's room above the panel for a speaker that sticks out an inch or so, and where the panel is quite flat—for curved panels, separate speakers are best.

Some speaker systems mount a separate tweeter and woofer on a plate resembling the front panel of a mini-speaker

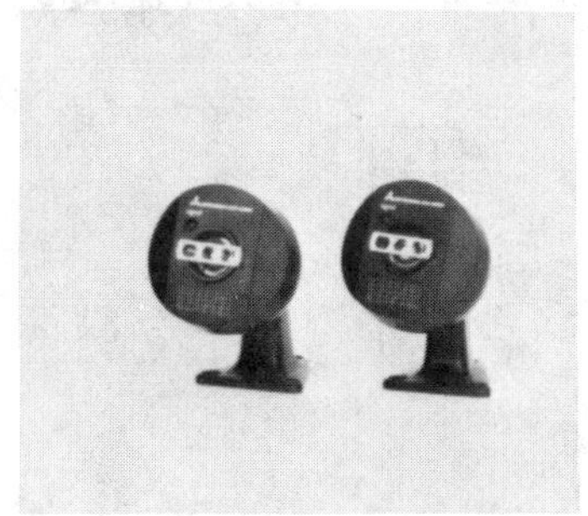

Supplementary tweeters, which mount on the car's interior surfaces, can be used to extend high-frequency response, or to aim the highs where they're needed

FREQUENCY AND DIRECTIONALITY

Add-on tweeters and flush-mount systems with separate drivers let you put your highs in one place, the rest of the sound in another. If the distance between the two is fairly short, and if both lie in the same general direction for you, their sounds will blend and seem to come from one place. If the distance between them is too far, though, or one lies ahead of you while the other's at your side, you get unnatural effects, as if the music were smeared over the space between the speakers or—if the separation's very large—as if the music's coming from two different places (as indeed it is). The bigger the angle between the two sound sources and your ear, and the higher the crossover frequency between them, the more likely you are to hear this effect (though not all listeners notice or are bothered by it).

Subwoofers can be put nearly anywhere without this effect being too apparent, because the crossover frequency is so low. Some makers, though, have used this principle to suggest putting the tweeter and midrange in the front of the car for good directionality and the woofer in the back for better bass. Unfortunately, though, the crossover point between the woofer and tweeter in most two-way car systems is somewhere between 1,000 and 2,000 Hz, which is high enough for the separation to be noticeable.

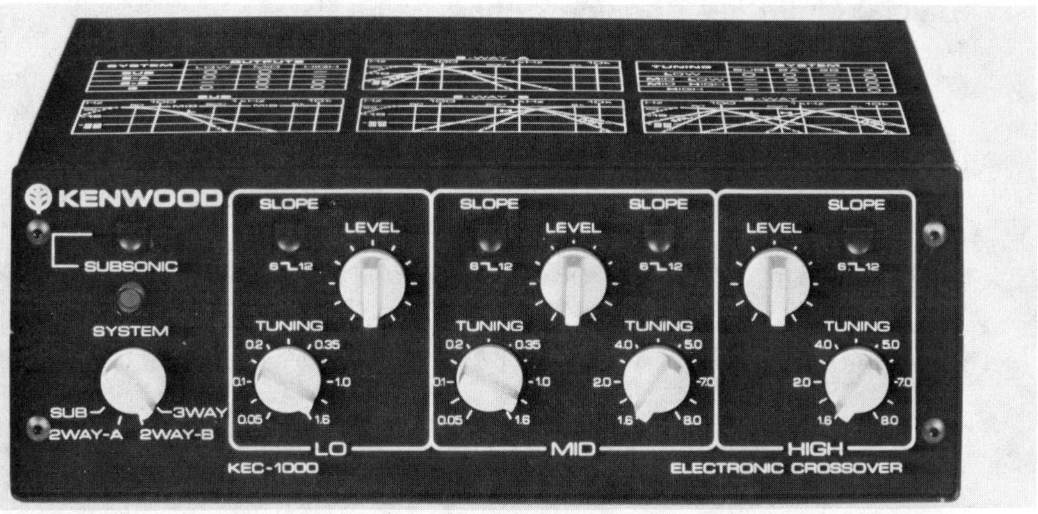

Electronic crossovers go between the in-dash unit and two or more amplifiers, so that woofer, tweeter (and sometimes midrange) can each be powered separately (Courtesy Kenwood)

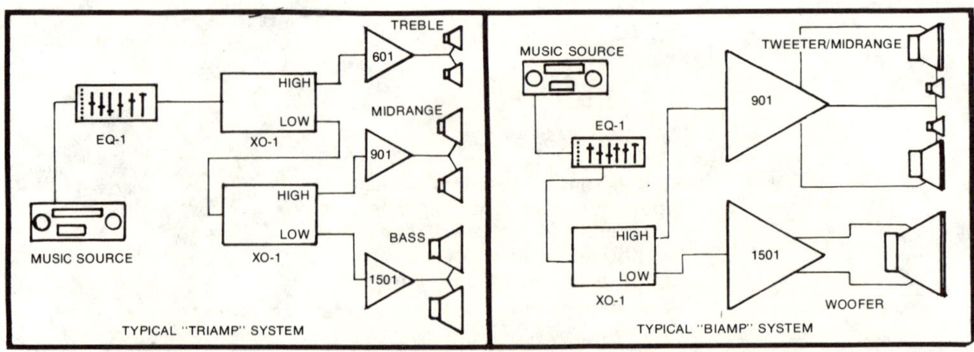

A bi-amplified system (left) has one electronic crossover, feeding an amplifier for the woofer, and one for the rest. A tri-amplified system (right) has two crossovers, and separate amplifiers for bass, midrange and treble

BI-AMPLIFIERS

One amplifier can power an entire speaker system. But you don't have to do it that way.

You can also "bi-amplify" your system, using one amplifier to power the woofer or subwoofer, and another to power the higher frequencies. In that case, you'll also need an "electronic crossover", a frequency divider that goes between the preamplifier (preamp) and the amplifier (amp), not between the amplifier and the woofer and tweeter. Some systems are even "tri-amped," with a separate amplifier for the mid-range as well—not to mention the possibility of an additional amplifier for the subwoofer.

The advantage of bi-amping is cleaner sound. Most distortion in the speakers and amplifiers is caused by strong bass signals, but is heard at higher frequencies. In a bi-amped system, any upper-frequency distortions caused by power demands on the bass amplifier will only go to the woofer, which can't reproduce them very strongly, and the output from the midrange and tweeter will stay pure and clean.

Special Mounting Considerations

There are ways to mount speakers where they theoretically don't fit. Shallow speakers, with mounting depths of about one inch, are available for spaces where the room behind the speaker hole is limited. Deeper speakers can be mounted on stand-off rings, which reduce mounting depth by pushing the speaker out more into the passenger compartment.

Cars with small rear decks often have holes only for narrow oval speakers, such as 4 x 10-inch models. Adapters are available which fit beneath these openings and flare out into large sizes (such as 6 x 9).

Speakers for rear-deck use should be as plain looking as possible; and if they match the color of the rear deck, all the better. Shiny surfaces and flashy chrome trim look fine in the showroom, but they get annoying if you see their reflections in the rear window whenever you look back into your mirror.

Speakers for use near the floor should have very sturdy, firmly-attached grilles, since they're likely to be kicked a lot.

Door speakers should be shielded against rain dripping down the window channels. Some speakers come shielded or with add-on shields, but well-stocked auto parts stores and care stereo installers carry shields separately.

Some listeners find that they get a better stereo illusion if their rear-deck speakers work on opposite channels from the front ones, the speaker in the right rear

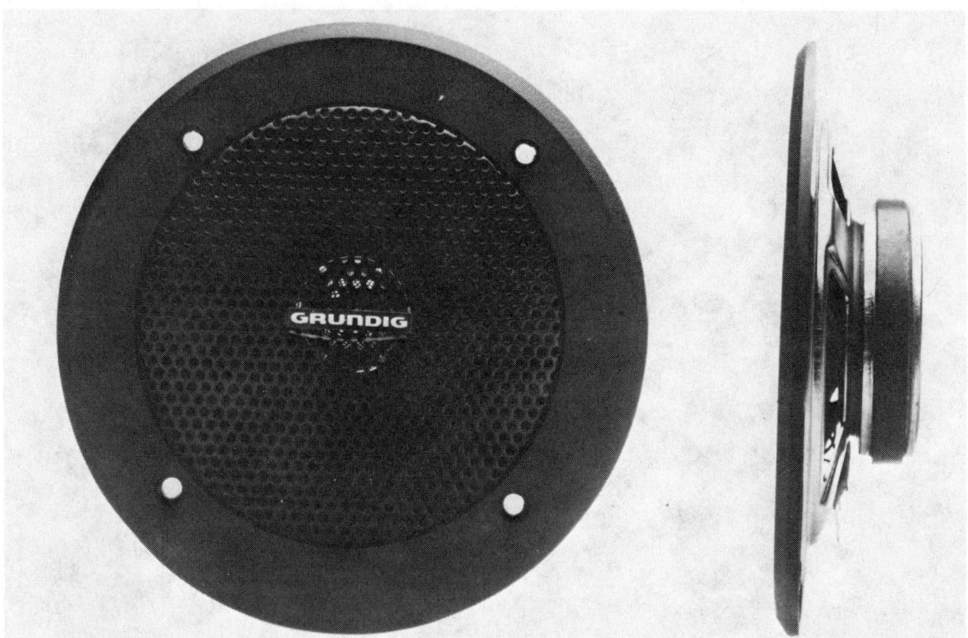

Some speakers are made extra-shallow, for mounting where space behind the panel is cramped (Courtesy Grundig Autosound)

corner of the car playing the same signal as that in the left front, and the left rear speaker playing the right front signal.

Rear speakers can also be used for augmented spaciousness by feeding them delayed signals. This makes the sound from the back seem more like the delayed echoes coming from the rear of a concert hall. Not all delay systems are equally effective, though; get a demonstration before buying, to see whether you find the effect worth the money.

Another way to deal with shallow mounting spaces is to mount the speaker on a standoff ring (Courtesy Sony)

Speakers come in a variety of sizes and shapes, to fit a variety of mounting situations (Courtesy Clarion)

JUDGING HOW CAR SPEAKERS SOUND

With home speakers, judging the sound you'll hear is less of a problem, since you can hear those speakers in their own enclosures and in surroundings somewhat like those in which you'll listen to them. With car speakers, the enclosure will vary with the car it's mounted in, and the showroom is nothing like the interior of a car. Some dealers do have demonstration cars where you can hear perhaps two or three different speakers (there's rarely room for more), or car-like enclosures in their showrooms. Those help make listening tests more meaningful, if still not as useful as those you can make for home speakers.

Still, there are some things you can learn about a speaker both from its specifications and from showroom listening.

Speaker Specifications

SIZE

The most important speaker specification, and the most reliable one, is size. Self-enclosed speakers come in a wide variety of sizes (though the range of variation is small). Flush-mount speakers come in more standard sizes, though there are a lot of them: round ones with nominal diameters of 3½, 4, 5, 5¼, 6, 6½, 8, 10 and 12 inches (8-inch and larger ones are usually subwoofers), and oval ones in such sizes as 4 x 6, 4 x 10, 5 x 7, and 6 x 9 inches.

Engineers differ over whether round speakers sound better than oval ones. The most un-biased answer is that the problems of both shapes are different, but equal.

FREQUENCY RESPONSE

Frequency response should be taken with a grain of salt. There's no universal way of measuring it—and for flush-mount systems, at least, the response will vary from car to car.

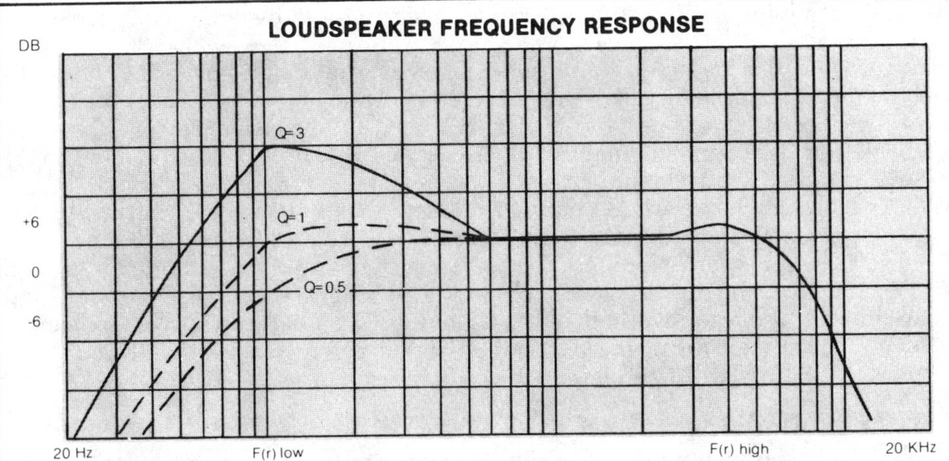

Fr (low) is the frequency of the fundamental resonance.
Fr(high) is the upper rolloff frequency which often has a resonance associated with it.

The useful range of a loudspeaker is usually limited to the region between Fr (low) and Fr (high). Below Fr (low), the suspension stiffness resists further output, this resistance causes a 12 dB/octave rolloff. Above Fr (high), inertial losses due to the weight of the moving mechanism causes a high frequency rolloff also at 12 dB/octave.

The "Q" of the loudspeaker affects the response at the fundamental resonant frequency. High "Q" (underdamped speakers tend to have smaller magnets and exhibit a peak before rolloff. Low "Q" (overdamped) loudspeakers tend to have large magnets and show no peak at resonance. A medium "Q" (factor= 1) loudspeaker is a good compromise between maxiumum extended low frequency output and lack of response peaking of transient ringing

More magnet weight is not necessarily better. Too small a magnet makes bass boomy and unnatural (upper curve)—though some listeners like it that way. Too large a magnet cuts down bass response (lower curve). With correct magnet, response is fairly flat (middle curve) (Courtesy Audiomobile)

MAGNET WEIGHT

Magnet weight doesn't tell you much, either. Magnet performance depends on magnet weight, material and construction. Speakers with strong magnets tend to be more efficient, needing less amplifier power for a given sound output. A strong magnet also helps get good bass, by damping it so that response rolls off smoothly at low frequencies, without a resonant hump above the roll-off point. But too strong a magnet rolls the response off too fast, and you'll actually lose bass.

IMPEDANCE

The impedance (resistance to electric currents) of most car-stereo speakers is 4 ohms. That helps car-stereo amplifiers feed the speakers more power. But, some speakers have impedances of 3.2, 8 or 16 ohms. In automotive use, the higher-impedance models are probably best used with higher-powered amplifiers.

AMPLIFIER POWER

Though there's no standard way to specify and measure them in car speakers, amplifier power requirements are a very important specification. Since high volume is sometimes needed to overcome road noise, it's best to use amplifiers in the upper half of a speaker's recommended power range. More powerful amplifiers can also be used, if they're used cautiously. The chief benefit of this is lower distortion from letting the amplifier loaf—maximum volume is still limited by what the speaker can take.

Bear in mind that doubling an amplifier's power won't make the system twice as loud. In the first place, it takes ten times the sound power to make something sound "twice as loud" to our ears. Merely doubling the power increases volume by 3 decibels (dB)—about the smallest difference we can detect without comparing two sounds directly to each other.

What's more, if your present amplifier delivers four watts at your normal listening level, your new one, regardless of its power, won't be called on to deliver more unless you change your listening habits. (You just might change them, though, if your old amp was operating near its limits. The loudest listening level you find comfortable is as often governed by distortion as by actual sound volume; if the new amp doesn't start distorting until much higher volume levels than the old one did, you may find yourself suddenly liking louder sound.)

LISTENING TESTS

Many dealers offer demonstration facilities where you can get some idea—sometimes even a very good one—of how a given car speaker will sound. Some dealers will have such demonstration setups for every speaker they handle, others will have them for only a few models.

A speaker is likely to sound different in your car than it does on demonstration. But there are ways of predicting some of the main differences beforehand.

Resonance and Bass

The biggest difference is likely to be bass. The bass tones a speaker delivers depends quite a lot on the volume of the cavity behind it, that will vary unpredictably from car to car. The bigger that enclosure volume, the deeper the bass will go.

Bigger enclosures also mean a lower resonant point. Every speaker/enclosure combination responds far more readily to amplifier signals at some single frequency—its resonant point—than it does to signals at all other frequencies. Above that frequency, response usually slopes down a bit, then flattens out. Below it, response usually slopes off and keeps on sloping.

Since response rolls off this way below resonance, the lower the resonant frequency the deeper the bass can be—one reason why bigger enclosures are better for low-frequency performance. But there's another effect, too: the higher the resonance, the more likely it is to be in the midrange, where the signal will excite it most often. That's what makes door speakers sound boomy.

The enclosure volume of most dealer demonstration boards tends to be greater than a door's and lower than a trunk's; so the odds are that a given speaker will have a higher resonance and less bass in your door than in the showroom, while a rear-deck speaker will have more bass and lower resonance in your car than in the store.

Even so, you should pay special attention to speaker resonances in the store. Try and identify where and how pronounced each speaker's resonance is. (The noise from an un-muted FM tuner set to a frequency between stations will help you with this test. It contains a random mixture of all frequencies from about 50 to 15,000 Hz; any frequencies that stand out consistently from that jumble are frequency peaks and resonances in the speaker.) If one speaker has a lower resonance than another in the same display, it's also likely to go lower in your car, but you can't compare speakers in different displays this way, because their enclosure volumes may be different.

Some speakers have pronounced resonances, others have their resonances better damped. This difference is usually easiest to spot if you first compare two speakers from the same manufacturer whose main difference is magnet weight; the heavier model should have less noticeable resonance. (This test isn't valid with speakers of different makes, since their magnet structures and efficiencies may also differ.)

The less resonant speaker may well sound as if it has less bass. That's because the hump above the bass roll-off makes bass at or near the resonant frequency sound louder, even if bass below that frequency can't be heard. If you listen carefully to both speakers, with material that contains some truly deep bass notes, you'll hear the more damped speaker going further and further down the scale as the music does, but losing loudness as it does so; the less-damped speaker will keep thumping away loudly, but that thump will all be at one frequency, regardless of what the music's doing.

Rock listeners often prefer more resonant bass, if the resonance is low enough, since rock bass's main function is rhythm, not melody or harmony, and since rock bass rarely goes down much below about 150 Hz. Classical and jazz listeners will usually prefer the less resonant bass for its greater accuracy and ability to deliver the low notes as notes, not just as thumps. If you listen to both, get the less resonant speaker, then use an equalizer to restore the thump when listening to rock.

Treble, Dispersion and Absorption

Dispersion—the ability to spread high frequencies evenly over a wide area—is even more important in car speakers than in those for home use, since it's often necessary to install car speakers at oblique angles to the listener. This is an easy one to test for: just play a signal that's fairly rich in highs (inter-station FM noise is perfect

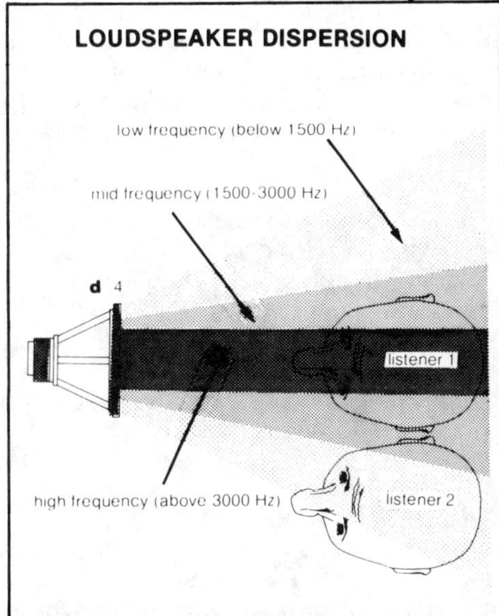

The outermost circle shows wide dispersion at low frequencies where the wavelength of sound is longer than the cone diameter "d" (below 1500 Hz for a 4 inch speaker). Both listeners 1 and 2 hear these lower frequencies clearly. The next region inward shows a narrowing of the dispersion pattern emitted by the loudspeaker. These frequencies, where the wavelength of sound is close to the diameter of the speaker (1500-3000 Hz for a 4 inch speaker), are clearly heard by listener 1 and much more difficult to detect by listener 2.

The inner most region tends to really squeeze the high frequency dispersion pattern into a narrow beam. Listener 1 hears high frequencies clearly while listener 2 hears nothing above 3000 Hz.

The lower the frequency, and the smaller the speaker, the more evenly sound is dispersed through the listening area. Figures shown are for a four-inch speaker; typical one-inch tweeters would disperse highs far more widely (Courtesy Audiomobile)

for this test, too), then walk back and forth across the speaker's sound field. It's normal for the highs to fall off in intensity as you move away from the speaker's axis. On good speakers, though, the fall-off will be gradual and even, with no sudden peaks and dips in the response as you move. That FM signal will also let you check for peaks in the speaker's high frequency response, by listening for any high frequencies that the speaker emphasizes consistently.

These defects in high frequency response will not change with installation in the car. What you hear in the showroom is largely what you get. The one thing to watch out for is installations where the treble tones are swallowed up before you hear them because the tweeter is firing into the car's upholstery or the passenger's socks. Soft surfaces absorb highs. Hard ones, like glass, reflect them. Bear those points in mind when trying to figure how a given speaker's high end will sound when it's in your chosen mounting spot.

How high the speaker will go is important—but less important than these other factors. The higher the frequencies the speaker can deliver, the more likely they are to be drowned out by noise on the road (though you can still hear them when the car is quiet). Peaks and dips in frequency response, or response you can't hear because you're too far off the speaker's axis will have a much greater effect on how your system sounds to you.

Middle Frequencies

Speaker ads don't say much about performance at the middle frequencies; they're usually too busy trumpeting their makers' real achievements in the more difficult areas of reproducing extreme bass and treble frequencies. Mid-frequencies are probably the most important of all in governing the quality of what you hear: most musical notes and most speech fall in the mid-range.

The things to listen for in mid-range sound is clarity and balance. A well-recorded piece of choral music (not easy to find, since choral music is hard to record well) makes an excellent test for clarity. Solo speaking voices (especially male ones) make good tests for balance, since we know pretty well how voices really sound. Avoid speakers that make announcers sound as if they're broadcasting from inside a barrel (though check a few stations if you get this effect—some stations broadcast their announcers that way).

Again, what you hear is usually what you get. The main difference you may find between mid-range performance in the showroom and in the car is the mid-range hump that can occur when a speaker is mounted in a small enclosure (such as some doors and most kick panels).

THE ANTENNA SYSTEM

If your system has a radio, it needs an antenna. Even if your car already has an antenna built into its windshield, you can improve your radio reception noticeably by using a good, whip-type antenna instead. Windshield antennas tend to be directional, making the signal quality and strength you get change every time you turn the car.

If you have a CB radio in your car, you may be tempted to get a combination antenna covering the AM, FM and CB bands. That will discourage theft, since it doesn't advertise the contents of your system as separate antennas can. But it will also greatly diminish the amount of signal for both radio systems.

Antennas may look streamlined when raked back at an angle, but they tend to work best when vertical. FM stations used to transmit signals which required horizontal antennas; but as cars, with their vertical whip antennas, became equipped for FM, the stations equipped themselves to transmit properly to those antennas.

Antennas come in several configurations: fixed whips, telescoping antennas which

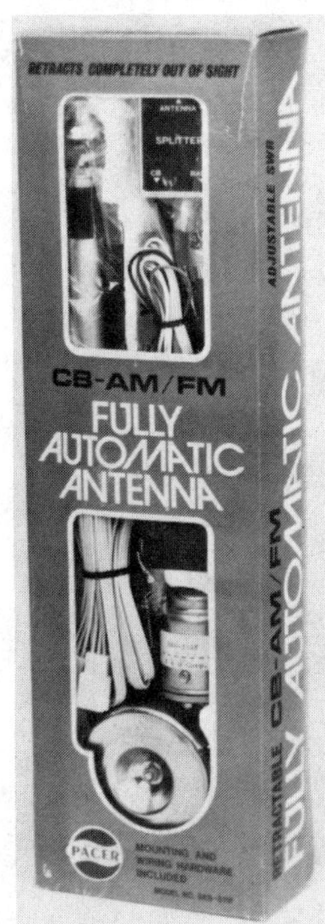

A power antenna can be easily retracted out of harm's way, and can be raised as you drive for better reception. They also come in combination AM/FM/CB (Courtesy Pacer)

can be retracted manually, and both manual and automatic powered antennas. Fixed whips are least expensive and sturdiest, though they can be damaged by playful children or automatic car-washes. If the antenna is mounted on a spring, it's far less likely to suffer damage, though FM reception may be affected by its swaying. The fixed whip requires almost no mounting space behind the panel it attaches to. If it's mounted on a ball joint, it can be attached to almost any body panel, however that panel may be angled.

Manually telescoping whips are easier to damage when they're up, but safe from damage when retracted. Some models lock into their retracted positions, and cannot be opened without a special key, for still further protection. If you mount such an antenna as near to the driver's door as possible, you're more likely to remember to put it up when you get in the car and push it down again when you get out. Antennas which attach to the front windshield pillar fulfill this requirement nicely, but may cause increased wind noise at highway speeds.

With power antennas, you don't have to remember to raise and lower the whip when you're outside the car. Manual power antennas can be raised and lowered by a switch on or under the dashboard. Automatic antenna raise themselves when the radio is switched on, and lower themselves when it's switched off—at least if the radio has automatic antenna terminals, and most modern stereo receivers do. Manually-controlled models, though, can be partially retracted when operating where the signal is too strong for the tuner; this problem is an increasingly infrequent one with modern tuners, however.

In most power antennas, the motor is at the bottom of the housing into which the whip retracts. In some installations, though, there is no room for this; so several manufacturers have two-piece models whose motors are connected to the main housing by flexible cables.

Most retractible antennas, powered or unpowered, can be mounted at a variety of angles, so that you needn't try to find perfectly level body panels to mount them on. Special models are available for mounting on steeply sloped body panels.

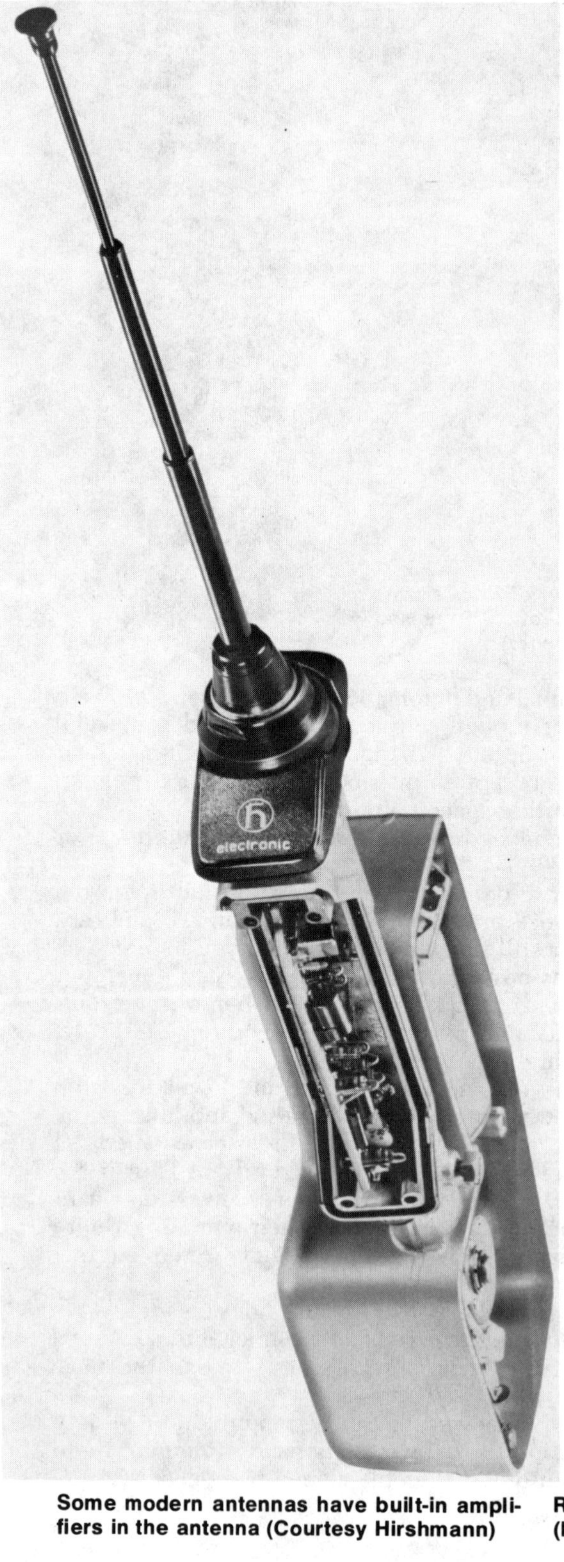

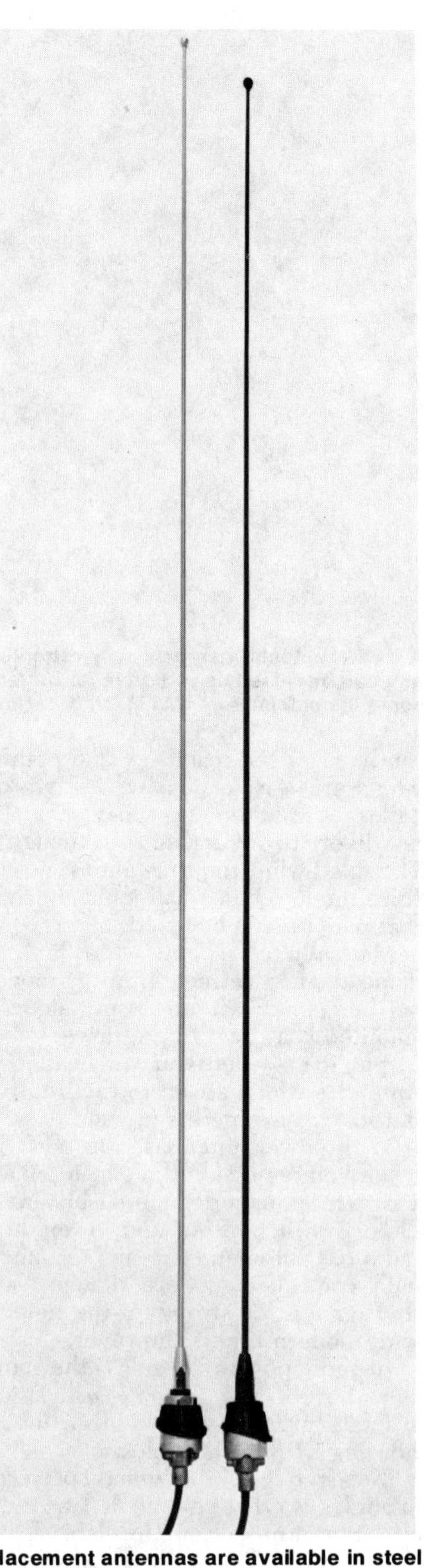

Some modern antennas have built-in amplifiers in the antenna (Courtesy Hirshmann)

Replacement antennas are available in steel (left) or fiberglass (right) (Courtesy Harada)

"Unbreakable" antennas are made of rubber, specially treated with metal particles for good conductivity (Courtesy Pacer)

One new antenna type is the amplified antenna. It's smaller than the normal type, and therfore picks up less signal. But circuits built into these antennas amplify the signal back to normal strength, or even a bit more. Amplified antennas come as fixed whips (often flexible, rubbery shafts) or as manually retractible models.

The signals from regular antennas can also be amplified this way. Several companies make FM boosters which connect between the antenna and the receiver. It's best to buy one with a by-pass switch, so that you can feed an un-amplified signal to the receiver when no boost is needed. Unfortunately, there are no standards or common specifications for such boosters. Some models, therefore, may add noise to the signal as they amplify it, may actually reduce signal strength when switched off, and may interfere with FM reception. However, if picking up distant FM stations is important to you, boosters may well be worth a try; they don't cost much.

FM boosters boost the signal from the antenna to the receiver (Courtesy Antenna craft)

ADD-ON COMPONENTS

Just as with a home systems, it's possible to start with a moderately-priced system, and improve it later, or to incorporate some of those improvements and extras from the start. Some of these were mentioned in previous sections: equalizers, boosters, higher-powered amplifiers, and electronic crossovers for bi-amplification, noise-reduction systems, FM boosters, faders and amplifier balancers, time delay/reverb systems, and other components.

Equalizers

Equalizers let you adjust your system's frequency balance far more flexibly and elaborately than your system's tone controls do. If the tone controls are not enough to help you get the sound exactly as you want it, then equalizers will certainly help.

Separate equalizers, with no power amplification built in, can be used only with systems having preamp-level controls between the in-dash unit and the amplifier; the equalizer plugs in between the in-dash unit and the amp. Booster/equalizers, with speaker-level inputs, can be used with any system, but are best used with systems having only speaker-level outputs—if you have a choice, a separate equalizer and booster will usually give you better sound.

Equalizers are often combined with boosters, because it takes a fair amount of power, more than most in-dash units have, to get full benefit from an equalizer. That power is only needed when you use your equalizer to raise the system's output in one or more frequency bands, especially when raising the bass. But since bass output is frequently a problem in the car, raising the bass output is one of the first things most equalizer owners do. It's not enough to feed more bass into the amplifier; the amp must be capable of putting out more bass as well, and that takes power.

Keep that in mind when planning a system from scratch, too. If you plan to include an equalizer, consider getting a more powerful amplifier to go with it.

The first feature to consider when shopping for an equalizer is the number of frequency bands it controls. The more bands, the more flexibly you can control the sound, but the more you'll have to fiddle with those controls to adjust them properly. If you like to readjust the sound for every broadcast and recording, then you'll probably prefer an equalizer with compartively few bands. Five-band equalizers are most popular, for just that reason. If you want to adjust your system's overall sound once and leave it alone, then the more bands you have, the more precise your ultimate adjustment can be.

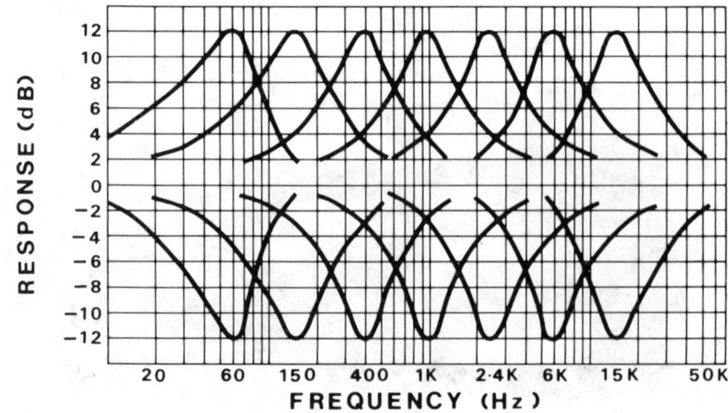

Equalizers let you adjust frequency response in many, narrow bands (Courtesy Audiobahn)

Slanting this equalizer's sliders left plenty of control room without taking much panel space (Courtesy Sony)

Most equalizers have sliding controls for each band. A glance at the position of these sliders will show you what frequency change the equalizer is making, which is why these are called "graphic" equalizers. The longer the slide, the more precisely you can adjust the sound.

Long sliders take up space, though. One solution to that problem is to slant the sliders, to keep them long while leaving the control panel shallow. Another (less commonly used) is to restrict the control range to perhaps ±6 dB instead of ±12. A one-inch control covering the former's 12–dB range gives the same precision as a two-inch slider covering the latter's 24 dB. If there's a switch to choose ranges, you can make either precise adjustments over a narrow range or more sweeping adjustments over a wider one.

Some newer equalizers use buttons to raise and lower response in each bank, with lights showing the settings that result. Such systems can offer precise control and compactness. However, you cannot set them by feel as you can with ordinary sliders (especially sliders with firm click-stops at their center points); when you're driving, that could be a problem.

An equalizer should also have a by-pass switch, so you can take it out of the system entirely. This lets you compare the sound with and without the equalizer settings you've made, to be sure that the frequency compensation you've added is actually an improvement. Theoretically, the by-pass can also make the sound a little cleaner when you're not using the equalizer, since every added circuit, no matter how well made, adds something to the system's distortion and noise. But if the equalizer is good enough, that difference may be too small to be heard.

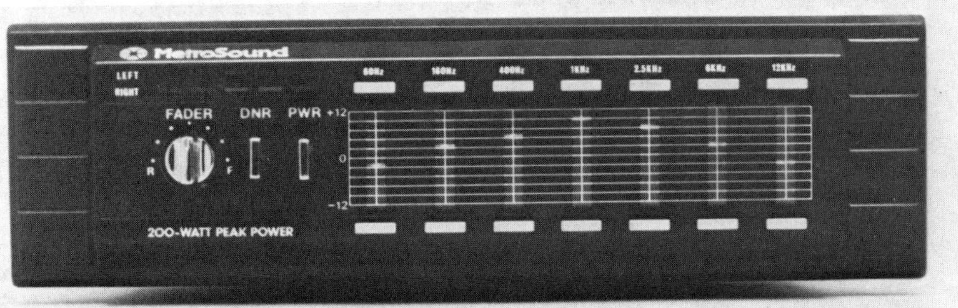

Some equalizers have no moving sliders; you press buttons to raise and lower response, and lights indicate the setting (Courtesy Metrosound)

Boosters

Boosters obviously can make a system louder. But they can also make its sound cleaner and less distorted. It all depends on how you want to use the extra power. As we saw previously, all amplifiers distort when driven hard, but more powerful amplifiers start distorting only at higher power levels. So you can use this added power in two ways. If you listen at the same sound levels as you did before you got your booster, the sound will probably be cleaner because the booster won't be working as hard to produce that volume. If you want to listen louder, however, you can do so with no more distortion than you had before.

Boosters have some limitations. You'll rarely find one that delivers more than 10 or 20 watts per channel, and you won't hear very much improvement unless your original sound system's amplifier delivered less than about half the power that the booster can. (When comparing figures, make sure that the power measurements for both the booster and the system's built-in amplifier were made under similar conditions—see the section on types of equipment for more details.) Boosters, however, are usually designed for use with all-in-one, in-dash systems, which normally deliver something like 2 to 4 watts per channel. Starting from that power level, you should hear a definite, if not dramatic difference.

The other limitation of a booster amplifier is that it works from a signal that's already been through the in-dash unit's built-in amplifier. This signal will have somewhat more noise and distortion than signals taken from preamp-level outputs

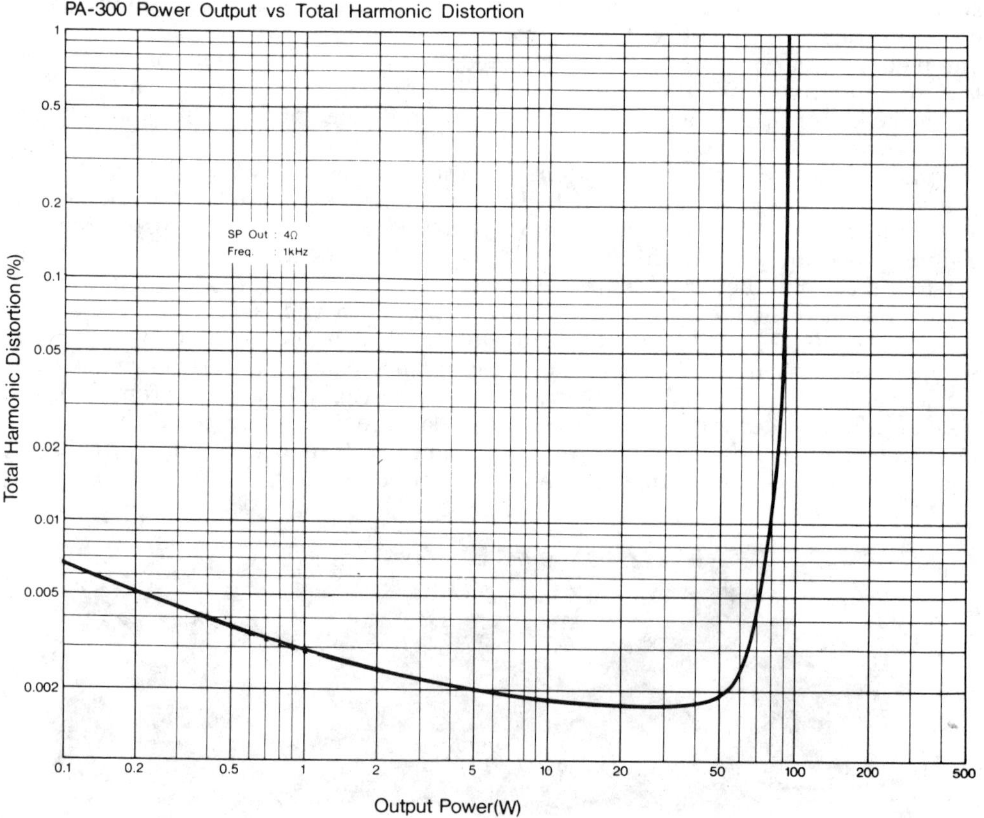

Demanding more power than an amplifier can give makes the sound distorted; but a booster amp can add power without such drastic sound deterioration (Courtesy Nakamichi)

would, and the booster will amplify that noise and distortion, as well as adding some of its own. Even so, the sound will probably be cleaner than it would have been without the booster—but not as clean as if a preamp output were feeding an amplifier of equivalent power.

If you're buying a booster for use with the sound system you have now, you might consider getting a "booster/amplifier"—one which has both speaker-level and preamp-level inputs. You can use that unit as a booster with your present system, then use it as an amplifier with a new in-dash unit in your next car. If you're keeping your car long enough, you might even want to replace your present in-dash receiver someday with a new receiver having preamp-level outputs. Booster/amplifier units are often available with more power than plain boosters, too.

How do you tell if you need more power in the first place? If turning up the volume control until the sound is loud enough for you makes the sound audibly rougher, too, then you probably do need more power; if turning up the volume only increases the roughness, not the sound level, you definitely do. If you get adequate volume long before the sound gets even marginally irritating, then you have enough power now.

If you already have a pretty hefty amplifier, and still get distortion when you turn the sound up, the amplifier might not be the problem. Check to make sure you're not overdriving the speakers instead; if you are, then you should replace them, not the amplifier. If neither speakers nor amplifiers are causing it, check the sound system's wiring to make sure that the wires and connections (especially those between amplifier and speaker) are not frayed, partially broken, or making contact with the car body or each other. Wire is cheap—if in doubt, replace it. The heavier the wire you use the better, too.

Many boosters and booster/equalizers have arrays of LEDs (light-emitting diodes) as a sort of "meter" to indicate how much power the amplifier puts out from moment to moment. These may be fun to look at, but they convey little useful information (you can tell what the amplifier's doing by listening to the speakers), and they can distract the driver. Look for a unit whose dancing lights can be shut off—or mount the unit so the lights don't show.

Bi-amplification

Using a separate amplifier to power each driver in a multi-speaker system will usually improve the system's sound, sometimes dramatically. But it also raises the system's cost considerably, since it requires more amplifiers and an "electronic crossover" to channel the proper frequencies to each amplifier, and usually adds to the installation cost as well. Despite that high cost, many systems are bi-amplified or even tri-amplified, sure evidence that the technique yields a real improvement—for those who care to pay its cost.

If you're among that number, there are several points to keep in mind while selecting the pieces of your system. Your speaker should have separate connections for each driver or set of drivers which will operate from a given amplifier. For a bi-amplified system, you'd need one connection for the woofer, one for the midrange and tweeter; for a tri-amplified system, woofer, midrange and tweeter connections should be independent of each other. Speaker systems made up of separate drivers always fulfill this requirement; co-axial or multi-axial speakers and speaker systems built into their own enclosures often don't, a point to check when shopping.

Your crossover's frequency divisions must also match those for which the speakers were designed. If they don't, the system's frequency response will be irregular. Mis-matched crossover frequencies can even damage speakers, if the tweeters or midrange are fed frequencies too low for them to handle. Some manufacturers offer matched speakers and crossovers, or speakers plus amplifiers or in-dash receivers with matching crossovers built in. Other companies sell crossovers whose frequency divisions are adjustable to match most speaker combinations.

Noise Reduction Systems

Just a few years ago, about the only noise-reduction system in home use was Dolby B (Dolby A is just for use in recording studios). Nearly every cassette deck made had it, some FM stations and FM tuners used it, too. And by now, most car-stereo manufacturers offer it in at least some models.

But Dolby B is no longer unique. Its first challenge came from the dbx noise reduction system, which in turn was soon challenged by an improved Dolby, Dolby C. Each of these is an "encode/decode" or "closed-loop" system, designed to be used both in recording (the encoding phase) and in playback (decoding). For best results in playing recordings made with any of these noise reduction systems, you must use the same system in playback.

What happens if you don't? It all depends. When played back without Dolby decoders, Dolby B tapes may sound as if their highs are a bit overemphasized, but rarely to the point where you can't restore them nearly to normal by turning down the treble control. On systems with weak high-frequency response, in fact, undecoded Dolby B tapes may sound better than normal ones.

On Dolby C tapes played without proper decoding, the highs are even more pronounced. You can play them on Dolby B machines with about the same treble-control settings and get pretty good results; but if your system also lacks Dolby B, you may have trouble cutting the highs back to normal with just tone controls.

Tapes made with dbx encoding sound even worse when played back un-decoded. Their high frequencies are emphasized, and their dynamic range sounds squashed.

The obvious solutions to these problems are either to make only tapes whose noise reduction systems match your car's, or to give your car system whatever noise reduction facilities it lacks. At this writing, dbx and Dolby C are both available in in-dash systems, but add-on decoders are available only for the dbx system. It's likely that Dolby C decoders will also be available separately by the time you read this. Decoders for dbx and Dolby C can both increase your system's dynamic range, if you're equipped to make appropriately encoded tapes at home. (Add-on encoder/decoder boxes for both Dolby C and dbx are available for home systems.)

Another noise-reducer coming into car-sound use is "DNR", or "Dynamic Noise Reduction." This is an open-loop, or decode-only system: it requires no special preparation or encoding of the tapes you play, but can reduce noise on all types of program material, both on tape or from FM and AM broadcasts. Again, this is only available as a built-in feature on some stereos, so far, but could be available as an accessory by the time you read this. If it is, see if any DNR accessories have controls to vary their action; such controls (not needed on the other systems) let you adjust for the best possible hiss reduction with the least possible effect on the music.

Other Sound Controls

For all the benefits of having speakers front and rear (see the section on Speakers), not all receivers are set up to control two sets of speakers at once. If yours is not, you can add either a fader or an amp balancer. Faders are used when both sets of speakers are driven by a single amplifier, and are connected between the amp and the speakers. Amplifier balancers are used when front and rear speakers have separate amps, and are connected between the receiver and the amplifiers. Systems with a single amplifier and fader cost less, but the fader does waste some of the amplifier's power, and may have a minor effect on the sound.

Time delay systems are used to make the car sound larger, by simulating the

Faders balance the signal from a single amplifier between front and rear speakers

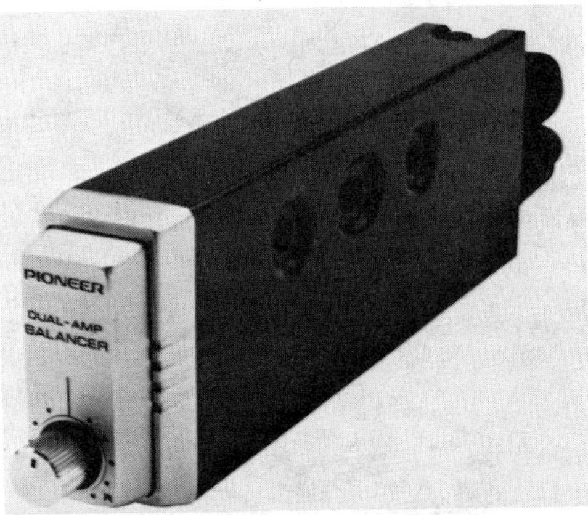

Amplifier balancers are used for separate amps for front and rear

long-delayed echoes heard in large spaces such as concert halls. Depending on the system, the delayed sound may be mixed with both front and rear speaker systems, mixed with the rear speaker sound, or fed to the rear speaker instead of the undelayed sound. Systems which mix delayed with undelayed sound in the main speaker channels tend to reduce the clarity of the sound.

Delay systems should allow the amount of delayed sound, or the delay time, to be adjusted. While a lot of delay or reverberance can add substantially to the impact of music designed to be heard in large spaces (such as organ solos), it can make other soloists and small groups sound as if they're performing in a well.

SHOPPING FOR YOUR SYSTEM

Shopping for car stereo is a matter of deciding what to buy and where to buy it. Both decisions are important.

What to Buy

What you'll buy will depend on many factors. The four main ones your tastes in sound, your desire for features and conveniences, your budget, the kind of car your sound system must fit, and what equipment will work best together.

So far, we've mostly been concerned with the kinds of equipment available, and what sonic and convenience advantages they offer. Now it's time to consider the remaining factors.

We have not given specific price guidelines, because prices are subject to wide fluctuation. Not all those prices will have risen, either. While consumer prices in general were rising feverishly in the past few years, many features (such as digital tuning and automatic tape reverse) became available in ever less expensive equipment. During the same period, other products have improved in quality with no rise in price.

To see what is available in your desired price range, consult your local dealers, advertisements, annual directories (published by several of the major hi-fi magazines) and the catalogs of mail-order car-stereo specialists. Bear in mind that many dealers will offer lower prices than those shown in the directories. But bear in mind also that the prices shown in most of these sources are for equipment only, not for installation. Unless you're prepared to install your system yourself (covered in the next section), you'll find that installation will usually increase the cost somewhat;

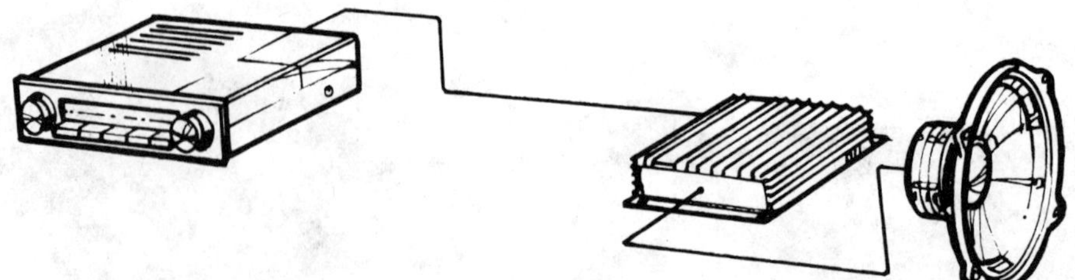

AM/FM Cassette deck (w/ or w/o separate amplifier) and pair of speakers

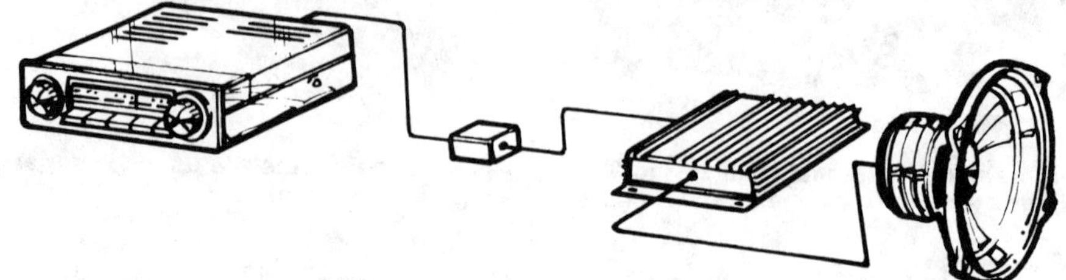

Adding a preamplifier cleans up the sound and gives more precise control of sound

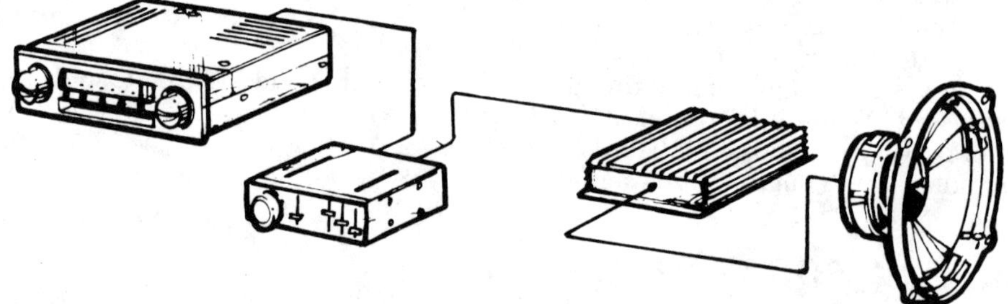

Adding an equalizer lets you dial in your preferences over the entire frequency range

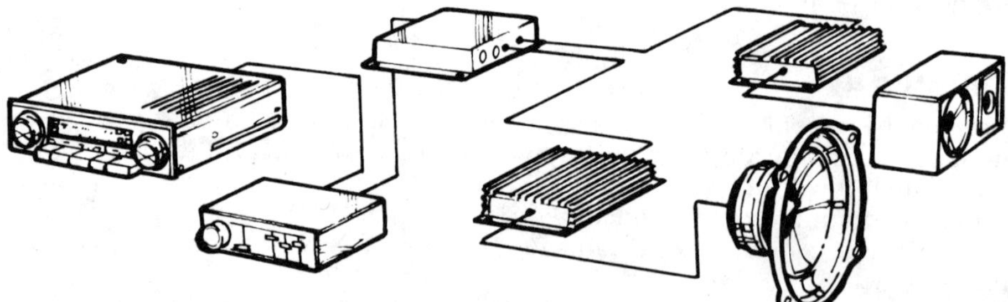

Add an amplifier, cross-over and additional speaker and you begin to truly hear highs and lows

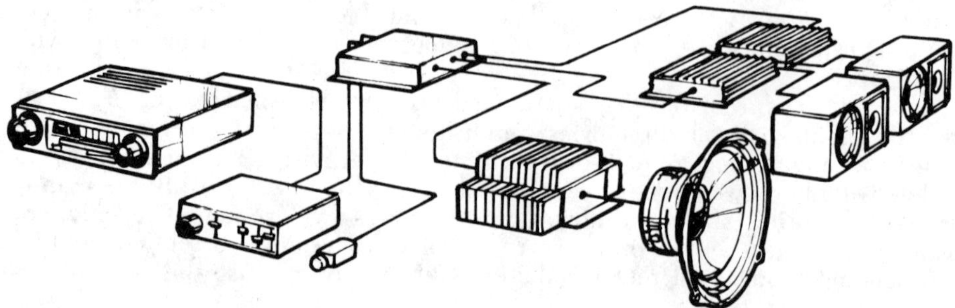

The top-of-the-line with sub woofers, satellite speakers, multiple amplifiers and custom speaker enclosures can run into thousands of dollars

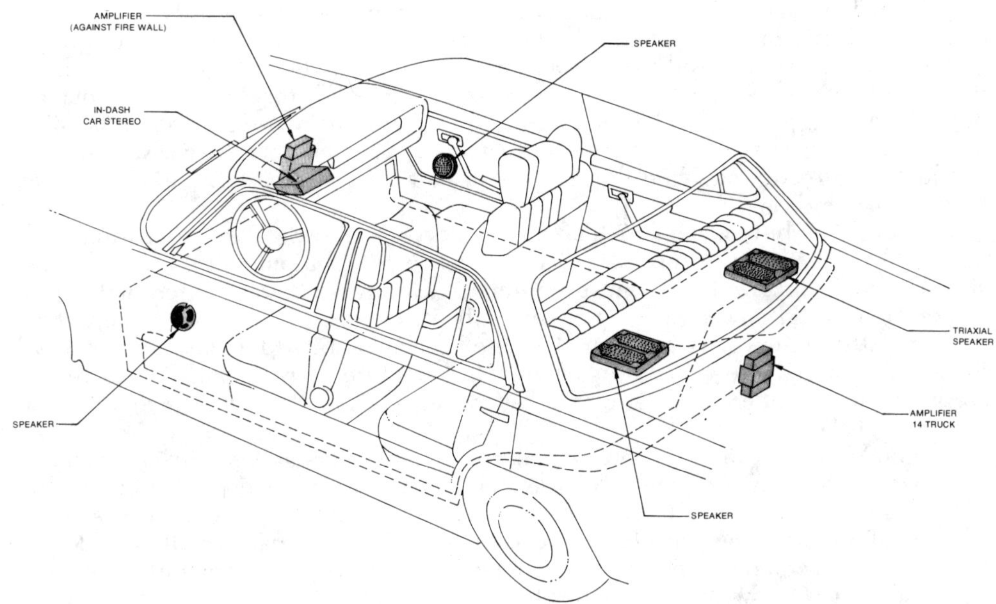

Typical component locations

your local dealers and installers should be able to tell you just about how much it will cost to put your prospective system in your car and what potential problems you may encounter on your vehicle.

By this point, you should have some idea of what type of system you want in your car, what level of performance you expect and what features you'll need or are prepared to pay for. Whatever your needs, you'll find a good many systems which will answer them, leaving you the task of narrowing down the possibilities enough to make your final choices.

The possibilities narrow fast, though, when you restrict yourself to that equipment which will fit your car; and the smaller the car, the faster they will narrow. The first problem you'll have to face is finding a receiver to fit your dashboard. In-dash radio slots come in a variety of sizes and, sometimes, in unusual configurations (on some cars, for instance, they run vertically instead of horizontally). To find what fits your car's dashboard, you'll need to know the size of the dash opening and the distance between its control knob shaft holes. Dealers and some manufacturer literature can help you identify some systems that will fit; learn the dimensions of those systems, and you'll be able to find others that fit, too.

Equalizers are easier to install, because they needn't be as handy as the main controls in the receiver. Few if any cars have slots pre-cut for equalizers, but many have panels which can be cut to accomodate them, either in the dashboard or in a console below the dash. Equalizers may also be hung beneath the dash on brackets or in housings which look like extensions of the dashboard. Consoles, available to go beneath many dashboards, can be used to hold equalizers, receivers, and accessory instruments (such as voltmeters or tachometers).

Amplifiers are fairly easy to place, because there's usually no need for their controls to be accessible. You can use nearly any space, as long as it's not so cramped that the amplifier lacks air circulation for cooling. The more powerful the amplifier, the more space it will usually need. Large amplifiers, or multi-amplifier systems, are frequently mounted in the trunk.

Speakers take a bit more thought, since where you place them affects your sound.

Many cars have mounting holes or cavities built into their dashboards, rear decks, or interior door panels which you can find with some investigation. If you use those mounting spots, you'll need to use speakers which match the hole sizes. If you have your heart set on speakers of some other size, or if the factory mounting spots are not where the speakers will sound best, you'll have to investigate other possible locations. Many of the more successful catalog houses and car stereo supply specialists have already cataloged the various speakers, installation kits and dimensions by car make and model.

Whatever you buy, make sure all components of your system are compatible with one another. Even if several manufacturers made the equipment you select, most speakers will work well with most amplifiers, as long as the amplifiers fall within the recommended power range. It's generally a bad idea to use an amplifier which delivers either more or less power than the speaker is rated for, and not too good to use one right at the very limits of the speaker's rated power range. Best results are generally obtained with amplifiers in the top half of the range recommended for your speakers.

Incompatibilities can arise between receivers, amplifiers and equalizers of different brands. The most frequent problem is mis-matched connections. Several different types of plug are used to connect car-stereo components and not all companies who use the same plugs wire them the same way. If you're handy with a soldering iron, or know someone who is, this problem is fairly easy to surmount—just wire up an adapter cable with the proper plug at each end.

Signal voltage levels must also match. If the receiver puts out a higher signal voltage than the equalizer or amplifier is designed for, it will overload the amp or equalizer's inputs, and you'll hear distortion. If the receiver's output voltage is too low for the next component's input, you may not be able to get sufficient volume from the system. The system may be noisier than normal, too. Adapters to match signal voltages exist, but they are usually sold only to installers, not at retail sales counters.

Where to Buy

The least expensive way to buy a stereo system is to shop around for the lowest equipment prices, then install it yourself. That analysis ignores a few factors, such as the value of your time in doing the installation, the cost of any special tools you'll need to do the job, and the possibility of damage to your car, but, car stereo owners have successfully installed millions of systems themselves, and saved themselves the expense of having it done. If you're handy, but have never tried an installation before, use the section on installation as a guide.

If you're buying a new car, you can get a stereo system installed at the factory. If so, you'll probably be able to hear a similar system installed in a similar car before you make your decision and you'll be assured of an installation that really fits the car. If your car's base price includes a radio, you may also be able to upgrade to the factory stereo for less than the cost of ripping out the standard radio and having a stereo system of your own put in.

Before deciding to do this, though, ask your car dealer what happens if you order your car without the radio. Many car manufacturers lower their prices if you order the car this way, but dealers may not discuss this "delete option" if you don't ask. The real cost of a factory stereo system is not the difference between the stereo and the standard radio cost (although many manufacturers leave the wiring and speakers and delete only the radio for credit), but the difference between the price including stereo and the price less radio. Often, you'll find that other stereos offer equal or better value—even if extra installation costs are included.

Finding out what constitutes an "equal value" isn't always easy, though. While independent stereo makers publish comprehensive feature lists and specifications, this information is infrequently available for factory-installed equipment. Try to find out at least what types of speakers are included in the factory setup—they're often single-cone or whizzer-cone types with light magnets rather than two-way or three-way systems with more powerful magnet structures.

Your car dealer may offer alternatives to the factory equipment, often made by major car stereo companies whose names you know, and with full specifications available. You can usually be sure that such systems will fit your car properly, and careful shopping will reveal if that equipment (including any installation costs) matches the values available elsewhere.

Whether the system is installed by the dealer or the factory, if it comes with a new car you can probably finance it as part of your car loan. This spreads the payments out over a fairly long period, and raises each car payment by a small amount. But those small amounts add up, in time, and you may find the extra finance charges on the stereo system outweigh the convenience of stretching out the payments.

Car stereo equipment is available in a wide range of locations—from auto parts stores to electronic specialty dealers to mass merchandisers and department stores to factory authorized dealers. Wherever you shop, you'll probably have to choose between dealers who charge less and dealers who do more for you. At any price level, some dealers will do more for you than others; but the lower a dealer's prices, the less money he has available to pay for services you may want or need.

If you buy from a mail-order house, for instance, you will frequently pay quite low prices. But you'll have to either install the system or arrange an installation yourself. And if parts of the system need repair, you'll have to remove that equipment and either ship it back to the mail-order house or find a factory-authorized service center near you. Local dealers will generally help with removal (or you can remove it yourself and save the money) and will either repair it themselves or get it to a factory service center.

Local dealers will vary in their car-sound expertise, in the range of equipment they stock, and in their display and installation facilities. Car-stereo specialists will most often be able to discuss your car and its problems in detail, guide you to equipment which will fit your car and your needs, demonstrate it for you adequately, and install it. Other dealers, however, may well have what you want, sometimes at lower prices.

If you buy the whole system from one dealer, he's more likely to stand behind the system as a whole than if you buy the receiver from one store and get the amplifier and speakers in two other places. Buying this way can save money, too: the more you buy from any single source, the more leverage you have in bargaining for better prices.

Car Sound Checklist

TUNER/TAPE PLAYER

- In-dash mounting is best
- AM/FM/cassette tape player
- Does it fit the space available?
- The tuner/tape deck should cost 40–50 percent of the total you can spend
- Is it styled to blend with the dash

Tuner

- Are the controls easy to use

Specifications

- IHF useable sensitivity: FM sensitivity of 1–5 mv and stereo sensitivity of 5–10 mv at 30 dB, AM sensitivity of 20–25 mv at 20 dB (lower is better)
- Image rejection ratio or band selectivity of 40 dB (higher is better)
- "Local/Distance" switch or automatic gain control of 50 dB (higher is better)
- Stereo separation of 25 dB at 100 Hz (higher is better)
- Frequency response of 50–15,000 Hz (broader is better)

Features

- Pushbutton tuning (nice, but not at the expense of audio features)
- Digital or continuous readout (no performance difference)
- Electronic tuning (no performance difference)
- "Muting" switch
- "Mono/stereo" switch or automatic switching circuit
- "Loudness" switch
- Power antenna lead
- Separate bass and treble controls
- Balance control, side to side
- Fader control, front to back
- Preamp Output Jacks (necessary for the best quality sound)

TAPE PLAYER

- Cassette player (unless you already have an eight-track library)
- Front or side load (no performance difference, side load has less frontal area)
- Chromium dioxide metal tape capability (nice, but not necessary)

Specifications

- Frequency response of 50–15,000 Hz (broader is better)
- Wow and flutter of 0.25 percent (lower is better)
- Signal-to-noise ratio of 55–60 dB (higher is better)

Features

- Power off/eject
- Auto-reverse (no performance difference)
- Locking fast forward and rewind
- Dolby noise reduction (necessary for the best quality sound)

AMPLIFIER

- Separate component amplifiers usually give better sound
- Amplifiers are better than power boosters
- The component amplifier should cost 25–30 percent of the total you can spend
- Is amplifier compatible with tuner for impedance and input sensitivity
- Will it fit in my car
- Biamplification (requires 4 speakers)

Specifications

- Average power output per channel of 15–20 watts at 1 percent total harmonic distortion (higher output is better, lower distortion is better)
- Signal-to-noise ratio of 70 dB (higher is better)

Features

Internal short and overload protection circuit (absolutely necessary) Automatic power equalizer

EQUALIZER

• Integral with amplifier or separate (be wary of getting a power booster instead of a true amp)

• Will it fit in my car

• The equalizer should cost about 5–10 percent of the total you can spend

• Is it compatible with my amplifier and speakers

Specifixations

• Frequency bands adjustable to ±12 dB

Features

• Five to seven band equalization
• Balance control, side to side
• Fader control, front to back
• Dual amplifier fader (necessary in a two-amp biamplification system)

SPEAKERS

• Will they fit in my car

• Is the total speaker system compatible with my amplifier for power handling capacity (cautious types will get speakers rated for slightly more maximum power than the amplifier)

• The speaker system should cost 25–30 percent of the total you can spend

• Is the total system compatible with the amplifier for impedance

• Are the speaker grilles styled to blend with my car

Specifications

• Frequency response of 60 to 18,000 Hz (broader is better)

Features

• 20 ounce magnet or smaller "super magnet" on woofers
• Foam or cloth hinge
• Acoustically neutral speaker grilles

ANTENNA

• Will it fit on my car

• A manual retractible antenna can cost less than $5, a signal-boosting or automatic power retracting antenna will cost about $50, a power retracting signal-boosting antenna is $100

• Is it styled to blend with my car

• Is it made just for AM/FM

Specifications

• The best antenna is a signal-boosting electronic antenna, next best is a 31 inch whip, everything else is third

FEATURES

• Automatic power retracting (requires a power antenna lead on the tuner)

INSTALLATION

Installation consists of 3 basic parts—electronics, mechanical and speakers (which combines a little of each). Every installation is unique with its own problems, but the following guide will help you avoid many pitfalls.

Following this section are photographs of an actual installation illustrating many of the principles discussed and found in a typical job.

Read these sections and Chapter 1 on Tools before proceeding with the installation.

Electronics

Your system will neither look nor work its best unless it's properly installed. And getting it installed takes time, careful work and at least a modicum of knowledge. The more complex the system, and the more critical you are of the results, and the more time and work it takes.

If you install it yourself, you'll save money. If you have it done, you'll pay that money—but you'll save yourself the time and effort.

If you want to spend the money to have someone else do the installation, how do you find a good installer? Ask around, especially among people whose car stereo systems you admire. Check the work done by the dealer who sold you the equipment—or by the installation shop he uses, if he has no facilities of his own. Look as well as listen—you want an installation that's neat and convenient.

Check prices, too. Not all shops charge the same. The store that sold you the equipment may make you a better price if you buy the installation with it. Don't dismiss the higher-priced shops out of hand, either. Ask them what more you're getting for your money—it might be worth it.

Ask for an estimate, in writing, before you authorize the job. Be sure the installer knows both your vehicle model, what equipment you want installed and any special requests you might have. Even with this knowledge, the unexpected can always occur. But if the charges substantially exceed the estimate, there should be a reason why.

Do It Yourself

Good installations are not cheap; and once you've gotten estimates, you may prefer to do your own. You also might prefer to do it yourself for other, equally valid reasons: the challenge, a love of tinkering, or an excuse to use your new power tools. Whatever your reason, the following tips will help you on your way to a good installation.

PRELIMINARY PLANNING

If you just pick up your tools and start to work, you're likely not to get everything right. Read this section and the installation that follows before starting.

Every car model poses different problems, and it's well to get as familiar as possible with those posed by yours. Ask around among other owners (especially those who have installed their own systems) to see what works and doesn't work. Ask your car dealer's service manager. Get and study a shop manual for your car, if you can. (It will come in handy if you ever need or want to service your car, too.) If you can't get the manual, at least get the car's electrical schematic and learn how to read it (See the section in this book on general electrical work.).

Decide in advance what circuits you'll want your system to draw power from. Cars contain three types of power circuits: those which are always on (such as the ones powering the clock, cigarette lighter and interior lights); those which are on when the key is in its "Accessory" position or when the ignition is on (such as heater fans, or the headlights in some foreign cars), and those which are only on when the ignition is switched fully on.

High-power amplifiers are best connected to circuits which are only on when the ignition is. Such amplifiers can draw enough current to drain the car's battery if they're used when the engine is off and not running the alternator or generator.

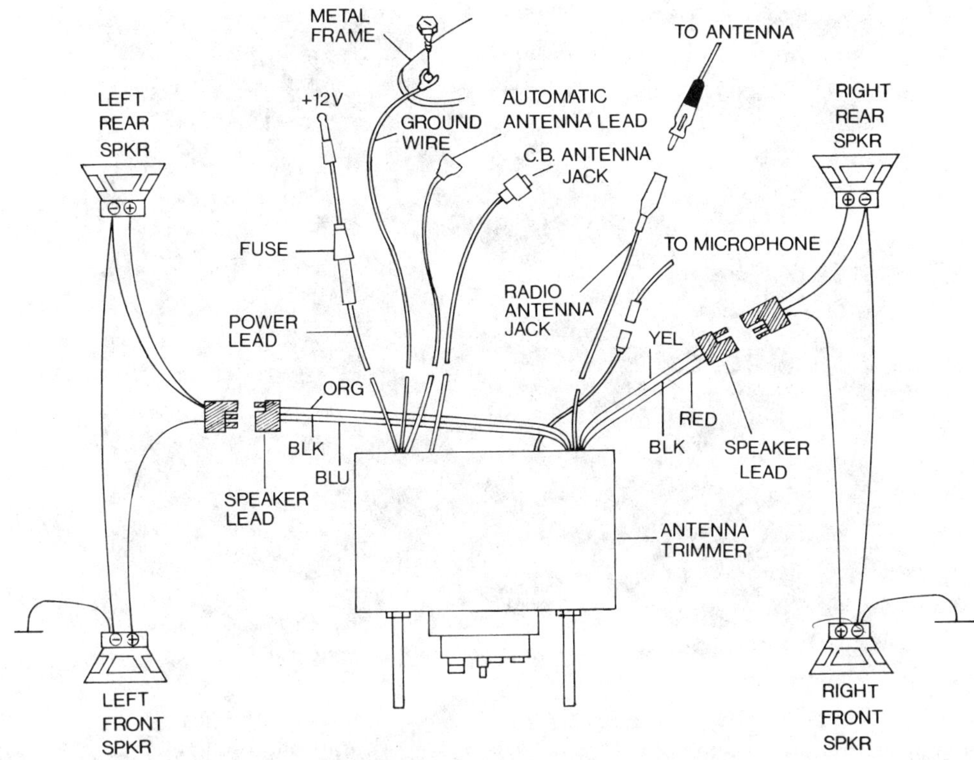

Wiring diagram for a typical (and fairly simple) installation (Courtesy Pioneer)

You could still run the system by turning the ignition on without starting the engine, but you shouldn't—not only to protect the battery but to protect the ignition points on cars without all-electronic ignition. Some high-powered amplifiers shut themselves off if the battery voltage lowers beyond a preset point; such amplifiers could be used safely on Accessory-switched circuits.

Radios, and tape systems which automatically eject the tape when the power is shut off, are usually best operated from switched circuits, ensuring that they won't be left on to drain the battery when you're not in the car. If the system does not draw much from the battery, you'll probably prefer to connect it to Accessory-switched circuits, so you can run it without starting the engine and wasting gas.

Tape players without automatic ejection (which includes most players) pose a bit of a dilemma. If you connect them to a circuit that is always hot, you risk draining your battery by leaving them on. But if you connect them to a switched circuit, you might forget and switch off while a tape is playing. This could damage both the tape and the player. Tape damage isn't too serious, unless the cassette warps in place (not unlikely if the car is parked in the sun, especially in summer). You can not remove it without taking the player apart. The player damage occurs because the rubber roller is left pressing the tape against the rotating capstan, and develops flat spots where the pressure is applied. This causes it to turn unevenly, causing wow and flutter when you next play back the tape.

Receivers with digital tuning frequently have two power feed lines, one to go to a switched circuit, and one to feed from an unswitched one. The latter operates the memory for the station-selector buttons, and the clock if there is one.

Unswitched, accessory-switched and ignition-switched circuits may usually be found both under the dash and at the car's fuse box. Study your car's schematic

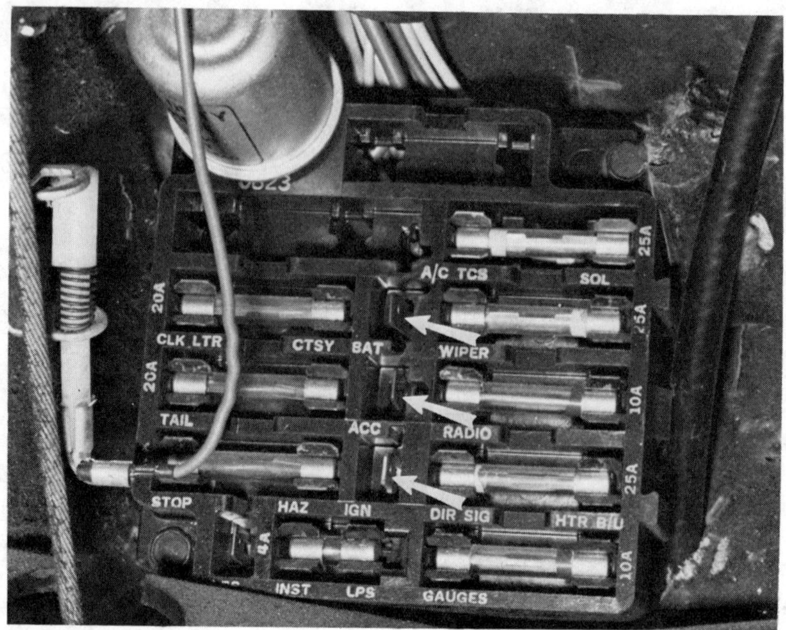

Most fuse boxes have extra terminals like this, which makes tapping in for power easy

diagram to identify and locate these circuits and to find what color codes are used for their wires. Also check the load already on each line with the load your stereo will add to it. If the total of both loads runs uncomfortably close to the rating for that circuit's fuse, look for another power source, or consider dividing your system's power feeds between several such circuits.

If interference is a problem, it sometimes helps to run the system's power feed directly to the battery. If you're worried about draining the battery by leaving your system on, consider putting in a relay which will only switch this line on if an accessory or ignition circuit is on, too. Or you might put a switch with built-in pilot light into the dash, whose glow will remind you to shut the system off.

Reading the instructions which came with your equipment should be an integral part of the pre-planning process. Find out what connections you'll have to make, and where they'll go. Determine what mounting hardware is provided, and if you'll need anything else. (The time to start driving around in a search for extra parts is before you've started taking it apart to put your stereo in.) Find out where the manufacturer recommends placing the equipment, and how much ventilation it will need.

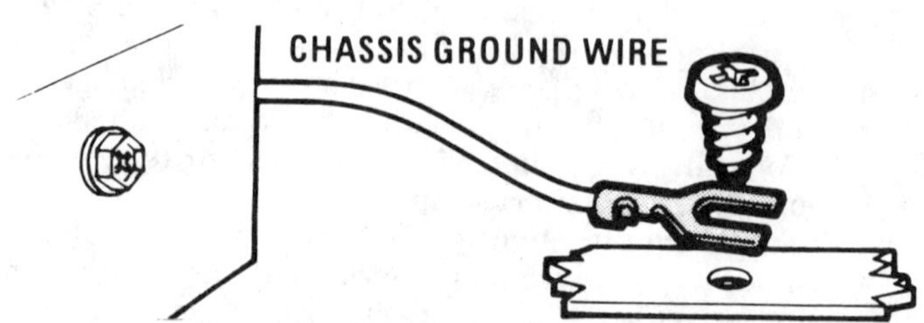

For correct grounding, screw the main unit's chassis ground wire to the car's sheet-metal

Installation kits are available for virtually all cars and trucks

Examine the Equipment

Now examine the equipment itself. Learn what each connection and control is for. Try plugging the parts together to make sure they mate. If the receiver and amplifier are of different makes, double-check the plug diagrams included with each piece, to make sure the plugs are compatible. If not, re-wire one plug to correct the situation. See where all mounting brackets and bolts go, and try the brackets on for size beforehand. Find out if there's an installation kit available for your particular; there's a good chance there is one available from manufacturers specializing in radio mounting kits.

Temporarily connect the equipment to a 12-volt power supply or the battery, and try operating the system, to make sure all its parts work. It's easier to get something fixed before installing it than after—and it's easier to tell whether problems are due to the equipment or its installation if you've tested the equipment first.

Tools and Supplies

Check to see if you have all the proper tools (see the chapter on Tools), and get them together before you start to work. You're certain to need a drill (preferably electric), some sort of saw for cutting speaker holes, regular and Philips-head screwdrivers, wire strippers, wire cutters, pliers, a center punch, a hammer, a variety of sheet-metal screws (usually #10 or #8) in several lengths, several sizes and shapes of metal file, an assortment of washers and lockwashers, a volt-ohmmeter or continuity tester and some electrical tape. You'll probably have use for a soldering iron (there are 12-volt models you can run from your car's battery), rosin-core solder (NOT acid-core), a drafting compass (for marking speaker holes), a tape measure (preferably the stiff, metal type), a crimping tool and crimp-on contact lugs, a flashlight, wire nuts, heat-shrink tubing and tape, a saber saw or keyhole saw and socket wrenches. Safety glasses or goggles are also recommended. You'll want clean rags to wipe your hands and work areas; and unless it's rather chilly, you'll probably want a towel to help you mop the sweat from your brow. Touch-up paint to match your car's interior and exterior colors may also come in handy.

Look for a good place to work on your car, too. The ideal one would be sheltered from the elements, large enough so you can stick your legs out of the car without getting them run over, and preferably near an outlet for your power tools. If you can keep the neighborhood's small kids away, you'll save the time you'd otherwise spend answering their questions; but kids old enough to have some interest in electronics can be a help.

Prepare the car, too. Clean excess junk out of the passenger compartment, and from the trunk if you'll be working there. It's easier to work if you can lie down under a panel without getting a back full of junk, and it's easier to find any small parts you drop if the area is clean.

Component Placement

Scout the territory. Look inside the dash, and double-check that your receiver will actually fit there (although you should have done this before purchasing the equipment) with room for its connections and any support brackets required. Find out where you can attach a brace (usually a perforated steel strap) to support the back of the receiver. Check any places where you plan to put the amplifiers, to be sure there's not only room enough for the amp but some room for air to circulate around it, too. Try for a spot which will let you place the amplifier's cooling fins upright, to work like chimneys, unless the amplifier instruction manual advises differently. If you plan to mount any components (such as the equalizer) beneath the dash, make sure there's a solid mount for the support brackets; see if there are any places where the equalizer can be placed in the dash, for both neatness and security.

While the dash is usually the best place for the receiver, it's hardly the only one. Some prefer to put it out of sight, beneath the seat—not all that inconvenient to reach, on some cars, if you can operate the system by touch. Units have also been installed in glove compartments (it's seldom difficult to cut out the back of the

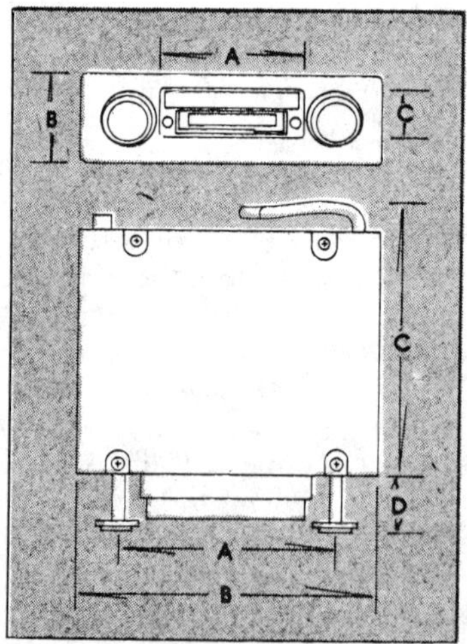

Critical radio fit dimensions: top: A—width of nosepiece; B—housing height; C—shaft hole size; Bottom: A—distance between shaft centers; B—housing width; C—depth of housing; D—shaft length

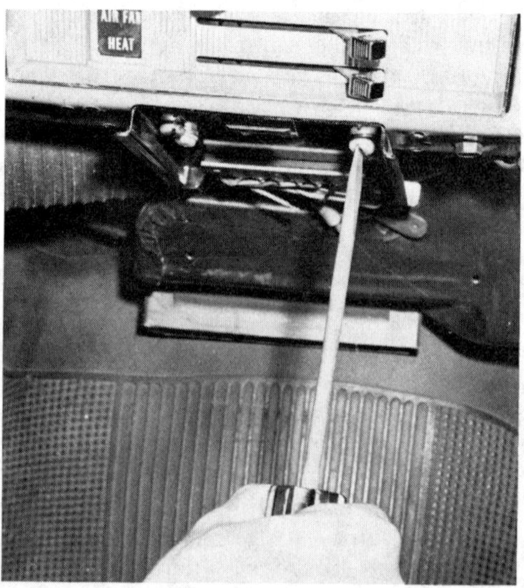

Slide mounts make the system more versatile

compartment if it isn't deep enough), between front bucket seats or in the rear compartment (most commonly in limousines). The ashtray position is sometimes used—you can put "beanbag" ashtrays on top of the dash, when needed.

Slide mounts contribute nothing to a system's sound, but they can make it more versatile and secure. The security is obvious—if you can easily remove the system, you can put it in a safe place when you park. The versatility works two ways: If you equip two cars with slide mounts and speakers, you can then transfer your stereo to whichever car you're using.

Underdash mounts are reversible, so you can mount your stereo above the transmission hump, too. Van installations often use the space above the windshield; housings or consoles are available for this, but you can make your own. Some manufacturers make "Cockpit" models which mount on the ceiling of the car between the two front seats.

Tape units are usually designed to be mounted horizontally. If you're planning to mount one more than 30 degrees from the horizontal, check first with the manufacturer of the model you're planning to buy.

If you're mounting your equipment anywhere but in the dashboard radio slot, make sure you pick a place where it won't get in your way when entering or riding in the car, and where you're not likely to injure yourself on it at any time.

Antenna Mounting

Experts differ on where the antenna should be placed. Some feel it should be in the back of the car, away from the engine's interference. Others feel it should be in the front, so there need be as little cable as possible to pick up interference between the antenna and the radio's input. Some even feel that front-mounted antennas should be on the side of the car away from the spark plugs.

Solid whip antennas give you a wide choice of possible locations, since they require very little mounting depth. Whips with ball-joints give you even more choice, as they're not restricted to horizontal surfaces. Telescoping antennas must telescope into the car, so they can only be placed where the car presents a suitable cavity. That's even more true of motorized antennas, which need motor space as well. If mounting on or near a movable body panel such as the hood or trunk lid, make sure the antenna won't get in the way of its opening or closing.

Wiring Basics

An electrical circuit is, as the name implies, a loop. What goes out through the "hot" or "+" lead must come back through the "ground" or "−" one. Both leads are equally important. The car itself usually serves as the ground, at least for power circuits, though less frequently for speakers. Most cars, today, have 12-volt, negative-ground systems with the hot leads nominally 12 volts above ground; in practice, voltages in a normal car may vary between about 11.6 and 14.4 volts under normal operating conditions.

Power leads generally have fuses, which are designed to blow if the current flowing through the line exceeds safe limits. The fuses for circuits which came with the car are usually collected in a single fuse box beneath the dash or under the hood. Car stereo components and other add-ons will have fuses of their own. Receiver fuses are usually in "pig-tail" holders built into the hot power leads. Amplifier fuses may be either in the leads or built into the body of the amps themselves.

If a fuse blows, never replace it with a larger value. On rare occasions, fuses blow for reasons of their own; but if a fuse blows more than once, it's a sign there's trouble in the circuit which should be cured before it gets worse or damages something.

Before you tie your stereo into the car's electrical system, check the car's wiring carefully. Do the color codes on the wires you plan to use actually correspond to those on the car's wiring diagram? The diagram may not reflect production changes

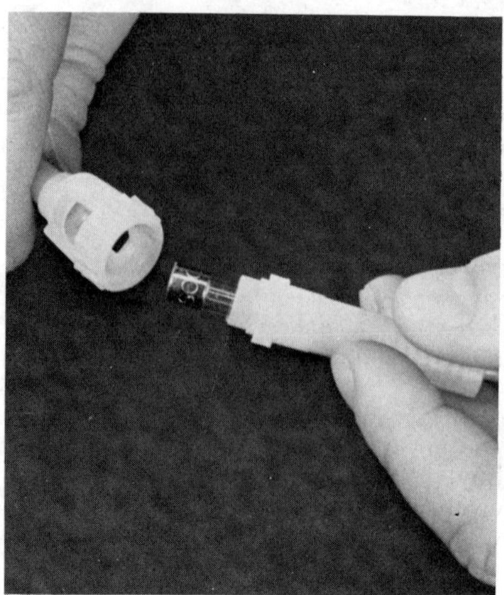

Components are usually fused in-line or in a holder built into the component body

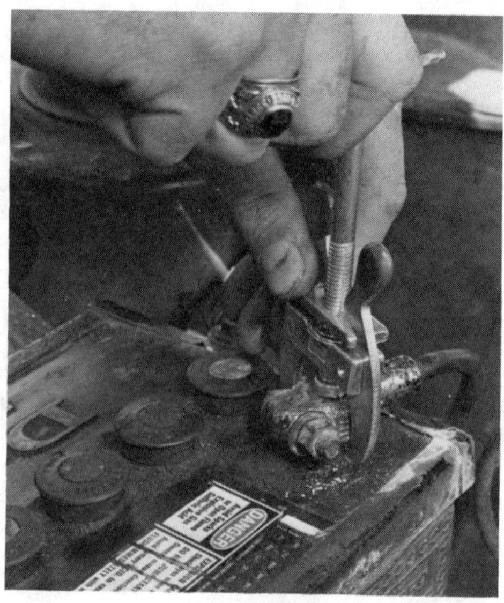

Disconnect the negative battery cable before beginning any wiring

that took place after it was printed; but it's also possible that you've mis-identified the wires. Wires in the car can become filmed with dirt (especially when the wires are near the engine), and color codes of even clean wires can be hard to read in the dim light which prevails under the dashboard. A good, bright flashlight with fresh batteries, or a plug-in trouble light can help ensure you get things right. A voltmeter or 12-volt neon tester can help you check to be sure whether and when a line is hot, or whether it's grounded.

It's a good idea to disconnect the power before working on the wiring. If the line you're tying into is switched by the ignition key, turn off the switch; if it's fused, remove its fuse, and if it's always hot, remove one lead from the car's battery. Be very careful not to short-circuit the battery with your tools.

Follow your equipment's grounding instructions carefully. Some car stereo components have separate ground leads which must make contact with the car's metalwork. Others make contact by grounding their chassis against the car, usually through the mounting screws. Still others may have ground leads which connect to another component in the system. Where separate ground leads are used, it's usually best to run them all to the same point on the car.

A good ground must contact bare (not painted) metal. One good way to do this is to drill a hole at the desired ground point, run a self-tapping sheet-metal screw into it, and tie the wires to the screw. Crimping "spade" terminals to the wire ends will help keep them under the screw head; match the terminal size to the wire gauge and the screw size, for tight connections. A bit of conductive silicone grease or petroleum jelly in the screw hole will help prevent corrosion at that point.

It's sometimes hard to tell by eye what parts of the car are actually grounded. Some non-metallic panels are metal-backed, while some metal structures (especially under dashboards) may not actually be electrically connected to the rest of the car. It's always best to check possible ground points: check with an ohmmeter or continuity tester for connection to a known ground point, or use a voltmeter or neon tester to make sure there's proper voltage between your ground and a hot line. Use your meter to check all power circuits against short circuits (inadvertent connections between hot and ground lines) or broken connections.

Wire splices can be made in several ways. Screw-on "wire nuts" are provided

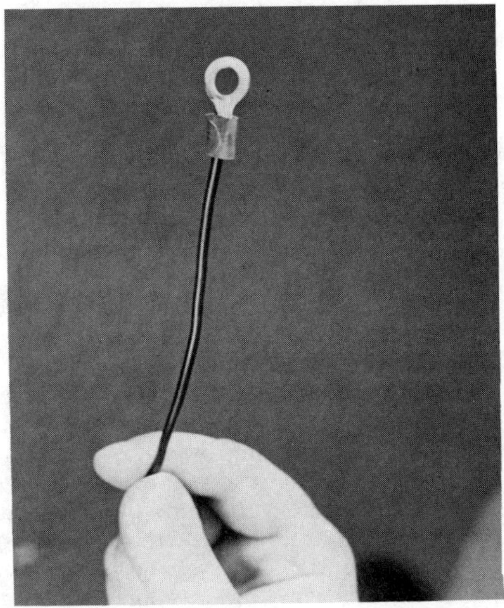

Crimp-on lugs make good ground connectors

with many car stereo components, and are available at hardware stores; make sure the bare portions of the wire are not long enough to stick out past the skirts of the wire nut, or they may short against some other wire or the car's frame.

Soldering makes a more secure connection. Twist the wires together securely before soldering—the solder is not a glue but a permanent "wetting" of the wire connection to ensure proper contact. Heat the wires till they melt the solder, rather than heating the solder till it drips onto the wires. Use just enough solder to flow in a thin coat over all wires involved, not enough to make lumps on the joint. Hold the joint absolutely still while it cools. A good joint will have a clean, silvery appearance; if it looks clouded or filmy, the joint shouuld be re-done.

Insulate the joint after soldering it. You can use electrical tape, but tubing, especially heat-shrink tubing, is more secure. The tubing should usually be slipped over the wires and pushed some distance from the joint before you solder, then slipped back over the joint once it's cooled.

If you use heat-shrink tubing, be especially sure to push it far enough down the wire to ensure it won't get hot when you solder. Use a tubing size just big enough to fit over the joint. Never use a match or other open flame inside the car to shrink the tubing. Use an electric hair dryer if you have a power source handy.

Clamp-on connectors are also available for a variety of uses. They're especially handy for making a "tee" connection to tape into an existing power lead without cutting it. Slip-joint pliers, opened at least one notch are usually the best tools for clamping these connectors together. Be very sure to match the connector to the wire gauges involved, or you may not make good contact. Check with a meter or tester in any case.

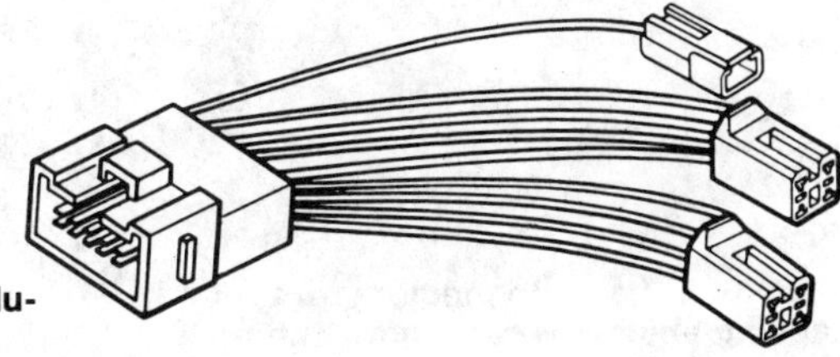

OEM wiring harness adapters are easy solutions to wiring problems

Do your wiring before the equipment has been bolted into place. This leaves you more room to work, and also ensures that you will leave enough slack in the wires to allow the equipment's removal later. Don't leave extra slack, though, even if you have to cut leads. And make sure that any slack is out of the way, where you or your passengers won't snag themselves on it.

Wiring should be concealed as much as possible, not just for neatness's sake but to prevent accidental snagging. You may run wires under carpets or floor mats, but be sure to run them where they won't be stepped on. Foot pressure can break wires, or wear through the insulation and allow short circuits. One commonly used wiring channel is the trough beneath the car's doorsill plate, usually one of the few easily-removed panels in the car.

If you have to fish a wire through a narrow passage or use a stiff wire as your "needle", follow that with a strong, thin cord (such as a fishline), and pull the wire itself through with that. Put rubber grommets into metal panel holes which wires pass through. This will prevent the panel from chafing through the wire's insulation, or the wire itself, over the years.

Try to run your system's wires (those carrying signal, as well as power leads) as far as possible from the car's other wiring, and not parallel to the car's wires. This will frequently reduce interference pickup.

Antennas must also be grounded. Scrape some paint from the underside of the panel your antenna mounts to, so the antenna mounting bolts will make good contact. Use petroleum jelly or silicone grease to prevent rust.

Mechanical

You'll have to make some holes in your car's body panels. Do it carefully. Never drill into any panel without checking to be sure what your drill will run into on the other side. If there are wires back there, tape them out of the way. If there are tubes or hoses carrying your car's fluids, or mechanical components which the drill might injure, find another spot.

Cover the spot with tape and mark it with a center punch before you drill. That will give your drill a good, initial bite, so it won't skitter all over the panel before digging in. If the surface is carpeted, cut an "X" in the carpet at the drilling spot, and pull the carpet flaps away from the hole. Otherwise, your drill bit may catch a thread and unravel part of the carpet.

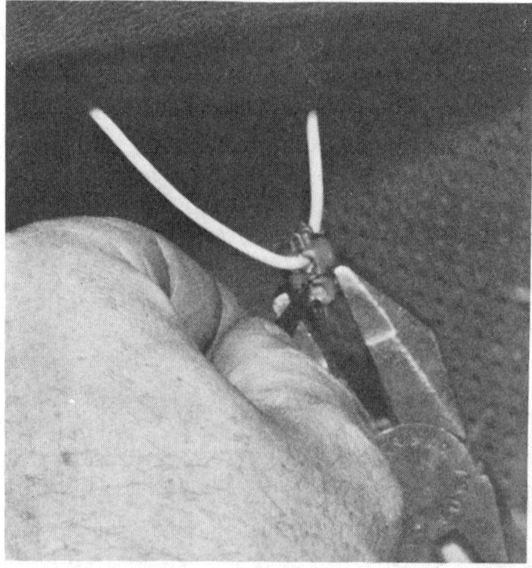

Clamp-on (tap) connectors are handy for tapping another wire without cutting it

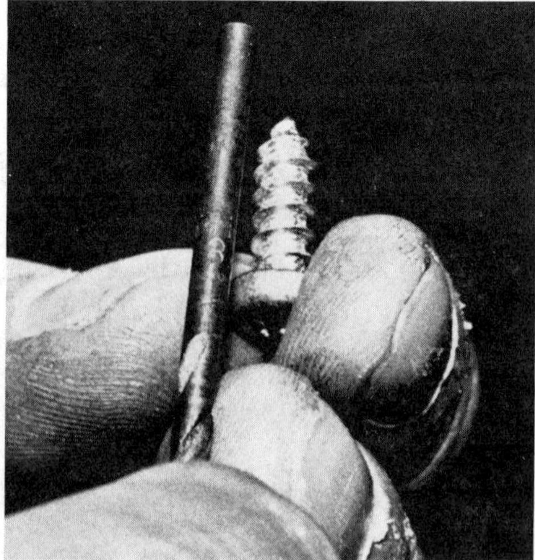

Use a drill of the same diameter as the "root" of the screw

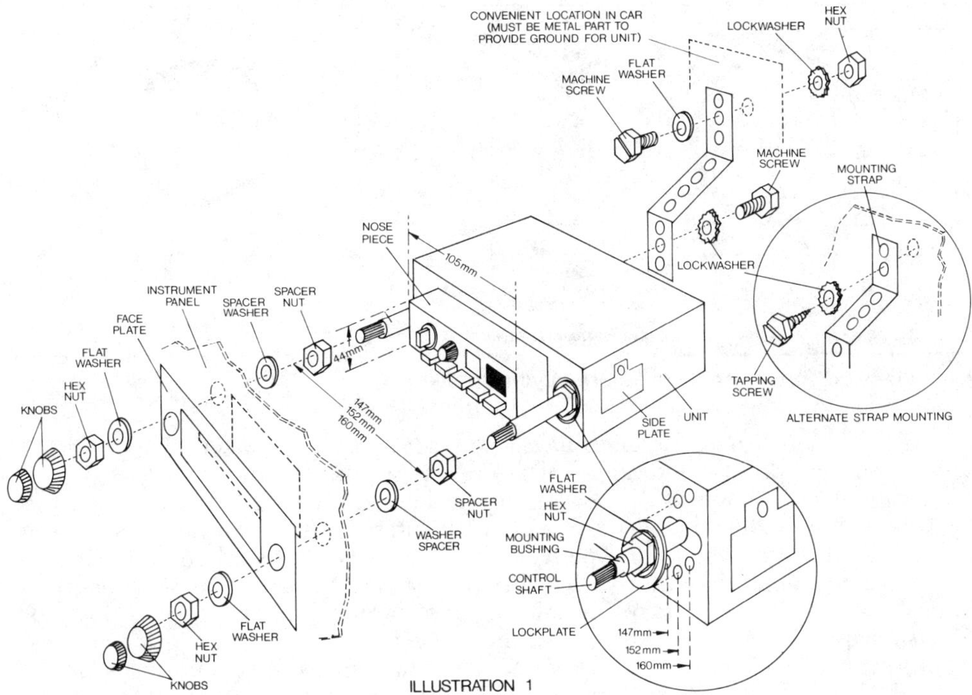

Typical radio installation

Use any mounting templates supplied with your equipment, to be sure you get the holes properly shaped and positioned. When in doubt, make the hole a bit small—you can always make it bigger, but you can never make it smaller again.

If your receiver has adjustable spacing between its control shafts, make sure they're properly positioned for the holes in your panel and the face plate your using. Those shafts usually have two sets of nuts and lockwashers, one to lock down against the top of the face plate, the other to snug up against the back of the panel. Try to adjust these nuts so that the threaded portions of the shafts are all behind the panel, out of sight. If you can't (if you lack mounting depth, for instance, or if such mounting buries the radio dial out of sight), use rigid black plastic tubing to cover the exposed shaft ends; the receiver's knobs will hold the tubing in place.

Protect your eyes from flying chips when you're drilling and falling dirt when you're lying under the dash. Don't solder directly over yourself, lest you be hit by falling drops of molten solder. Wear work clothes.

Retouch any paint you've chipped, whether on the car or on your stereo equipment.

The Speakers

Your speaker installation, like the mechanical and electrical portions of the installation, should begin with careful planning. Your first consideration—preferably even before you pick your speakers—should be where those speakers will go.

The ideal system's front speakers would be as far forward and as near to eye level as possible, with the woofers, midranges and tweeters cheek by jowl. The rear speakers could be just ahead of the rear seat passengers (which would give those passengers the clearest sound and sharpest stereo imaging) or on the rear deck (which would give the deepest bass). But these locations are rarely practical. Far

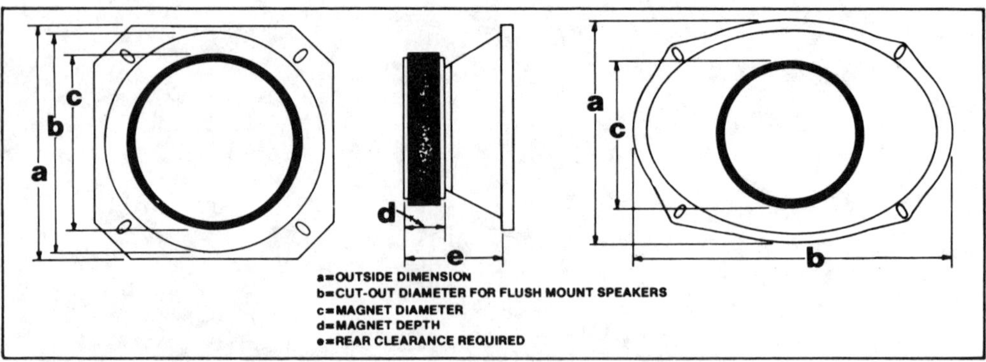

Check these critical dimensions before buying speakers

forward at eye level there's a windshield—no place to install speakers there. There's rarely a spot for speakers just ahead of the rear passengers, either.

So examine your car closely to see where speakers actually can go. Examine other cars of the same model which have already had systems installed in them, and listen to them, if you can, to find out exactly what will and will not work in your car.

Most systems wind up with rear speakers in the rear deck, and front speakers in the dashboard, doors or kick panels. Kick panels aren't used as often as doors or the dashboard, so unless otherwise specified, the following assumes that your system will have to be rear-deck and door or dashboard speakers. (Procedures for the door or kick panel are very similar.)

Dashboard mounting isn't easy unless the dash has speaker mounting wells built in. Today's car dashboards usually hold 3 to 4-inch or only slightly larger ones. It is possible to adapt other speakers, such as the tweeter and mid-range of a three-way system, to fit into these holes, though.

You may also find pre-cut speaker holes in your rear deck. (If they're not the right size for the speaker you want to use, a wide range of adapters are available to let you use speakers that are smaller or larger than the hole.) But while the dashboard speaker mounts are usually easy to spot because of their external grilles, rear-deck mounting holes will probably be concealed from casual view. It's common for the metal panel which supports the rear deck to be pre-cut, but for the deck's visible fiberboard or similar trim panel to conceal the fact. If that's the case, it's usually pretty easy to make a matching cutout in the upper panel. This is usually

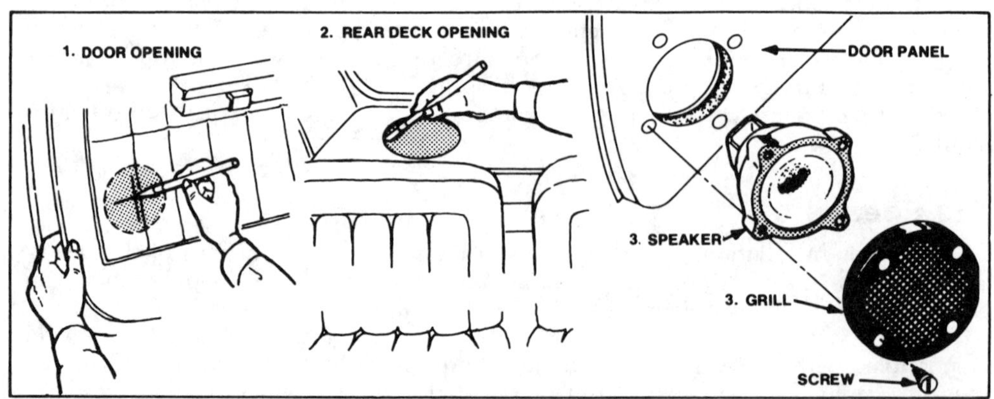

Mark the hole pattern with a template (1). Cut the fabric with a knife (2) and finish the hole with a saw or other cutter. Install the speaker and grille (3)

done with a keyhole saw from inside the trunk, where there's usually a bit more room to work and where the hole in the sub-panel can serve as a guide. The job is easier if you clear out the trunk before you start, and if you drill a pilot hole, big enough to admit the first inch or so of the saw blade, before you start. In a few cars, the upper panel has holes drilled into it at the factory to form a speaker grille; in that case, you can often mount the speaker from below, with no need for cutting.

CUTTING SPEAKER HOLES

In most other cases, you'll have to make your own speaker holes. The job can be time-consuming, but is basically simple.

First, find a spot where you can mount your speaker freely. To do that, you'll have to get a look at what's behind your chosen mounting spot. For rear-deck mounts, look inside the trunk to see if there are holes in the metal under-panel through which the rear of the speaker can protrude. There often are, even when there are none deliberately designed for speaker use. Try to find a speaker position which will allow at least two, diametrically opposite speaker mounting screws to bite into metal or some other substantial structure, rather than just fiberboard.

For door mounts, the picture gets a bit more complicated (though at least you have the convenience of working outside the cramped environs of the car. You'll have to open the door's inner skin to see what lies behind it—not just to look for holes, but to make sure the back of the speaker won't obstruct the window or lock mechanisms. You must also make sure that the front of the speaker won't be in your way when you wind the windows up and down, or open the doors; don't just measure the arc traversed by the window crank, either—leave yourself a bit of knuckle room.

Looking inside the door is not as hard as it sounds, but if you're in doubt, ask your local car dealer, stereo installer or body shop how to do it on your car. You'll first have to remove the interior door handles and window cranks. These may be fastened by clips around their shafts, by screws (sometimes hidden behind pry-up trim discs), or by other methods.

Next find out how the door's inner panels (or kick panels) are fastened. They may be held by screws, by screw-like fasteners, or by tension clips. Be sure you know what holds your panels on—you can bend or break panels if you try to remove them the wrong way. When you think you've found likely spots for your speakers, re-attach the window cranks for a moment and wind the windows up and down to be sure your speakers will clear the window glass and mechanism.

Measure carefully from identifiable points outside the panel area to the place

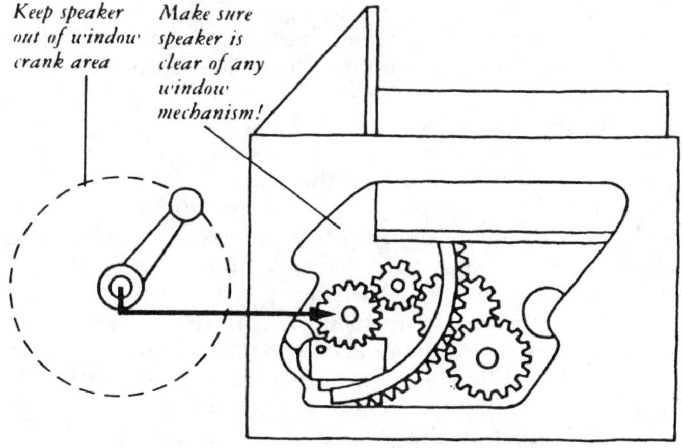

Look behind the door panels for any obstructions

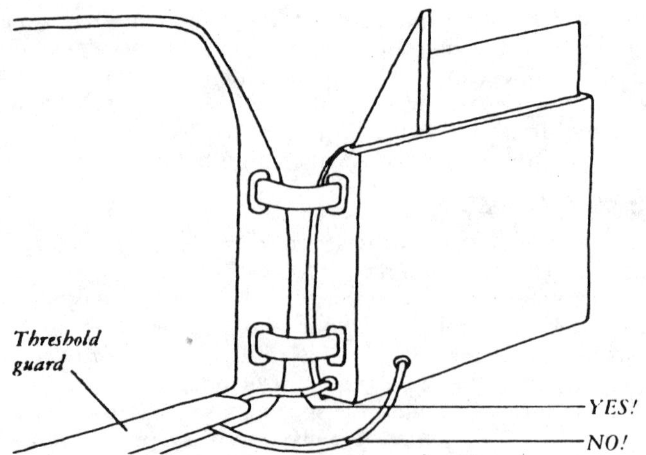

Route speaker wires through the edge of the door with enough slack

where you want your speakers to go. Now replace the panel and use your measurements to find and mark the spot where you'll cut for your speakers. Don't mark the hole's dimensions by tracing around the speaker itself—the resulting hole will be far too large, and you'll have to replace or patch your door panel before going further. Instead, use the mounting template supplied with your speaker to mark the dimensions and location of the holes for the speaker and for the screws which will fasten it.

Cut carefully. When in doubt, cut a hole you think is too small rather than one which might possibly be too big. Replacement panels are expensive, and your local salvage yard may not have one in a matching color.

Most door panels are of relatively soft material, over a metal frame. Cut the non-metallic skin with a razor blade or knife if it's of relatively soft material, such as vinyl, carpet or leather; or use a keyhole saw, hacksaw blade or tin snips if it's of a relatively stiff fiberboard, cardboard or plastic. Electric saber saws are good for both types of surface, if you have power and the room to work with them. If the surface is carpeted, cut through the carpet fibers with a razor blade before attacking the panel with a drill or saw, which could cause runs.

Once the trim panel has been cut, use it to mark the underlying metal with a crayon or chalk. Wind the window up before proceeding, so you'll be in no danger of breaking it. Here, a power saw can be a big help—metal can take a long time to cut or file by hand. Try to cut the metal so as to leave the speaker as much room as possible, while still leaving as many points as possible into which the speaker's mounting screws can thread securely. If the trim panel is in place, it can serve as a drilling guide for the screw holes; if not, be sure to dimple the metal with a center punch so the drill won't skitter off the mark.

When you're done, file all rough edges smooth, and clean up as much of the debris as possible. A vacuum cleaner with a crevice tool helps, and you may be able to fish out some metal chips with a magnet on a rod or string. Shavings can damage your speaker—and your speaker's magnet can attract the metal ones.

Some experts advise damping the inside of the door cavity to minimize resonances. Rust-proofing substances applied to the inside of the door's outer metal skin will help, and will also help rust-proof the panel. Fibrous insulating mats can be set into the tar, for even better damping; but there is then a chance that the fiber will hold water, increasing the chance of rust or corrosion.

If your speaker comes with a rain shield, mount it above the speaker to deflect

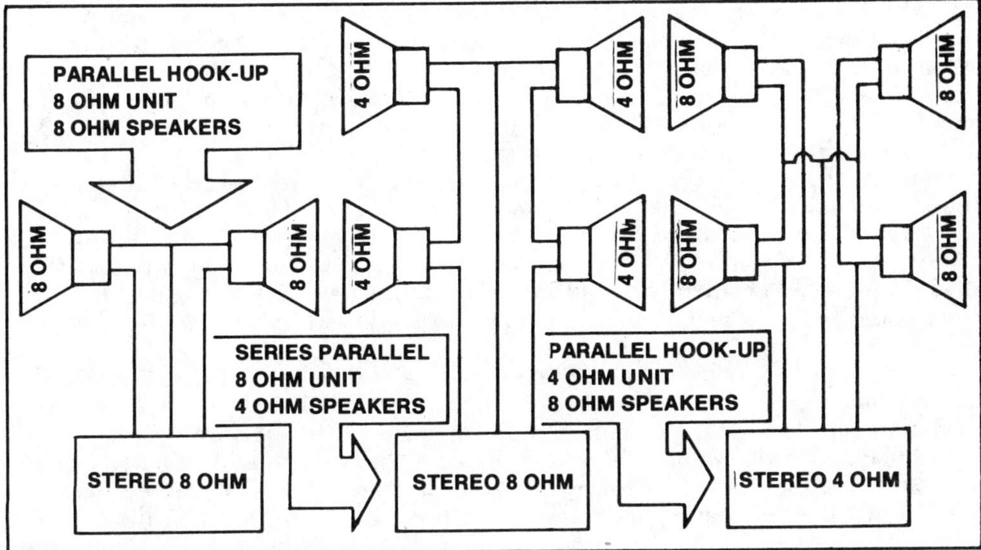

Typical speaker wiring

any water which might drip down the window channels. Make sure the drain holes at the bottom of the door are open, too, especially as stray chips from all your cutting could clog them.

WIRING SPEAKERS

Wire is usually supplied with speakers. The wire is usually more than long enough to reach between speakers and amplifiers almost anywhere in the car, usually has connectors mounted on it for slip-on connection to the speakers (and, often, for plug-in connection to the stereo system), and is clearly marked so you can tell the two sides of the wire apart. It's also thin, so it can be easily slipped between panels, under floor mats or through small holes.

Some authorities, however, feel that heavier wires would yield better sound. Special cables are available, but much of their effect can be had at far lower cost by substituting ordinary lamp cord of a heavier gauge than is normally supplied. The thicker the wire gauge, the lower its gauge number: #12 wire would be quite thick (and sometimes awkward in the car's close confines), but 16-gauge wire would be noticeably thicker than the #24 or similar wire normally supplied, and still fairly manageable. Make sure the cord you select offers some easy means of telling one wire from another. Some cords have one coppery and one silvery colored wire—made easier to identify, in some cases, by transparent insulation. Others have wisps of green thread accompanying one wire, red thread with the other. Most common of all, however, are cords with a rib molded into one wire; if you're selecting a cord with only this identifier, make sure you can tell unambiguously which wire is which.

The reason for this emphasis on identifying wires is that speakers must be wired so they operate in phase, all pushing or sucking air together when they're fed the same signal. Otherwise, both bass response and stereo imaging will suffer.

CHECKING POLARITY

You'll find a polarity marking (such as a red dot, or a plus or minus sign or some other identifying mark) distinguishing one terminal of each speaker. For proper phasing, the same wire should feed the same terminal on each speaker, and be fed by the same amplifier terminal.

If your speakers are of different makes, their polarity dots may not match. You can check that with two wires and a flashlight battery: Connect the battery for an instant to each speaker in turn, connecting the same battery terminal to the marked terminal of each speaker. The speaker cones will move in or out when you first connect the battery; if they all move in the same directions, then the speakers have the same polarity. If they don't, then wire one pair opposite to the other.

No matter how heavy the wires you use, they should be kept as short as possible. There is such a thing as making them too short, however. The wires must be long enough to reach from the speaker outputs of your receiver or amplifier, by some route that will prevent their being tangled or trodden on, out through the speaker holes. You'll need about six or eight inches of slack where the wire comes through the speaker hole, so you'll have something to work with when you connect the speaker to it.

Wiring to in-dash or kick-panel speakers is usually simplest. To wire door speakers, you must drill into the hinge side of the door (preferably not too near the hinges, as the door is often reinforced at that point). Many cars have pre-drilled holes filled by a grommet for this. From the door, the wire should go into a matching hole in the doorframe, or down under the sill plate. Make sure there is enough slack so that the door can open all the way without putting a strain on the connections, but not so much that the wire might get snagged. Wind the window up and down to make sure it doesn't touch the wire.

Where the wire goes through holes in the panel, file the holes smooth and line them with rubber grommets, so the hole edges won't wear through the wire's insulation. If there's any possibility of strain on the wire, knot it on the side of the panel away from the source of strain. That way, the knot will take the strain instead of the connections at the wire's end.

When wires must pass from the front to the rear of the car (to feed rear speakers, or to pass signals to and from trunk-mounted amplifiers), most installers use the same route: From the dash, the wires go under the doorsill to get to the rear passenger compartment. Then they're usually routed under the edges of the rear floor mat (where feet rarely tread) and under the back seat to the trunk.

You may have to remove the rear seat for this. Getting it out is often fairly easy, but getting it back in place is frequently a two-man job. Plan to have help available when you get to that point and be careful not to pinch the wires when you replace the seat.

The standard way to connect front and rear speakers is to feed left-channel signals to the front and rear left speakers, right-channel signals to the front and rear right ones. Some listeners, though, prefer to cross the channels in the rear, feeling that it distributes the stereo image better in a space where listeners are usually far closer to one speaker than to all the others.

With some amplifiers, it's also possible to adopt the "Hafler" or "Dynaquad" configuration, wiring one rear speaker between the "hot" speaker terminals of the two channels. The sound coming from this speaker will represent the difference between the two channels, which often consists of reverberant information. This simulates (or, to some minds, improves on) the effect of a delay system at a far lower cost. There are two catches, though: the difference signal rarely contains any bass, so the bass advantages of rear-deck mounting will be lost unless you add a subwoofer system or two normally-wired rear-deck speakers; and some amplifiers cannot be wired this way without damage (check with your amplifier's manufacturer before trying this).

Some amplifiers also let you use the car's chassis as one side of the speaker connection, requiring only one wire between the amplifier and each speaker, rather than a two-wire cord. Many amplifiers, however, do not allow this; never do it unless the amplifier instructions specifically sanction the idea.

If you have trouble getting your wire through tight spots, fish it through: tie a thin string or cord to a thin, stiff wire, and use that wire as a needle to thread the cord through your trouble spot. Then use the string to pull the wire through. If you're replacing existing speaker wires with heavier ones, you can use the old, thin wires as your string.

Try not to run speaker wires near or parallel to your car's existing electrical wires. While speaker wires are not as interference-prone as the cables between receivers and amplifiers, they have been known to pick up interference.

MOUNTING AND CONNECTING YOUR SPEAKERS

Where there's insufficient room behind the mounting panel for the speaker's magnet, you can stand it off from the panel with spacers. Some such spacers are even angled, to help you aim high frequencies where you want them. If you're using spacers, check that the speaker won't get in your way if extended into the passenger compartment, and be sure to pass the speaker wires through the spacers before connecting up.

The wires that came with your speakers usually have connectors which slip onto the speaker's terminal stubs, and similar connectors can be crimped or soldered onto any heavier wires you substitute. These connectors are fairly secure, and are unlikely to shake loose from the speaker unless pulled off. Nonetheless, many installers prefer to solder the wires to the speaker terminals.

If you're soldering your speaker wires, there are a number of rules to follow: Double-check that you've phased the speakers properly—soldered connections are a nuisance to change once they're made. Wrap the wire around the terminal securely before soldering. See the section on Tools, for an explanation of how to solder. Be careful not to burn either your car's or your own upholstery with solder drips or a hot iron.

When mounting a speaker in its hole, make sure its terminals are not contacting the car's metalwork. If you think they may, you can insulate the connections, bend them gently back (be careful not to break them), or rotate the speaker in its hole to a position where there will be no such contact.

Wherever possible, screw the speaker's frame to the car's metal structure. Where you can't, don't just screw the speaker to a trim panel; instead, put spring nuts (usually supplied with the speaker) over the panel at the mounting points, and bolt the speaker to those nuts.

Speaker mounting screws should be tightened evenly. Tightening one corner all the way before tackling the next will often warp the speaker frame. So tighten each screw a bit at a time, till all are equally snug.

Make sure the speaker seals tightly against its mounting panel. If there are air leaks on any side, bass response will suffer.

Try to match the grille to its location. Rear-deck and dash-top grilles should be the color of the panel they're mounted on, so as not to reflect into the driver's forward or rear view. When in doubt, use flat black grilles in these spots. Low-mounted speakers should have metal grilles, to withstand accidental kicks. Chrome plating seems to stand up better than paint, here. Some plastic grilles will warp if subjected to direct sunlight, which makes metal grilles a better bet for deck and dash installations.

RADIO, SPEAKER(S) AND ANTENNA INSTALLATION

Following is a step-by-step installation of various common auto sound components in a 1982 Mazda GLC. The Mazda GLC was chosen because of its popularity and typical installation of average difficulty. It illustrates most of the procedures you are likely to encounter in a typical installation, except for removal of the factory-installed radio.

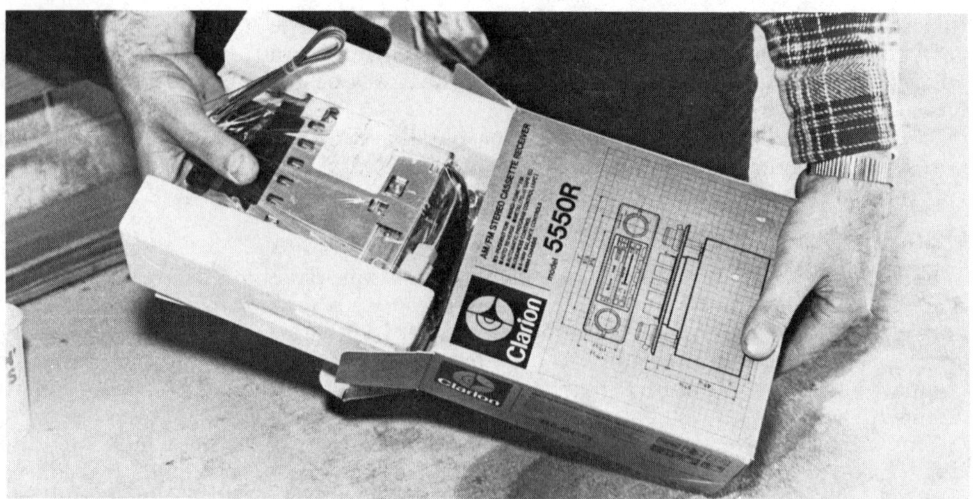

Assemble all the components and make sure you have all the pieces. Read the instructions before beginning

Remove the steering column shroud, parcel tray, ash tray and mount, and dash face plate

Pry the retaining plate from the dash lights dimmer switch. It snaps in place. Be careful because the wheel may fall out when the retaining plate is removed. Remove the switch from the back of the dash panel and reassemble the switch

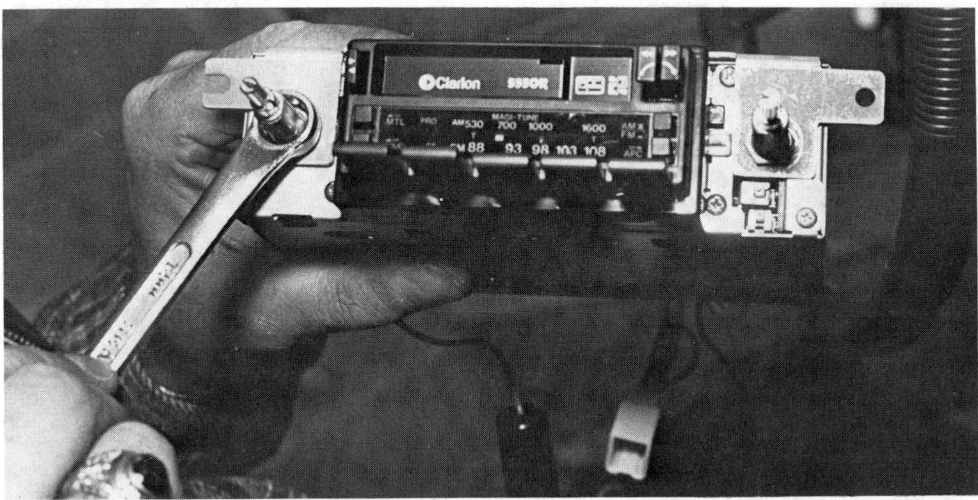

Assemble the metal support kit to the radio and temporarily install the radio. Check the fit of the dash trim plate

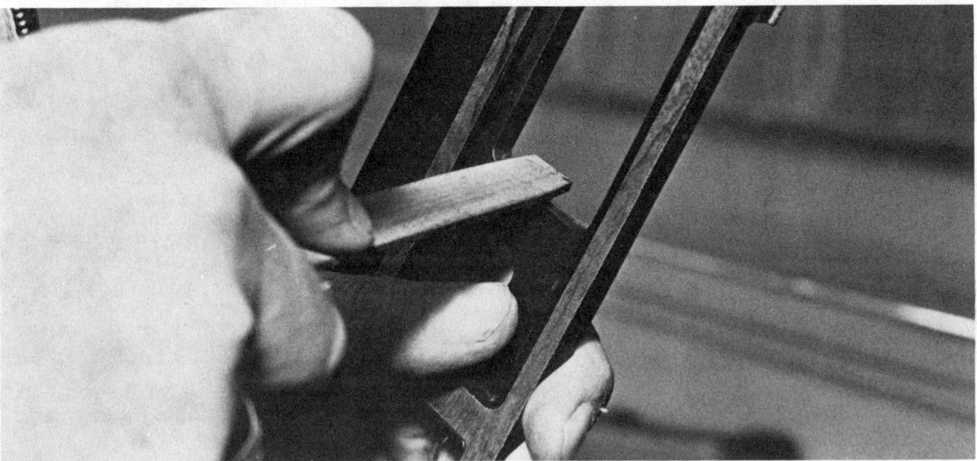

File away enough plastic to assure a snug fit, with no binding or interference. The GLC required minimal alteration. When the fit is correct remove the radio

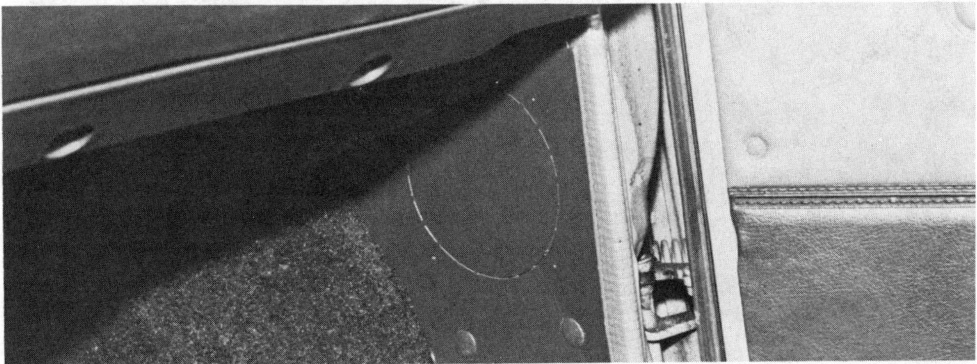

The speakers go into the GLC kick panels. The stock GLC panels have perforated cut-outs for 4″ speakers. Remove the panels from each side

The speaker openings behind the panels are sealed with rubber sheets. Remove the rubber covers

Pop the fiberboard ring from the speaker openings in the kick panel, using the perforations as a guide. It may be necessary to start the perforations by judiciously cutting a few perforations with a razor blade or sharp knife

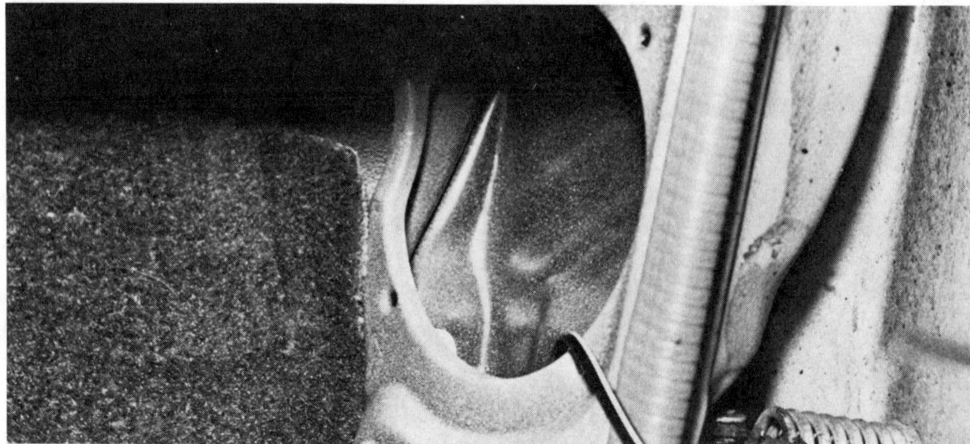

Route the speaker wires from the radio to the speaker cutouts. Leave enough slack in the wires to prevent binding and chafing

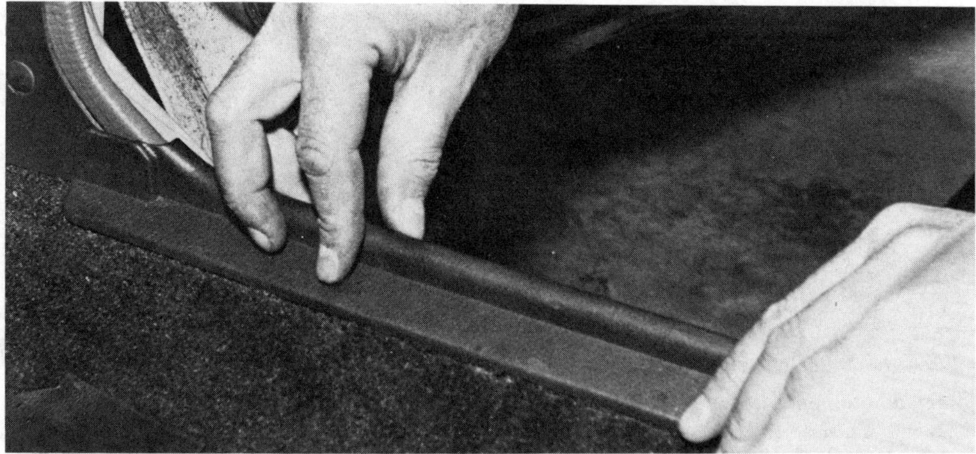

Route the wires to the rear speakers under the door sill trim plates

Speaker grilles for the rear speakers are provided in the rear parcel shelf. Holes are pre-drilled for mounting screws. Mount the rear speakers and connect the wires

Connect the speaker leads to the front speakers on the passenger's side. The speaker terminals should face the front of the car. Cutouts are provided in the car's sheet metal to accommodate the speaker terminals. Start the screws provided into the speaker, kick panel and tighten them into the pre-drilled holes

Replace the panel fasteners and install the speaker grille

Remove the antenna cover plate from the windshield pillar

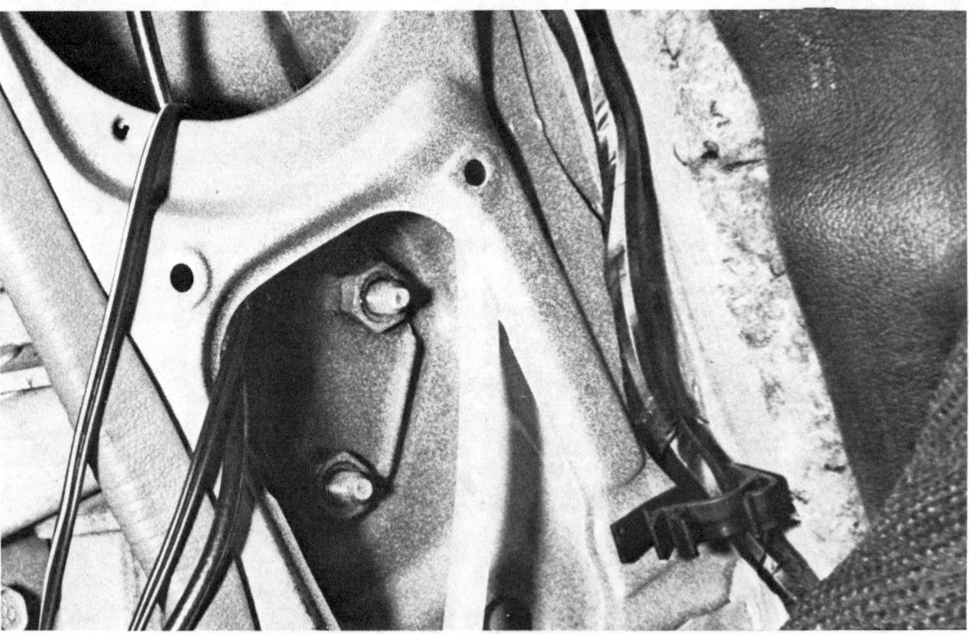

Route the plastic antenna housing down into the area behind the speaker cut-outs. Secure the antenna mounting plate with the 2 screws supplied. Attach the speaker leads and mount the speakers on the driver's side. Route the antenna cable and speaker leads (on both sides) under the rugs and up to the radio recess in the dash

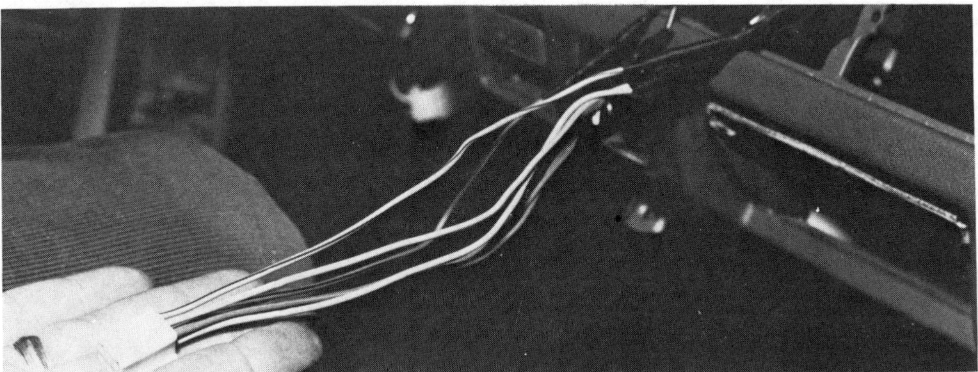

Cut the excess from the speaker leads and connect the wires to the female end of the wiring harness plug (supplied), using the wiring diagram in the instructions. Connect the fused power lead to a power source and ground wire to a good ground. Solder and tape all electrical connections

Connect the plug to the radio and test its operation. When everything is satisfactory, install the radio in the dash. Don't forget the rear brace

Install the dash light dimmer switch, the dash trim, radio face plate and knobs, ash tray, parcel tray and steering column shroud. The installation is complete

It also illustrates the ease with which you can improve your listening enjoyment with affordable, high quality, easily installed components, while preserving the car's original interior appearance. We chose a mini-chassis Clarion 5500R Stereo AM/FM/Tape, with Clarion 4" SD420 coaxial speakers, and a Metra 12015-7900 installation kit, which was a necessity. A Harada PM-60M factory replacement antenna completed the installation.

TROUBLESHOOTING

Radio/Tuner Performance

INTERFERENCE CAUSE AND CURES

Most car-stereo owners are rarely plagued by interference problems, even though they're operating sensitive electronic equipment just a few feet from a high-voltage spark generator and a variety of motors, relays, switches and electrical wires and in a device which generates static electricity as it rolls along the road.

The most common complaints about car-stereo installations are caused by interference from one or more of these sources and is usually curable.

Tracking Down The Cause

Finding the cure for any problem is easier once you know the cause. The causes of most car-stereo interference problems need not be mysterious at all. Tracking them down is usually an excercise in logic, with a touch of electrical knowledge thrown in.

Most noises are only heard when whatever causes them is working. If your radio moans in synchronization with the windshield wiper, for example, you know that's the cause. If you hear a noise that changes with the engine speed, you know the cause is somewhere in the engine's electrical system. The latter, however, is not as good a clue, since many possible interference causers lurk under your hood. We need to dig a little deeper to truly isolate the cause, in that case.

If the noise only runs when the engine does, then the engine probably has a lot to do with it. If the noise varies in pitch or intensity with engine speed, then it's probably the ignition (spark plugs, distributor, coil and wires) or the generator or alternator. In diesels, of course, it can only be the latter—diesels have no ignition.

The two are easily told apart: Ignition noise is a popping or crackling, which stops the instant that the engine does. Alternator or generator noise is more often a whine which sometimes intensifies when you switch on the headlights and which usually runs down for a second or so after you switch off the engine.

Voltage regulators can be a source of scratchy, irregular noise which also takes a moment to go off when you turn off the engine. Electric fuel pumps can cause similar noises, as can oil-pressure sensors.

Crackles or rumbles heard when the car is bounced (by rough roads, for instance) can have many causes: dashboard meters (try rapping on the dashboard to see if that makes the problem start or stop), fuel-level sensors, loose connections, oil-pressure detectors and intermittent wire breaks or short circuits. Noises heard primarily when restarting a warm engine are frequently caused by the radiator thermostat.

Other interference noises are more clearly related to their causes. Like the wiper motor we gave as an example, they only happen when the device that's causing them is turned on. The connection is not always obvious, though. Many noise problems are intermittent; so the headlight relay, for example, may not cause a problem every time you turn the headlights on—but you can usually count on its keeping quiet while the lights are off. Some puzzles may be caused by devices which are on when you don't expect it, such as thermostatically-controlled heater or air-conditioner fans, which may run even when you've switched them off, and thermostatic radiator fans which can even run when the motor is switched off, on some cars.

The wipers and headlights are not the only likely culprits, either. Interference has been known to come from the horn and horn switch, the turn-signal flasher, the windshield washer, and the heater or air-conditioner fan. It can come from static electricity generated within the car or by the tires' friction on the road, too.

Steps Toward Cure

Your next step is to determine how the interference is getting to your stereo, whether it's airborne, via the antenna, or is being conducted through your stereo system's power leads.

To check for antenna-borne noise, simply disconnect the antenna from the back of your receiver, and see whether the noise stays or goes. If that cures the problem, then check the antenna system carefully. Interference is likely to occur when the antenna's base is loose or poorly grounded. A break in the shield between the antenna base and plug can cause the problem, too.

If the system checks out perfectly but still makes noise, consider moving the antenna further from the engine; in that case, it may be simpler to install a second antenna at the other end of the car than to move your present one and be faced with the problem of filling the hole it leaves in your hood or fender.

It may also help to improve the car's grounding. Theoretically, all parts of the car are grounded to each other by normal, metal-to-metal contact; but in practice, that's not always enough. Grounding wires or straps between the engine, body

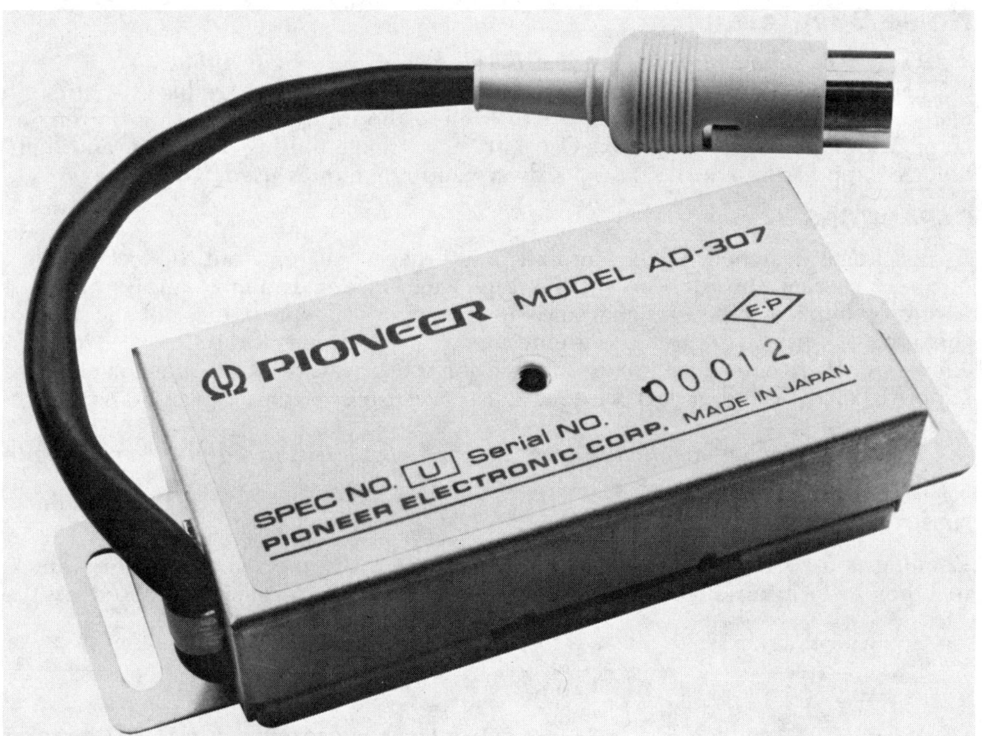

Total noise suppression system (Courtesy Pioneer)

structure, hood, fenders and inside fender wells can sometimes help. Some authorities also recommend grounding the tailpipe, steering column, trunk lid and any metallic tubes or parts which pass through the firewall.

The engine ground wire should be slipped under some bolt on the engine, preferably one which won't cause problems if it's backed off a thread or two to accomodate the wire. The remaining grounds should go to sheet-metal screws threaded into metal for a good contact; petroleum jelly in the screw holes can prevent corrosion at the holes. If possible, run all ground straps to the same point on the body; the firewall is generally convenient for this.

If the static is coming in the power line, you can filter that line to keep it out or at least reduce its intensity. These filters are of two general types. One actually is wired into the power line, with power entering at one end and emerging, hopefully cleaner, at the other. The other type is wired across the power line, between its hot and ground sides. In-line filters are generally rated to pass a specified amount of current or power; if so, make sure the one you buy is made to pass all the power your system will demand. If you can't get a large enough filter to handle all of your system at once, you can often put smaller ones in each component's power feed.

Check all your system's audio connections, too. Loose, intermittent or broken connections can pick up interference. Check, too, that your receiver and other components are solidly grounded to the car. In extreme cases, shield the power leads to prevent their picking up interference.

Keeping interference out of the system is of broadly-based but sometimes limited effectiveness. That is, it tends to help with many different kinds of interference problems, including those you haven't diagnosed; but it is sometimes less effective than getting rid of a problem at its source—annd certainly less effective than using both approaches together.

Noise Suppression

NOTE: *The following applies equally well to AM/FM or CB radios.*

There are two fundamental approaches used to suppress noise: reduce the strength of the interference at the source; or, to confine the interference, using the engine compartment as a shielding box. Capacitors, bonding, routing of wiring, and high-voltage suppressors are the basic hardware and techniques used.

CAPACITORS

A capacitor is designed to pass the flow of alternating current, but to block the flow of direct current. Interference of this type (man-made), is almost always an alternating or impulse type of signal and the capacitor will direct most of the flow of this type of current to ground without affecting the circuit of the direct current. A conventional by-pass capacitor is suitable for the broadcast band, but for effective suppression with higher UHF frequencies, the use of coaxial capacitors is recommended.

CAUTION: *Capacitors should never be used on transistorized or electronic ignitions.*

BONDING

Bonding is a particular technique used to connect the metal parts of the vehicle together to form an effective shield blocking RFI. Interference generated by the

CONVENTIONAL BYPASS CAPACITOR

COAXIAL CAPACITOR

Two types of capacitors (Courtesy Champion Spark Plug Co.)

ignition and charging systems will be kept from traveling throughout the vehicle and a common ground will be formed for all RFI signals.

WIRE ROUTING

Wire routing must be carefully done; if not, interference will be transferred from one circuit to another, particularly to the high voltage, or ignition cable side.

HIGH-VOLTAGE SUPPRESSORS

The ignition system is probably the greatest single source of RFI in a vehicle, and resistors are available to reduce the interference to a tolerable level.

GENERAL SUPPRESSION PROCEDURES

Anytime two-way radio or audio equipment is replaced or serviced, the following steps will help minimize the need for additional suppression.

NOTE: *Before attempting any of the procedures outlined in this section, disconnect the wires from the battery. If you don't, you could be seriously injured.*

1. Be sure that all of the original equipment for suppression is still intact and in good condition. It's possible that resistor cable could have been replaced by non-resistor cables, a bonding strap could have been removed, or a toothed lockwasher may have been lost.
2. Be sure that all components and connections are in good condition. A corroded connection will, in all likelihood, make interference worse.
3. Tune the engine or have it tuned by a specialist. Tune-up should include new spark plugs, points, and condenser at the least. Additional items which should be looked at, but require replacement less frequently, are the cap and rotor. Optimum radio performance will not be delivered unless the ignition system is in good condition.
4. Ideally, the radio should be connected to the battery. Connecting it to the accessory or ignition side of the ignition switch leads to interference in the radio from the car's electrical system.
5. Low-voltage wires should be kept away from the ignition system, as well as any other circuits which are suspected noise producers. Wires of suspected circuits should be laid flat against a grounded metal area where possible; they should not be bundled together.
6. Be sure that the antenna lead-in shield is grounded at both ends. Insulation, as well as all connections, should be clean and tight.

If you posses an ohmmeter, there are three checks you can make on the antenna. If you don't own an ohmmeter, try to borrow one to make these three checks.

a. Put the ohmmeter on the lowest scale and touch the prods to the antenna rod

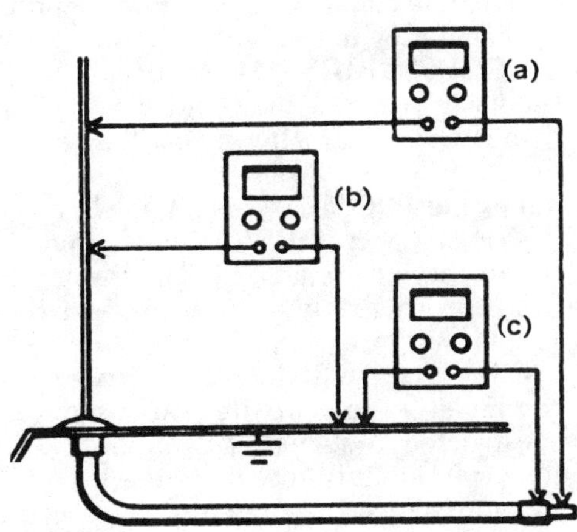

3 checks you can make on your antenna with an ohmmeter (Courtesy Champion Spark Plug Co.)

and to the center contact of the plug. The resistance should be a fraction of an ohm;

b. Put the ohmmeter on the highest scale. Touch the ohmmeter prods to the antenna rod and to the vehicle ground. Most antennas should read an open circuit, except for the few high "gain" type antennas with built-in transformers, which will be short-circuited;

c. Return the ohmmeter to the lowest scale. Touch the prods to the outside of the antenna plug and to the vehicle ground. Resistance should be zero.

If any of these tests don't turn out as they should, there is a serious fault or open circuit in the antenna system.

7. Above all, good suppression can only take place if all components are properly connected and grounded. All paint, oil, grease, or rust should be removed from all areas where good electrical contact is essential. Clean hardware and sharp-toothed washers should be used for mounting components. All places where lugs or eyes have been attached should be soldered to the wire, and all electrical connections should be taped.

If, after you have done all this and the evil noises still persist, you will have to conduct a step-by-step search to identify the culprit.

IDENTIFYING INTERFERENCE

Each type of interference you hear on the receiver has its own distinctive sound and characteristics. In order to find out what is causing the interference, you at least have to know where to start looking.

IGNITION SYSTEM: This is a popping sound which increases in tempo with the engine speed. It will also shut off immediately when the ignition key is turned off at fast idle.

GENERATOR/ALTERNATOR: These produce a musical whine, high-pitched, increasing in frequency with higher engine speed. It will not shut off instantly when the ignition key is turned off at fast idle.

VOLTAGE REGULATOR: Voltage regulator interference is usually heard in conjunction with alternator or generator noise, and makes its appearance as a rasping, ragged sound occurring at an irregular rate. It will not stop instantly when the ignition is shut off at fast idle.

INSTRUMENTS: Instruments in the dash produce hissing, crackling, and clicking sounds occurring at irregular intervals as the gauges operate. The condition is usually worse on rough roads and can be tested by jarring the dashboard.

The voltage limiter behind the dash, which is used with the fuel and temperature gauges, can produce a loud "hashing" sound at intermittent intervals. Bouncing the vehicle to activate the fuel gauge sending unit should verify RFI from the voltage limiter.

Disconnect the gauges or the sending units one at a time; the RFI should disappear if they are at fault.

ACCESSORIES: Make a preliminary check with all accessories turned off. Turn them on one at a time and listen for increased RFI. Intermittent noise from the turn signal or hazard warning flashers or windshield wipers can often be eliminated by the use of a capacitor, but most by-pass capacitors will have no effect on wiper motor noise. Coaxial capacitors should be used for this.

WHEELS & TIRES: Wheels and tires sometimes create a popping or rushing sound through radio while they operate on dry roads at high-speeds. Interference from the wheels and tires can be traced by lightly applying the brakes; the noise should disappear.

OTHER SOURCES: If a particular type of interference cannot be identified as coming from any of the sources described above, a test capacitor can be easily constructed as shown. A grounded capacitor touched to all "hot" electrical connections will identify the offending item if the RFI disappears.

Another test instrument can be constructed at home which is very useful in lo-

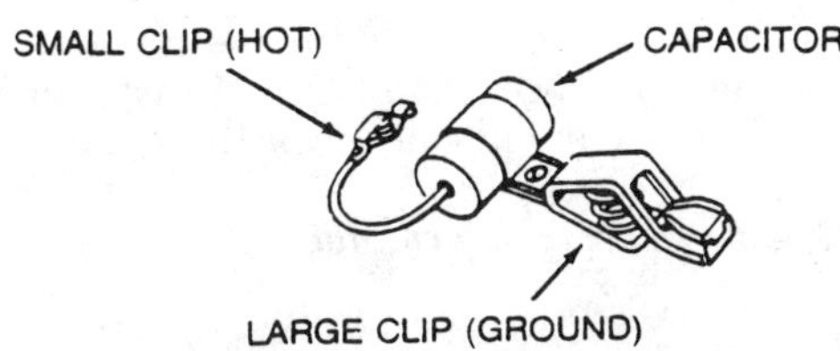

Using a grounded capacitor to identify the source of interference by the process of elimination (Courtesy Champion Spark Plug Co.)

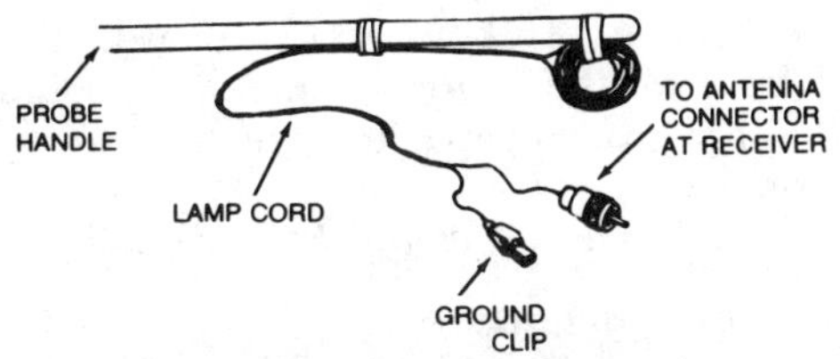

Home-made antenna for locating the source of interference by probing (Courtesy Champion Spark Plug Co.)

cating the source of RFI. Begin by disconnecting the antenna from the receiver. Wrap 50 turns of insulated, or bell, wire into a coil 2 inches in diameter, and tape the coil of wire to a broom stick or wooden dowel rod as shown. Using a few feet of normal lamp cord, connect one side of the coil to an alligator clip which will be used for the ground side. The other end of the coil should be connected to the center conductor of the antenna connector which can be purchased from any electronics store. Basically, what you have done is to construct a crude inductive antenna which will pick up interference. Connect the antenna to your radio, start the engine, and turn the radio on. Probe around the engine and wiring with your homemade coil. Interference will be the loudest when you are close to the source of the interference.

RFI SUPPRESSION TECHNIQUES

CAUTION: *Capacitors should not be used on transistorized or electronic ignitions.*

Alternator

The alternator slip-rings should be clean and the brushes should make good contact. A 0.5 mfd (microfarad), coaxial capacitor can be installed at the alternator output terminal. Be sure that it is rated to handle the alternator output current.

NOTE: *Do not connect a capacitor to the alternator field terminal.*

Generator

Most American (or import), cars and trucks these days are not equipped with generators. But, for the cars which are, the commutator and brushes should be making

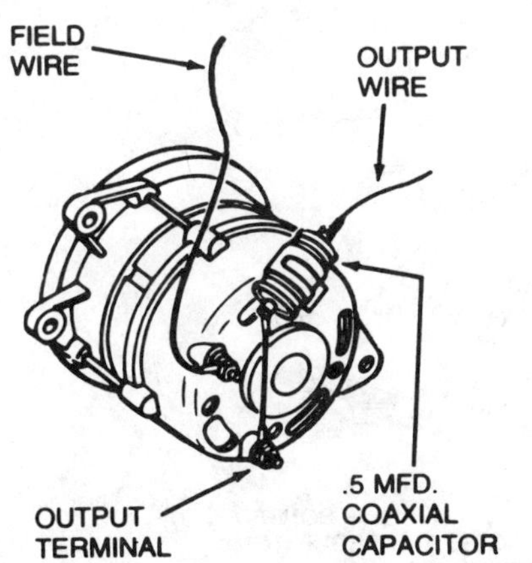

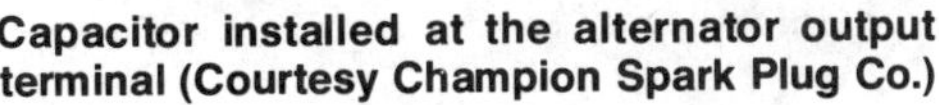

Capacitor installed at the alternator output terminal (Courtesy Champion Spark Plug Co.)

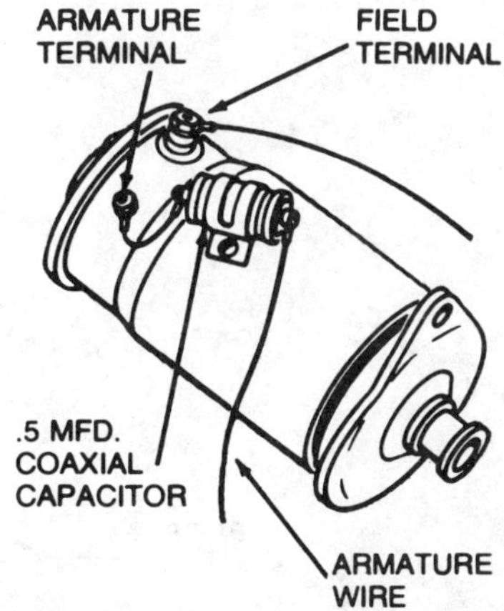

Capacitor installed at the generator output terminal (Courtesy Champion Spark Plug Co.)

good contact. If the commutator is badly worn, the generator should be overhauled.

Remove the factory-installed capacitor from the armature terminal and install a 0.5 mfd coaxial capacitor which is rated to handle the current output of the generator.

NOTE: *Do not connect the capacitor to the generator field terminal.*

Voltage regulator

Many of the newer cars are now using solid state regulators, often built into the alternator. But for those cars still equipped with the traditional external voltage regulator of the single or double-contact type, a 0.5 mfd capacitor can be installed as close as possible to the *armature* and *battery* terminals. On a single contact regulator, use a 0.5 mfd capacitor at the ignition terminal. Again, be sure that the capacitor(s) are rated to handle the generator or alternator current output. The rated output can be found in the electrical specifications of most any service manual for your car.

Capacitors should not be connected to the regulator *field* terminal. Unusual cases of interference may require that the FIELD wire be shielded. In this case, be sure that both ends of the shield are grounded.

If regulator noise is extreme or simply cannot be quieted, the wire from the "F" or field terminal can be replaced with a piece of RG-8/U coaxial cable. If you do this, be sure that the coaxial cable does not touch the engine block or any other accessory delivering a lot of heat. Also, be sure that the braid at the ends of the coaxial cable is securely grounded to the chassis or nearest ground point other than the engine.

Instruments

A 0.5 mfd capacitor installed at the terminals of the gauges or sending units will usually silence interference from these sources.

The voltage limiter can usually be quieted with a 0.5 mfd capacitor connected at the battery terminal of the voltage limiter. In place of this, a 0.1 mfd radio-type pigtail capacitor connected across the voltage limiter terminals also will work. Extreme cases of noise from the voltage limiter can be cured by installing a "hash choke" in series with the battery lead.

Accessories

Almost any accessory which is operated by a brush motor (turn signals, stop signals, electric windows, heater blowers, and the like), can be quieted with a 0.25 mfd capacitor installed at the accessory terminals.

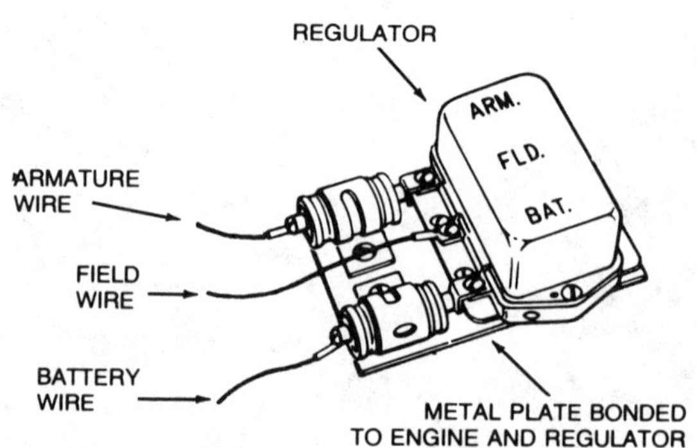

Capacitors installed at the regulator "Arm" and "Bat" terminals

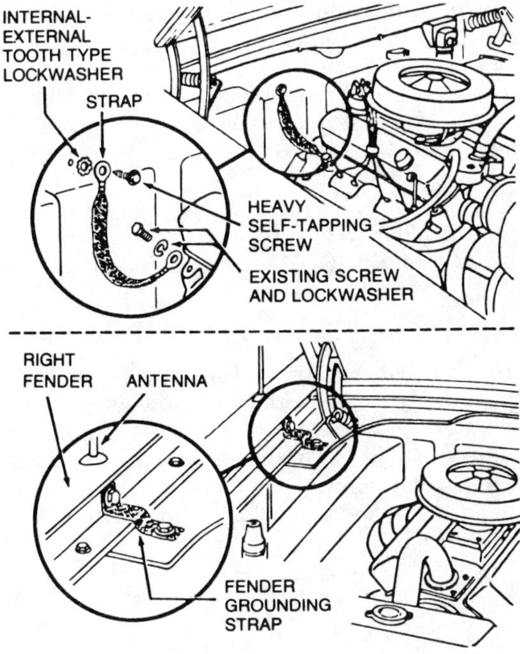

Examples of bonding (Courtesy Champion Spark Plug Co.)

Bonding

Bonding straps can be pieces of ½–1 inch wide copper braided strap for connecting components to ground, or pieces of metal for grounding fenders. Braided copper straps can be obtained from most well-stocked electronic supply stores. In addition, many car manufacturers and radio manufacturers offer bonding kits of this material. If you can't find the copper stuff, an alternative is to use the braided coaxial shielding from a piece of spare coaxial antenna cable. You can get this off by carefully slitting the outside insulation from the coaxial cable (without slitting the shielding). Peel away the insulation and slip the braided shielding off the foam insulation. Whatever type of bonding material is used, be sure that the lugs used to attach the cable are securely attached to the cable and soldered.

The art of "bonding" is largely a matter of luck and trial-and-error. The location of the bonding straps often plays an important role in its effectiveness, and experience will most times reveal the best location. An expert at CB installations can offer words of wisdom on this subject.

Some good places to begin installing bond straps are:

- Corners of the engine to the frame
- Exhaust pipe to the frame and engine
- Both sides of the trunk and hood lids
- Coil and distributor-to-engine and firewall
- Air cleaner-to-engine
- Battery ground-to-frame
- Tailpipe-to-frame
- Steering column, oil pressure gauge line and any other metal lines passing through the firewall
- Front and rear bumper supports
- Radiator-to-radiator supports.

Generally, any metal parts which are separated from the frame by any type of insulation (spacers, paint, noise silencing material), should be electrically connected to the frame, or connected together.

Use self-tapping screws in conjunction with toothed lockwashers to cut into surface layers of metal. Bonding straps should be as short and heavy as possible to be really effective, and should be checked periodically for corrosion and tightness.

Wheels

Static collector rings, installed inside the front wheel caps, will collect static build-up from the front wheels and prevent it from entering the receiver.

Primary Ignition System

IGNITION COIL

The first step is to remove the ignition coil and its mounting bracket. Clean the paint from the back of the bracket with sandpaper or a file and from the mounting point on the engine. Reassemble the bracket and the ignition coil tightly.

If this does not help, install a 0.1 mfd coaxial capacitor as close to the coil battery terminal as possible. Do not connect the coaxial capacitor to the distributor terminal, nor should a normal by-pass capacitor be used. In addition, a 0.005 mfd 1,000 volt ceramic disc capacitor installed at the coil distributor terminal will help eliminate interference.

Be sure to check coil polarity, or have it checked.

DISTRIBUTOR BREAKER POINTS

The distributor breaker points are not usually the cause of interference, although they cannot be totally ignored as a cause of RFI. Point condition determines to a large extent whether or not they will produce any interference. Points which have been well-maintained are far less likely to cause any interference problems than are those which have been poorly maintained. If the points are suspected of causing a great deal of interference, look for point bounce or deteriorated points.

Fleets and commercial trucks can reduce RFI and at the same time increase point life by determining the allowable condenser limits for the vehicle, and selecting condensers at the high limit for mainly stop/start driving or selecting condensers at the low limit for mainly high-speed driving. If the condenser limits are determined to be 0.18–0.25 mfd, use a 0.25 mfd condenser for stop/start driving or a 0.18 mfd condenser for high-speed use.

NOTE: *By-pass capacitors should not be installed at the coil distributor terminal.*

DISTRIBUTOR CAP AND ROTOR

The distributor cap and rotor should be replaced at the interval specified by the vehicle manufacturer. In terms of suppressing RFI, they should be replaced when the tip of the rotor and the contacts in the cap show signs of erosion or carbon tracking, which increases the gap over which the spark must jump, leading to higher RFI levels.

The rotor used with a GM V-8 distributor can be had in a radio suppression version, which is stamped with an "E" on the metal blade.

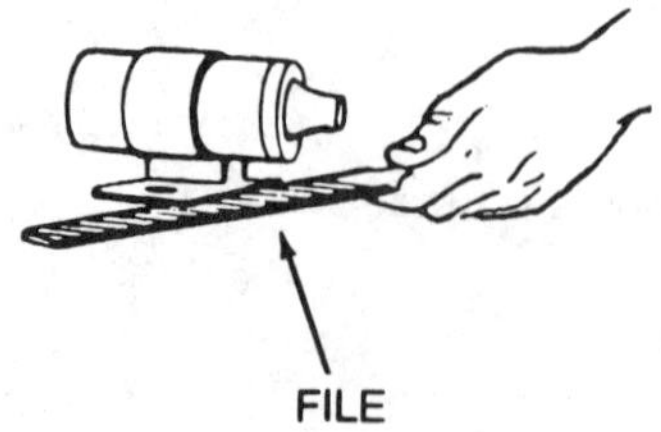

FILE

Clean the back of the coil mounting bracket (Courtesy Champion Spark Plug Co.)

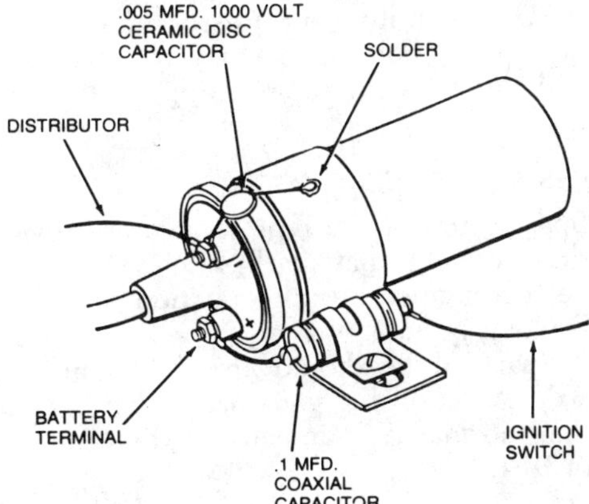

Capacitors installed on the ignition coil (Courtesy Champion Spark Plug Co.)

Secondary Ignition System

This is the high-voltage side of the ignition system and the worst producer of RFI. Radiated interference is reduced effectively by suppressor resistors of various types. Some are separate components, while others have been incorporated into the distributor rotor or spark plug towers on the cap. These are mainly service items for U.S. cars and trucks.

SPARK PLUG CABLES

SAE standards specify two resistance ranges for cable use on newly-manufactured vehicles:

LR—3,000–7,000 ohms per foot;
HR—6,000–12,000 ohms per foot.

Of the two, LR is the most common, but HR is sometimes used between the coil and distributor where short cables are involved.

Replacement wires of the resistance type are available from any of several manufacturers. The resistance data is generally available on the box or from the manufacturer.

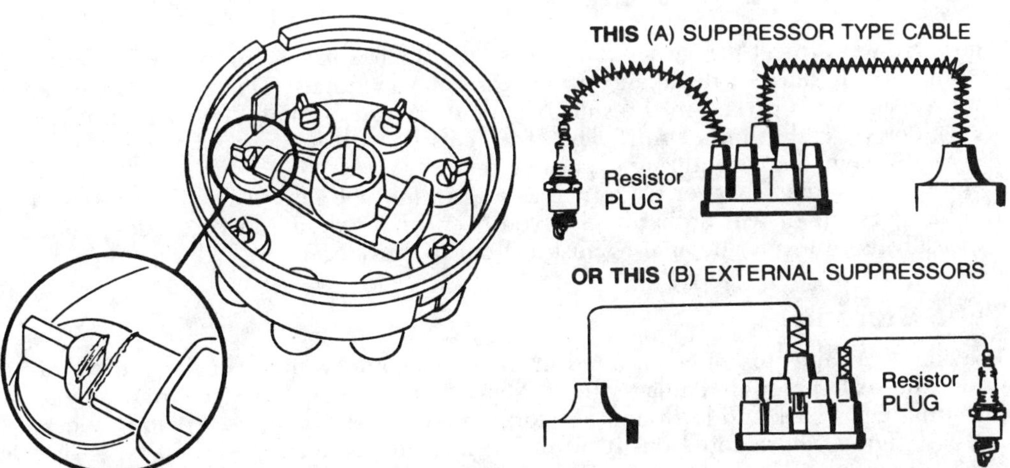

Replace rotor and distributor cap (on point-type ignitions) when they show signs of wear (Courtesy Champion Spark Plug Co.)

Do not combine spark plug suppression devices (Courtesy Champion Spark Plug Co.)

When handling suppressor cables, never pull on the cable; remove them by pulling on the boot. Never try to attach a screw-on suppressor to a suppressor cable and don't try to repair suppressor cables. Cables which are damaged should be replaced.

RESISTOR SPARK PLUGS

Spark plugs of the type known as "resistor type" afford better protection from RFI than conventional spark plugs. The use of resistor-type spark plugs is increasing in newer engines because of their ability to maintain their suppressive characteristic for long periods of time.

Spark plugs should also be maintained properly to provide protection against RFI. A wide plug gap, when the electrodes are burnt, or uneven, requires higher than normal voltage causing the ignition system to emit higher than normal levels of RFI.

COMBINING SUPPRESSION DEVICES

Some cars and trucks are equipped with resistor-type plugs and suppressor spark plug cables. Resistor-type plugs can be used in other vehicles where more suppression is desired, or some other suppression devices can be used, but combining the two is not a good idea. Choose between:

Resistor plugs with suppressor cables, OR Resistor plugs with 10,000 ohm suppressors in the center tower of the distributor and 5,000 ohm suppressors in the spark plug distributor towers.

SAFETY WARNING DEVICES

Federal safety regulations have required the addition of a variety of warning lights and buzzers over the past few years. These buzzers are to remind the driver to turn the headlights off, fasten seatbelts, remove the ignition key, etc. If necessary, these circuits can be suppressed at the primary power circuits.

Be careful when hooking up your transceiver to a power source—it is not a good idea to connect it to any source shared with a buzzer, solenoid, or flasher.

CARING FOR YOUR STEREO

There are ways to get the most from your stereo. One is to take proper care of your system, which starts with taking proper care of your tapes. Don't leave tapes in your car when it's parked in the sun. A parked car can become like an oven when its windows are shut on a sunny day. If it heats enough to warp your tapes, they can jam in your deck, requiring expensive repairs.

By the same token, never try to jam a recalcitrant tape into place. If it gives you trouble going in, it will probably give you even more when you try to get it out, especially as you won't be able to push it from the inside.

Tape Storage

Leaving your tapes to bounce around in the glove compartment, in the console or under the seat can easily damage them. Many tape cases and carriers are available for toting tapes back and forth and for storing them when not in use. Before selecting one, figure where you'll put it in the car and how convenient it will be to fish tapes from it while you're driving. Cases which hold tapes in their individual boxes protect the tapes best, but those which hold unboxed tapes are often more convenient when you're trying to retrieve and load tapes as you drive.

You may also want some sort of small accessory to hold a few tapes near the

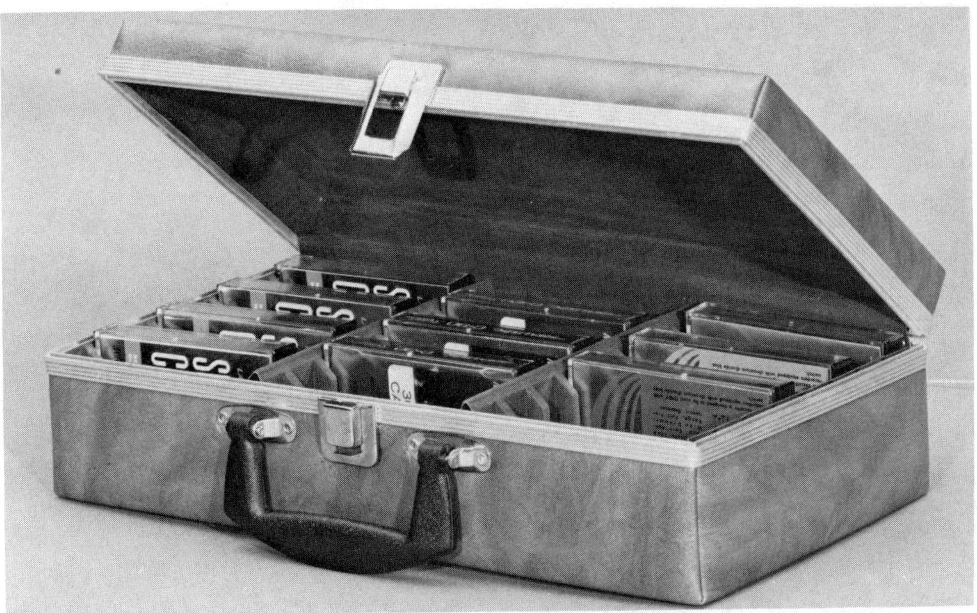

Tapes should be stored in a clean, dry place, away from heat with the open end protected

driver's seat. There are tape holders for the sun visor, the dashboard and for under the dash, as well as those which rest on the car's floor. Your tastes and the space available in your car will govern which is best for you.

Tape Player Maintenance

Clean your tape heads periodically. Twice a year is a reasonable minimum. Do it more often, though, if you play tapes often, live in dusty country, or drive much with open windows. If all three conditions apply, you might do it as often as weekly. Car-stereo tape heads are often buried in receivers or decks, where swab-type cleaners have trouble reaching them. There are, however, cleaners built into cassette shells, which can work with any cassette deck.

Similarly, the tape head should probably be demagnetized from time to time. Here, once or twice a year should suffice under normal circumstances. After all, experts disagree on how often heads should be demagnetized on recorders, and all agree there should be far less need on decks used just for playback. Demagnetizers which must be poked at the heads from outside may have trouble reaching them in many decks, but there are also demagnetizers built into cassette shells, which

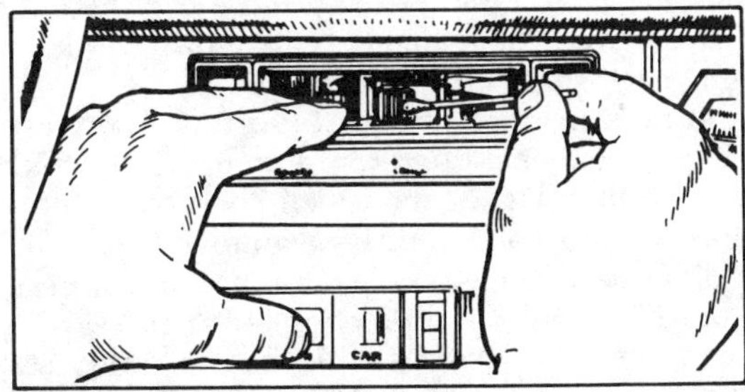

Clean the tape head and capstan every few hours of operation with a cotton swab and denatured alcohol

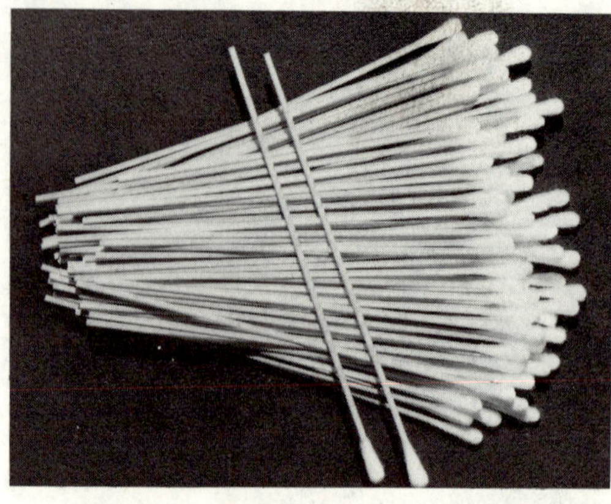

Cotton swabs are useful for cleaning tape player heads

will do the trick. Some of these even have the added advantage of running on battery power, so you need not drive your car up to a power outlet.

Aside from that, your system usually shouldn't need much maintenance.

Taping

Another way to get more from your system is to make tapes for it. That doesn't just mean making cassette copies of your favorite records, but making copies with your car's listening environment in mind.

For example, if your car system's response is a bit lacking in some part of the frequency spectrum, or if part of the audible range is often obscured by noise, you can use a home equalizer to boost that part of the range in the recording you make. (High-frequency boosts, though, should be extremely mild, if you attempt them at all—tapes distort more readily from excess high-frequency energy than from overloads in any other parts of the range.)

If your car is noisy, you might also compress your tapes a bit in the recording, by "riding gain" so that the loud passages in the record grow a trifle softer on the tape, and the soft passages grow a little louder. Do *not* do this by suddenly turning down the recording control when the signal grows loud, and vice versa. Instead, work gradually and in opposition to the music, turning the gain down little by little during crescendos, and turning it slowly up again as the music grows softer.

Theft Protection

The best protection you can have is the constant exercise of common sense. Try not to advertise the presence of your stereo in areas where your car will sit alone and unprotected. Such places include not only the proverbial dark alley, but also unattended, public parking areas, especially in troubled neighborhoods. If your stereo is on a slide-mount, take it off the dash and either take it with you or conceal it. If you're hiding it (or any other valuables) in your trunk, make the transfer to your trunk before you reach your final parking place.

There are gadgets to help protect your system, too. The least expensive are false fronts which fit over your expensive stereo and make it look like a cheap radio. Next in price come cast metal gadgets which lock over the stereo and make it harder (slower) to remove and harder, if it is removed, to sell. The bungling thief will also make more of a mess when he encounters one of these devices.

Alarms give you more expensive protection—not just for your stereo, but for your car and all its contents. Professional thieves are rarely stopped by alarm systems, especially if they have some particular reason to pick on your car. But they will discourage both amateurs and pros who are aimlessly shopping. Radio-page alarm systems can even notify you of trouble, if you're within their usually short transmission range. Some alarms will also do tricks such as signalling where the car is if you send out a radio command from a pocket controller—handy if you've lost your car in a strange parking lot.

Unless your car is stolen or broken into, you may never know whether your alarm has actually discouraged crime or whether your local crooks just passed you by for other reasons. But your alarm can pay off in less equivocal ways: many insurance companies offer discounts for cars with alarm systems, sometimes even enough to pay for the alarm in a year or three.

See the Chapter on alarm systems later in this book.

Troubleshooting

Radio problems are not normally caused by a defective radio. More often the cause is due to some less obvious fault. Follow the procedures in order before assuming the radio is defective.

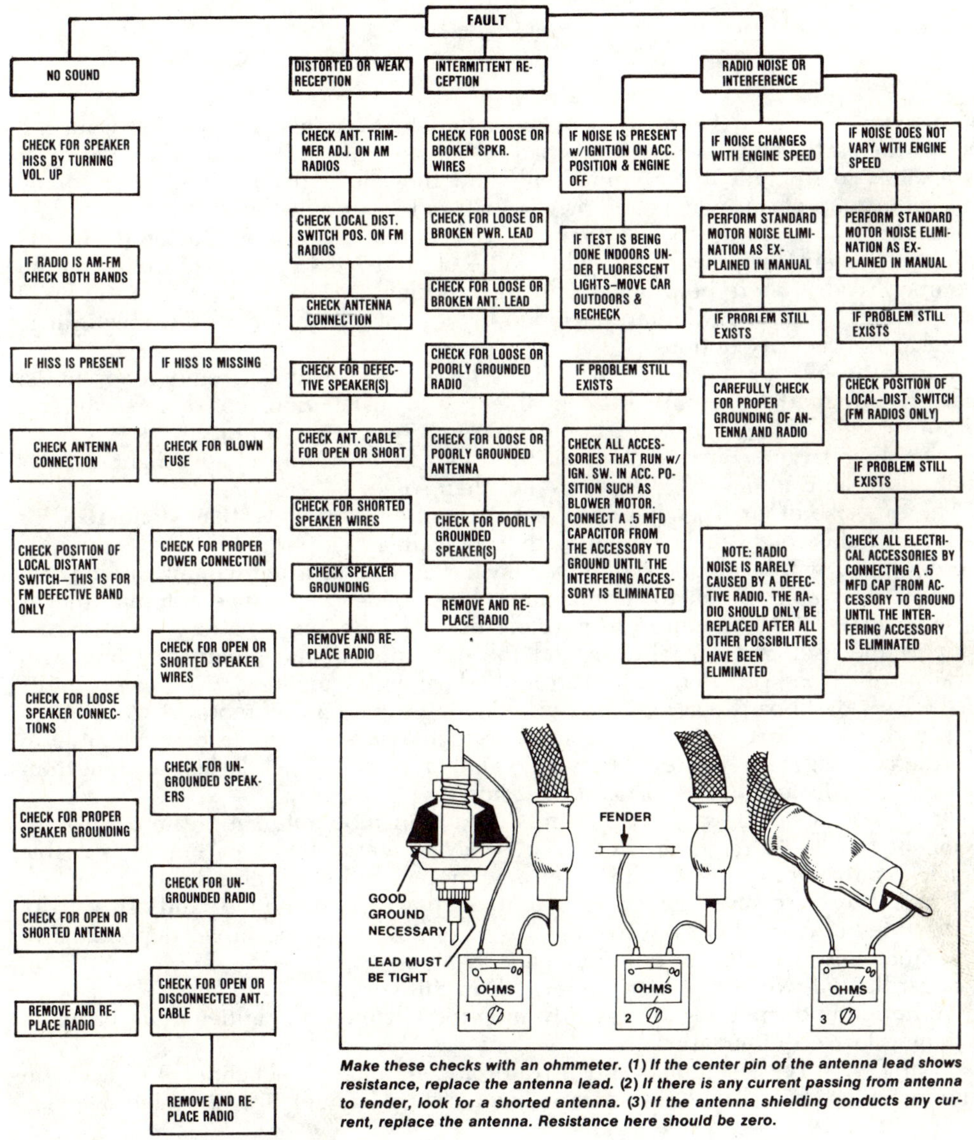

Make these checks with an ohmmeter. (1) If the center pin of the antenna lead shows resistance, replace the antenna lead. (2) If there is any current passing from antenna to fender, look for a shorted antenna. (3) If the antenna shielding conducts any current, replace the antenna. Resistance here should be zero.

3

CB and Emergency Radios

Remember CB radio? Contrary to popular belief, it has not disappeared from the face of the earth, or from America's roadways. There are still CB buffs who are just as anxious to upgrade their equipment, and they have been joined by a totally different group of car owners and drivers. CB radios are now being used as security items. Many drivers do so in potentially risky situations. Seven out of 10 drivers spend half their time driving at night, and 8 of 10 drivers spend half their time on the open roads, where help is not as readily available. Emergency radios can be of help in these situations, and are included by at least one major car manufacturer in a package of security options.

While the overall trend in CB radio is toward the compact, emergency units, that are designed to require little in the way of installation, consumers who are bitten by the CB bug may want to move up to a standard CB unit.

Like their larger cousins, many of the new, highly compact, 40 channel units offer all of the traditional CB features and then some.

The tiny size of emergency radios makes them less obtrusive than standard CB's and their light weight makes them easily convertible to a portable unit. Many units are equipped with a mobile mounting bracket as well as a telescoping antenna (to provide a portable option to the magnetic base high-performance antenna) that is easily switched from mounted to portable use. A lightweight battery pack is used for portable use, and can also expand the operation of the emergency unit in a variety of highway situations. The battery pack provides an alternative power source to the car's dashboard cigarette lighter, allowing the stranded motorist to summon help if the car's battery is dead or if an accident makes it unsafe or impossible to use the car's cigarette lighter. Many auto clubs report that nearly half of all of their emergency calls are for flat or dead batteries.

Other features of these versatile units usually include automatic gain control for excellent sensitivity, a superheterodyne receiver, automatic noise limiter, variable squelch control for quiet standby electronic meters and channel indicator.

Transmitters are rated for up to 4 watts of power as a mobile, and are usually switchable between about 3 watts and 1 watt of power as a portable, depending on how much power drain can be tolerated.

Regardless of which type you prefer, CB is still very much alive.

• Campground operators frequently monitor Channel 11, anticipating campers searching for accommodations.

• Garages, service stations, and private citizens monitor Channel 9 to assist in emergency situations or help stranded motorists. Channel 9 is the official emergency channel nationwide, which also includes such information as where to find food and lodging when traveling. Thousands of CB operators have banded together into organized groups and voluntarily monitor Channel 9 24 hours a day for the sole purpose of lending aid in emergencies. Among these are ALERT (Affiliated League of Emergency Radio Teams), HELP (Highway Emergency Locating Plan), REST (Radio Emergency Service Teams), and the largest, REACT (Radio Emergency Associated Citizens Teams), composed of over 1,000 teams and 40,000 members handling millions of emergency assistance calls annually. Members of these organizations have rendered invaluable service in almost all national disasters: earthquakes, floods, fires, tornados, and hurricanes. They are equipped to provide you with information or to route your call to the proper authority.

- Increasingly, state police are beginning to employ CB radio. Highway patrols in many states monitor Channel 9.

THE CITIZENS RADIO SERVICE

In the late 1940s, 2-way radio communication was mainly restricted to governmental agencies, police, and fire departments. But, in 1947, the Federal Communications Commission formed the Citizens Radio Service, to permit 2-way communications over short distances by private individuals or businesses.

Presently, there are 3 CB classes—Class A, C, and D—each serving a different purpose. Originally, there was a Class B, but it no longer exists.

Class D, or CB radio, as it is known today, officially was created in 1958, when the Federal Communications Commission allotted 22 channels (frequencies), of the formerly 11 meter amateur broadcast band to provide reliable 2-way communication for private citizens. Class D stations operate exclusively on these frequencies, and an additional 17 channels effective January 1, 1977, except for Channel 23, which was added later. Channel 23 is used on a shared basis with Class C stations.

The lower operating frequencies substantially overcame the line-of-sight transmission difficulties experienced with Class B equipment and the popularity of CB began its slow ascent as low-priced, reliable equipment was mass produced.

The FCC specifies radiotelephone only on the 40 Class D AM channels with maximum transmitter output power limited to 4 watts.

CBs and the FCC

No operator's license is required for CB. The Federal Communications Commission (FCC) used to require that you obtain a Radio Service Class D station permit before operating a CB. However, the permit requirement has been suspended.

You should however, pick up a copy of Part 95 of the FCC Rules and Regulations, which is the bible as far as CB is concerned. These rules can be obtained

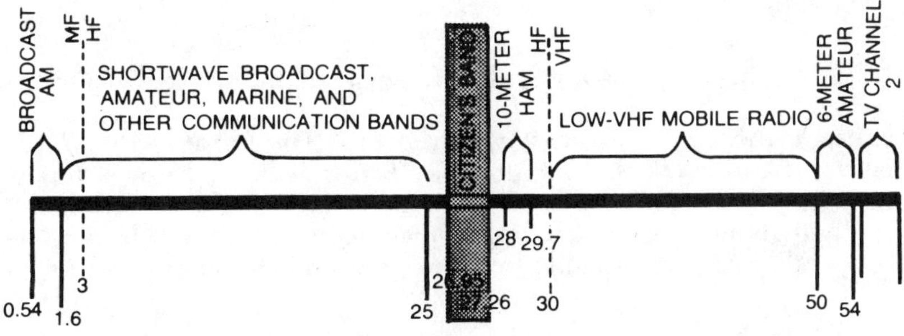

Location of Citizen's Band in the radio spectrum

Class D CB Channels

(frequencies in MHz)

Channel Number	Frequency	Channel Number	Frequency
1	26.965	21	27.215
2	26.975	22	27.225
3	26.985	23②	27.235
4	27.005	24*	27.245
5	27.015	25*	27.255
6	27.025	26*	27.265
7	27.035	27*	27.275
8	27.055	28*	27.285
9①	27.065	29*	27.295
10	27.075	30*	27.305
11	27.085	31*	27.315
12	27.105	32*	27.325
13	27.115	33*	27.335
14	27.125	34*	27.345
15	27.135	35*	27.355
16	27.155	36*	27.365
17	27.165	37*	27.375
18	27.175	38*	27.385
19	27.185	39*	27.395
20	27.205	40*	27.405

① Channel 9 is the national emergency channel
② Channel 23 is used on a shared basis with Class C stations
*Channels 24–40 were added on July 27, 1976 and available for use on January 1, 1977

from the Government Printing Office ($1.50), or are usually reprinted in any complete book on CB's such as Chilton's 40-Channel CB Handbook.

The FCC is empowered by Congress to establish and enforce the rules and regulations governing the use of CB radio. Many people did not understand the 20-odd pages of legal jargon that make up Part 95. To simplify things, the FCC made the following modifications, which are currently in effect:

• The "hobby" restriction is removed. Citations will no longer be given for idle "chit-chat" except in cases of profanity, playing music or selling merchandise on the air.

• The use of "handles" is now approved, provided the station call sign is also given.

• The station permit fee is no longer being collected and the permit requirement has been suspended.

• Effective Jan. 1, 1977, the number of channels was increased from 23 to 40. At the same time, the FCC stated that the 40-channel expansion was an interim measure, and that studies are underway considering the 220 and 900 MHz band for CB.

The FCC is concerned mainly with obscenity on the air and use of the linear (RF) amplifier.

Obscenity on the air is, fortunately, fairly rare. The linear (RF) amplifier is another matter. It can boost the output of a CB from 4 watts to over 100 and blank out large geographic areas, making it impossible for others to transmit. The FCC is so concerned about these that selling or owning one (it doesn't have to be hooked up) is a Federal offense punishable by a fine of up to $10,000 and a year in jail.

BUYING A CB RADIO

Transceiver Features

The word transceiver here is used synonymously with CB radio, although there are a few sets on the markets which are receivers only (they do not have transmit capability). These sets are rare these days, but if that's what you want, they are available.

RANGE

CB radios are not powerful transmitters capable of reliable communication across the country. Attainable range is dependent on terrain, weather conditions, antenna placement on the vehicle (in the case of a mobile), how many people are using any given channel at a time, and type of equipment utilized to name a few factors. For example, range is much greater over the water where it is flat with no obstructions, than in a large city with tall buildings around. You will also notice that range increases greatly on a "clean" channel, one where few people are using their equipment. Placement of your aerial also has a lot to do with it, since most mobile CB antennas are directional, that is, they radiate the transmitted signal better in some directions than in others.

As a general answer to the question, under optimum conditions, communication is reliable at 1–20 miles between base and mobile stations, and 1–3 miles between mobile units. Sometimes, however, conditions will conspire against you, and you won't even be able to communicate around the corner.

There is also a phenomenon known as "skip" or "DX-ing." Basically, this involves a transmitted signal which will actually bounce off the inonosphere, once (single skip), or more than once (multiple skip), and finally be received at a transmitter several hundred or even thousands of miles distant. This does not always happen. Depending on the conditions in the ionosphere, some 50–400 miles above the earth's surface, these radio waves may simply be bent or reflected back to the earth's surface. Constant changes in the ionized layers of the earth's atmosphere vary the effects of "skip" considerably, and these changes may occur at predictable intervals (season-to-season, night-to-day), or it may be completely random.

Operating Controls

The simplest transceivers have only 3 operating controls—a channel selector switch, a squelch control, and an on/off-volume control. The microphone has an additional control: a push-to-talk switch. You will find many more additional features, and before you buy a set, you should be aware of what these controls do, so that you can talk intelligently about them.

ON/OFF-VOLUME

This switch is usually combined into one control on the front of the set. Turning the switch clockwise turns the set on, just like any transistor radio.

SQUELCH

The squelch control is used to adjust the sensitivity of the receiver portion of the set. Normally, this is a single control, although on some sets it is the outer portion of the volume switch. Almost all sets made today have a squelch control. When it is set in the fully unsquelched position, you will hear a scratching static sound through the set which is being generated by the receiver itself. When a signal is received, it over-rides the noise and "turns off" the squelch circuit, allowing the signal to be heard. Normally, the squelch is set just beyond the point where background noise is silenced; nothing will be heard through the speaker until a signal

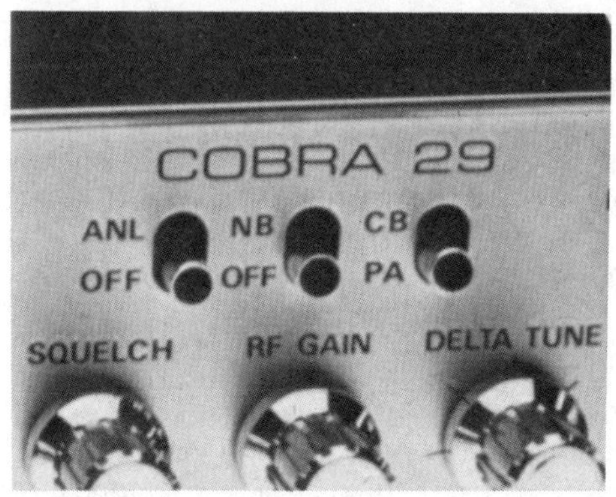

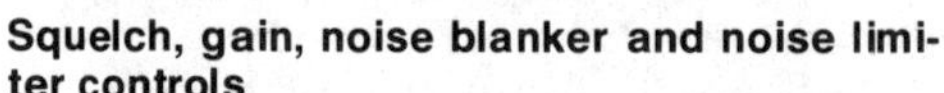
Squelch, gain, noise blanker and noise limiter controls

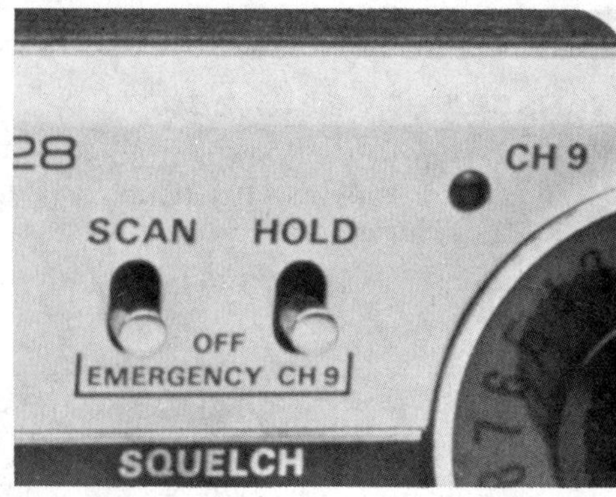

Channel 9 priority

is received. Rotating the squelch progressively toward the fully squelched position means that a stronger signal must be received to break the squelch. The converse is also true; the less the set is squelched, the weaker the signal it will receive, until the noise over-rides the squelch.

CHANNEL SELECTOR

The channel selector can be a rotating knob or a 3 position slide switch. A 3-position slide switch is normally used for sets equipped with only three channels, where a rotating knob is used for any more than 3 channels. You will notice that sets equipped with 3 or 6 channels, for example, are marked with letters instead of numbers. This is because the set generally comes equipped with only one set of crystals corresponding to given channels. In order to use it on other channels, you will have to install (or have installed), crystals for whatever channel you desire. Full 40 channel sets have the channel numbers marked on the knob, usually with a single light to illuminate the number of the channel in use, or light emitting diodes (LEDs) to show channel numbers, much like a TV set.

Most transceivers have the channel selector knob on the transceiver itself, making it necessary to reach down and change the channel although some manufacturers has solved this problem by putting the channel selector switch in the microphone housing, making one-handed control possible.

AUTOMATIC GAIN CONTROL (AGC)

Every receiver has an automatic gain control. The AGC is not really an operating control, but a feature of the circuitry to prevent overloading the receiver with an extremely strong signal. If the volume were turned all the way up to receive a particularly weak signal, your ears would be blasted when a strong signal was received. The AGC circuit prevents this. The smaller the AGC specification, the better; 5 db, for example, is better than 10 db.

CB/PA SWITCH

Most CB sets come standard with the capability to be used as a public address system. If so, the set is equipped with a CB/PA selecting switch and a PA jack, usually on the back of the set. By connecting the jack to an external speaker, you can flick the switch to PA, talk into the mike, and use your set for a PA system.

EXTERNAL SPEAKER JACK

The external speaker jack serves the same function on a CB as it does on your home stereo. If you are not satisfied with the sound from the CB speaker built into the set, you can by-pass it by plugging an external speaker into the jack, usually on the back of the set.

AUTOMATIC NOISE LIMITER (ANL)

The automatic noise limiter is usually an on/off switch located on the front of the transceiver. Its function is to act as a filter, chopping holes in the received signal and substituting periods of silence, thereby reducing the static that the receiver picks up from man-made sources, such as car ignition, machinery, etc. Switching the ANL on will cut down on man-made static noise and will also sometimes cut down on received signal strength, however, only to a minimal degree. The automatic noise limiter is sometimes built-in, and should not be confused with the built-in automatic gain control, nor with the noise blanker.

NOISE BLANKER

The noise blanker is really a more powerful automatic noise limiter; and if it is switchable, is used, when the ANL does not adequately suppress man-made noise. It will also suppress the pulsing noise of your set.

METER

If your set has a meter at all, it will probably be an S-meter, or, if a more expensive set, an S-RF meter. An S-meter indicates the relative strength of incoming signals in S-units, measured from 1–9 and in db above S9 when receiving. An S1 received signal would be very weak and an S9 received signal would be quite strong. Likewise, a signal metered at 40 db above S9 would be extremely strong.

The RF portion of the meter, if it has one, is a measure of the signal you are putting out. When this portion of the meter reads at maximum, it indicates that your rig is operating at peak efficiency.

The S/RF meter is an approximation only. Frequently you will hear someone ask for a radio check and a meter reading. This is OK for an approximation of how well your set is getting out, but modulation at the other receiver is a better indication. One S meter may read S7 for a received signal and another meter may read S5 for the same received signal.

Some meters also incorporate lights which glow in the meter to indicate various modes. For instance, a meter may glow red when you are transmitting or glow amber when you are receiving.

CHANNEL 9 PRIORITY

A Channel 9 priority is a device that enables the receiver to automatically override whatever channel is being utilized when a signal is received on Channel 9. Sometimes, a light will glow, alerting you to switch to Channel 9 or it may automatically do this when a signal is received. In this way, you can tune to any channel desired, and still monitor Channel 9. Normally, this feature is activated by means of an on/off switch.

DELTA TUNE

This control is a three-position switch on the front of the transceiver which allows you to correct your receiver for off-channel signals. Normally, it is left set at its center position, but when a signal is received with a high or low frequency error, the control is adjusted to either the plus (+) or minus (−) position. This allows you to receive off-frequency signals with a minimum of distortion.

DX/LOCAL SWITCH

This is usually a two-position slide switch, enabling you to only receive local or short range calls if you're on the local side of the switch, or to enable you to receive longer range calls if you're on the DX (distance) side of the switch.

MODE INDICATOR LIGHTS

Some transceivers are equipped with mode indicator lights; small lights, usually red and amber, which glow depending on whatever mode (transmit or receive) you happen to be in.

TONE CONTROL

Just as most AM radios are equipped with a knob to adjust the tone of the sound (treble-bass), some CBs are also equipped with a tone control.

MICROPHONE GAIN CONTROL

This is a knob that you will find on relatively few transceivers. Its use is to vary the percentage of modulation, thereby varying your talking power. Because the FCC limits the percentage of modulation to 100%, they are considering with holding type acceptance to receivers with a microphone gain control accessible to the operator of the set.

MICROPHONES

The microphone is your connection between you and your transceiver. As such, it should be a good one. Most stock mikes that come with the set are perfectly adequate and do a good job.

Basically there are two types of mikes—ceramic or dynamic. Either type is fine for the job, although the dynamic type probably rates an edge due to its greater reliability. Most microphones are plugged into the set, either on the front or side. A few standard sets and most emergency units have the microphone wired in directly. The advantage to a plug-in type lies in the ability to replace it with one of the many pre-amp types if you wish. Dynamic mikes are also least susceptible to damage from shock and to extremes of temperature and humidity.

Speak into the microphone holding it at a 45 degree angle, a couple of inches from your mouth. Don't speak directly into the mike, but hold it off to the side and speak past it. Voices spoken directly into a microphone at close range are received garbled and unintelligible. On the other hand, if the mike is too far away from your mouth, the modulation level will be too low and more background noise will be picked up, even though the S meter on the contact's receiver will indicate a fairly strong signal. When the modulation level is too low, your voice will sound weak and indistinct at the receiver. A little experimentation may be necessary at first to find the right spot for the best modulation but, a good rule of thumb to remember is: doubling the distance from your mouth to the mike decreases the mike's output by about 6 decibels or to about ¼ of its former output. This is one reason that the telephone handset and the headset were developed—to assure maximum modulation.

Speak in a normal voice, you don't have to shout. If you are using the mike properly, your modulation will be fine. Some sets are equipped with a microphone gain switch which can be adjusted for best modulation. Experimentation with individual sets is necessary to get best results.

Manufacturers' Specifications

Perhaps the greatest confusion in buying a CB is the manufacturers' specifications. Nearly everyone knows that there are such things, but hardly anyone knows what they mean. Bear in mind that many of the specifications listed on a spec sheet are strictly regulated by the FCC and manufacturers must comply with them in order to have sets type accepted.

INPUT POWER

Input power is usually given in watts, and prior to 1974, transmitter input power was limited to 5 watts. This is actually the amount of power applied to the final amplifier or stage. It does not include the power consumption required to run the transceiver and its various lights and meters. Some manufacturers advertise (and their spec sheets may indicate), that the input power is 5 watts. This is true, but it is the output power which matters to the performance of the set.

Emergency CB units are capable of being operated at different power levels. Typically, when in the mobile mode, output power is 4 watts. When in the portable mode, they can be switched to a lower output power level to conserve the batteries.

OUTPUT POWER

Output power is also given in watts and applies only to the transmitter. The FCC says that no Class D AM transmitter can put out more than 4 watts of carrier power without modulation. It seems logical, therefore, to look for a set which offers the highest output in watts. But, in actual practice, you will find that most transceivers deliver somewhere around 2½–4 watts, and you will notice little on-the-air difference between 3 and 4 watts. So, don't let this be the only judge.

In most cases, the wattage output is based on the power put into a 50 ohm antenna.

MODULATION

This is where the biggest difference in transmitters is found. FCC rules again limit the amount of modulation to 100%, and the closer to 100% the set is rated, the better its talking power. If there is a choice, get the one which is rated closest to 100% modulation.

SENSITIVITY

Sensitivity is a rating of the receiver portion of your CB. It is the ability of the receiver to pick up weak signals, and, with the crowded conditions found in most parts of the country, this becomes an important consideration when selecting a set. Sensitivity is normally given on the spec sheet in microvolts (uV), and the smaller the number, the greater its sensitivity. Look for something in the area of under 1.0 microvolt, down to about 0.30 microvolts.

SELECTIVITY

Selectivity is also a rating of the receiver portion and is equally as important as sensitivity. This is the ability of the receiver to reject transmissions on adjacent channels or channels other than that to which the receiver is set. Since signals are separated by small frequency differences, it is important that the selectivity be as good as possible.

The receiver's ability to reject signals on channels other than the one it's tuned to is expressed in dB (decibels) at ± 10 kHz of the channel frequency. The greater the number of dB, the more selective the receiver.

ADJACENT CHANNEL REJECTION

Adjacent channel rejection is similar to selectivity, and is measured in dB (decibels). The larger the number the better, but look for a set with a mimimum of 40 dB, but preferably 50 dB or better.

SPURIOUS REJECTION

Spurious rejection indicates the ability of your set's transmitter to keep its transmission on one channel. When you talk into the mike, if you over-modulate or put too much talking power into the mike, the undesired portion of your speech can "bleed over" onto adjacent channels.

On the manufacturer's spec sheet, this will be listed in dB (decibels). The better the set, the greater the number, but consider 40 dB an absolute minimum.

FREQUENCY RANGE

This is simply the frequencies of the highest and lowest channels at which the set will operate. Class D 40 channel CB equipment operates at 26.965 MHz-27.405 MHz and this is what should be listed under frequency range.

FREQUENCY STABILITY

The FCC requires that the set be able to transmit within 0.005% of the frequency on any given channel. This is the minimum tolerance allowed for the set to be type accepted by the FCC, although it is not uncommon to find tolerances of less than 0.005%.

SQUELCH SENSITIVITY

Occasionally, you will find this listed on a specifications sheet. The number given is the most sensitive setting to which the squelch can be adjusted. Putting too much squelch into the audio section will effectively drown out the entire signal, so that there are limits to sensitivity of squelch.

This is typically expressed in microvolts (uV), and the better squelch circuitry gets a lower microvolt count.

OPERATING VOLTAGE

Mobile units are designed to be operated from a vehicle electrical system which are typically given as 13.6 VDC, 13.8 VDC, or 12.6 VDC. They all mean the same thing. The only thing you will have to be careful of is polarity. Most mobile sets are designed to be operated from negative ground, and a few offer positive or negative ground operation. Check before you buy.

CURRENT DRAIN

Current drain is usually a miniscule amount in mobiles and will be given on a spec sheet in milliamperes or amperes. In a mobile you really need not concern yourself with current drain, unless you plan to operate from your vehicle's battery for extended periods, or plan to operate your emergency unit in the portable mode. The higher the number the more current it requires.

AUDIO OUTPUT

You want to look for the highest level of audio output you can find to be able to overcome natural noise. The audio output is the highest level of maximum clear volume which can be attained before distortion occurs; a good audio output rating would be 2.5–3.0 watts. Some of the best sets can go as high as 6 watts.

TRANSCEIVER CIRCUITRY

This subject could fill volumes and require the education of an electronics engineer to understand. Since all transceivers have to meet certain standards to be type accepted by the FCC, they are all fairly similar to those unversed in electronic circuitry. Unfortunately, there are also many variations.

There are, however, two basic types of circuitry in use today; single conversion receivers and double conversion receivers. Both are of the type known as superheterodyne. Without getting into a long electronic discussion of the differences, it all comes down to this: a double conversion superheterodyne improves its selectivity and gives itself a better chance to reject off-frequency signals. But don't by-pass a set just because it is not a double conversion receiver. The selectivity of a single conversion receiver can equal that of a double conversion if the selectivity filtering is good enough.

There are hundreds of sets to choose from and features are numbered in the teens. Your choice will probably depend on your needs, but here is a checklist to help you through the CB jungle.

1. Look for an "FCC Type Accepted" set. The set will be plainly marked as such, and type acceptance means that it meets or exceeds FCC standards for transmission and reception.

2. Don't expect your communication distance to be a function of the price you pay for the set, although you should expect the highest quality from the higher priced sets. Design specifications are limited by the FCC, and transmitters are basically equal. If maximum distance is important, spend your money on the antenna.

3. Learn to interpret the specifications, but don't let them be the sole determining factor.

4. Shop around for the best prices. Competition is very stiff and there are almost always sales in progress. Stick to known brands and the quality will be almost identical.

5. If at all possible, try the rig before you buy it. Most dealers have a watt meter for checking the transmitter. It should be at least 3.2 watts when transmitting. Check all channels for the normal CB patter. If it's not there, suspect the receivers' sensitivity. Check that other channels are not bleeding over onto any particular channel. If bleed over is present, the adjacent channel rejection is suspect. Check the squelch. Turn the squelch to a point just before it kills the signal. As it is slowly turned up and down, the audio should suddenly come on. If it acts as though you were turning the volume up and down, the receiver's sensitivity is suspect.

6. Look for a set with automatic noise limiter (ANL) and noise blanker (NB). Noise from your own ignition system can play havoc with your receiver.

7. Don't let the newest phase-lock-loop (PLL) circuitry be the determining factor. Crystal or digital synthesis will accomplish the same result.

8. Don't pay for SSB unless you can use it. It's too expensive and there are not enough SSB units for the average CB'er to pay the money.

9. Don't assume that all rigs will work with all cars, trucks and boats. Determine whether you'll be using negative or positive ground before you buy.

10. On mobile units especially, look for easily operated controls. Switches should leave no doubt as to their position and meters should be lighted and easily read.

The Antenna System

The antenna that you will use with your CB is going to determine its performance, for this is the most important part of the system. No matter how expensive or how good your transceiver is, it will not give peak performance unless it has a good antenna capable of radiating and receiving a strong signal. A poor antenna or poor antenna installation can make a $300.00 transceiver work like a piece of junk, just as a less expensive transceiver will work beyond expectations with a good antenna.

Because of the low power limitations placed on CB equipment, a good antenna becomes even more important. Normally, even though you have about 5 watts of input power to the transmitter, the set is only supplying about 3½ watts to the antenna and the output may even be less, depending upon the circuitry, transmitter efficiency, and energy required to run various lights and meters. In the case of small hand-held emergency unit the power may even be less in the portable mode, down around 1 watt. However, optimum performance can be obtained fromal most any set by carefully selecting and installing an antenna system which will be capable of using the limited power available to the best advantage. This includes not only the antenna, or aerial, but also the coaxial cable used to connect the antenna to the transceiver, various connections, and any matching devices which may be used. Failure of any part of the system will affect the performance of the entire system.

Many times a perfectly good transceiver is blamed for an inability to transmit effectively, when in fact, it may be the fault of the antenna system, which is the case in most instances. It is fairly easy these days for manufacturers of CBs to reach the legal design limits imposed by the FCC. The communicating range, therefore, lies in matching the antenna to the transceiver, for if the transceiver output remains a constant, it is possible to raise the communicating range of the rig simply by improving the antenna efficiency. An omnidirectional antenna used by almost all mobiles, can only radiate the amount of energy supplied it by the transmitter, but newer, more sophisticated base station antennas have a signal gain. This is accomplished through the ability to point or "aim" radio signals, making them appear to be much stronger than they actually are. A "gain" type of antenna can make 3 watts seem like considerably more as it leaves the antenna and can result in better overall performance simply by utilizing improved antenna efficiency.

TYPES OF ANTENNAS

It is not always possible to select an antenna that you want. Small walkie-talkies usually come equipped with a telescoping whip antenna, although more expensive walkie-talkies have provision for using a small portable-type antenna which fastens directly to the set with a standard PL-259 connector. These are also capable of using remote outdoor antennas, but this is rare. Twenty-three channel mobile and base sets almost always use remote antennas.

CB antennas come in all shapes, sizes, and prices, but there are basically whips, ground planes, coaxials, and beams, each with its myriad variations.

Whips

More commonly known as a vertical whip, it is used mostly for mobile installations. It derives its name from its whipping action, or flexibility, and is normally ¼ wavelength. A whip can be either base, center, top or continuous-loaded, depending on construction, to reduce its physical length and is available in steel or fiberglass. Marine antennas are generally of this type because of the abuse taken from the elements and from normal wer and tear on equipment.

Some of the advantages and/or disadvantages to whips are:

- CONTINUOUS LOAD: Easier to install, but less critically tuned.
- TOP LOADED: Most efficient, but harder to match. Their radiation characteristics frequently change due to the tendency of top weighted antennas to sway. The most fragile part (coil) is at the most vulnerable spot (top).
- CENTER LOADED: Efficient radiation patterns, but the weight causes a lot of sway.
- BASE LOADED: Offer slender profile and less susceptible to picking up inter-

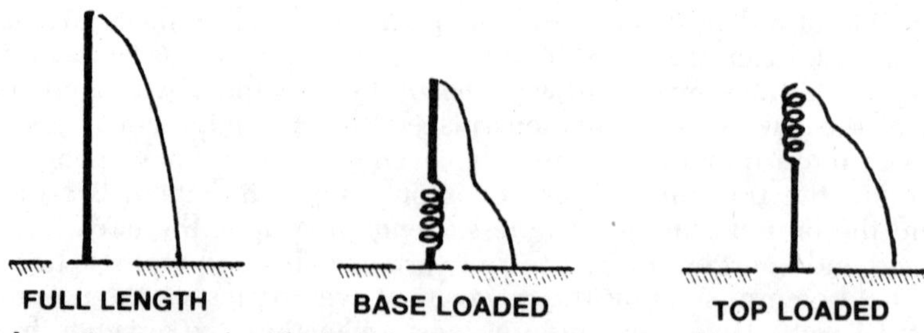

An antenna can be "fooled" into thinking it is electrically longer than it actually is with a loading coil (Courtesy Shakespeare Industrial Antenna Div.)

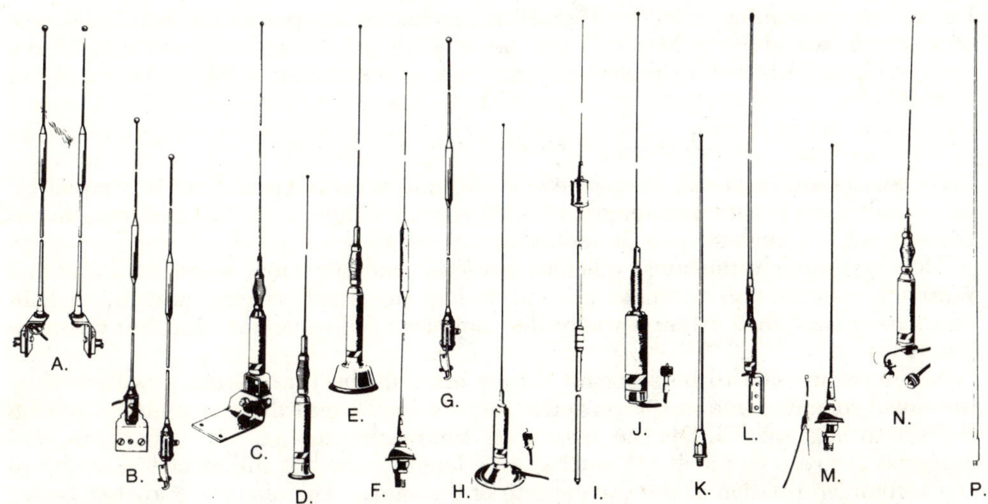

Most of the popular antennas: A. Twin trucker mirror mount B. Gutter mount flippers C. Base loaded for a motor home D. Base loaded snap-in roof mount E. Base loaded trunk mount F. Cowl mount center load G. Center load gutter mount flippers H. Temporary magnetic mount base load I. Bumper mount center load J. Center load K. Continuous load L. Non-ground plane (requires no ground plane, can be mounted on any surface) M. AM/FM/CB cowl mount N. Quick grip base load O. 102 inch whip

ference generated by passing vehicles. They are also more tolerant of the low capacitances between car and ground.

Keep in mind that no loaded antenna is as efficient as a greater wave one, although a center load is generally regarded as the best all-around compromise.

Ground Plane

Ground planes are by far the most popular in CB use. In its basic form it is omnidirectional and provides no gain, but in any one of its myriad variations, can give an omnidirectional gain or even be "aimed" to a slight degree. While ground plane antennas were designed primarily for base station use, they have found a large application in mobile use, using the roof or trunk lid of a vehicle for a ground plane.

ANTENNA FEATURES

Almost all two-way radio equipment uses the same antenna for transmitting and receiving. Switching within the transceiver is used to connect the antenna to the transmitter output side or the receiver input side. But not just any old hunk of wire will do for an antenna. The AM/FM car radio antenna is simply not suitable for a CB antenna, although there are several good combination AM-FM-CB antennas on the market. These types are tuned for optimum CB performance and will work just as well with the AM/FM receiver. About the only CB receivers which use the car radio antenna wre several models of converters which convert the AM/FM receiver into a CB receiver.

Antenna Length

There is a direct, scientific relationship between the physical length of an antenna and its electrical properties. An antenna will only function properly and efficiently when its own physical length is in a mathematical relationship with the wavelength of the signal which it is supposed to receive or transmit.

The wavelength of a radio wave, or the distance which it will travel in one complete cycle, can be calculated by dividing the velocity of the radio wave by its frequency, or number of hertz (Hz). Hertz means cycles per second and CB operates at approximately 27 MHz (27,000 hertz or cycles per second), and a CB radio wave will travel about 11 meters in one cycle. One meter is 39.37 inches, so 11 meters are:

$$39.37 \times 11 = 433.07 \text{ inches (36 ft. 1 in.)}$$

Since an antenna will not operate efficiently unless its physical length is equal to, or a multiple of, the wavelength at any given frequency, a CB antenna should theoretically be slightly over 36 feet long.

This is obviously the most efficient antenna, and the most impractical, so that most CB base station antennas are cut in half, to about 18 feet, and called half-wave antennas. They are essentially the same as a full-wave antenna, but far more practical.

Antennas are said to be resonant if they emit all the transmitted power. If they are not resonant, some of the power is reflected back into the transmitter, causing the set to heat up. This is the reason for tuning the antenna. It so happens that antennas are resonant at ¼, ½ and ⅝ wave length, which is the electrical length of the antenna in relation to the wavelength of the signal. The effective radiated power (ERP) is a measure of the strength of the signal. A ¼ wave has an ERP of 1, the ½ wave 2½ and the ⅝ wave 3. Multiplying the ERP times your 4 watt signal will immediately point up the advantages of a greater wavelength antenna.

But this still leaves the matter of mobile antennas. Even a half-wave, 18 foot long antenna hanging off the bumper is a precarious situation. So, for mobile applications, the ¼-wave antenna is far more suitable, presenting less of a danger to bridges, gas station lights, and low-flying birds. The ¼-wave antenna is only about 108 in. long ($433.07 \div 4 = 108$), also known as a "108 whip."

Loading Coils and Power Rating

For mobile CB application, people do not always want even 108 inches of fiberglass or stainless steel hanging from their car or truck bumper. The solution to this problem is to use an antenna which incorporates a loading coil.

The theory behind a loading coil is that, while using a physically shorter antenna, you can "fool" the antenna into thinking it is the proper length, usually ¼-wave or ⅝-wave. These antennas come anywhere from slightly under 18 inches long to

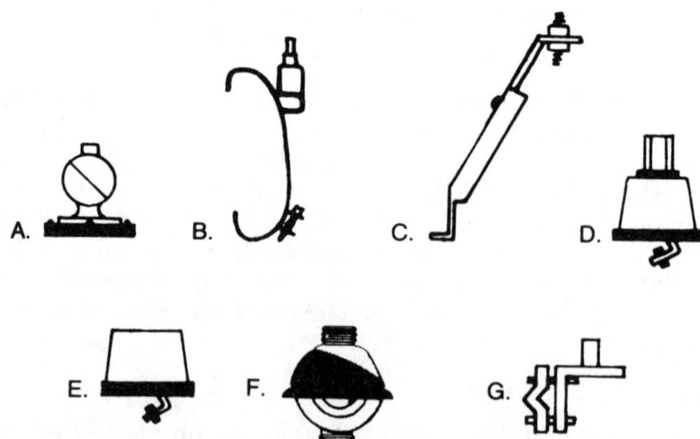

Most of the popular antenna mounts—(A) swivel ball, (B) bumper mount with ball, (C) trunk groove, (D) trunk lip, (E) trunk groove for snap-in antenna, (G) mirror mount and (H) cowl mount adaptor for base loaded antennas (Courtesy Hy-Gain Electronics Corp.)

around 4–6 feet long, with loading coils which are actually wire windings to increase the electrical length of the antenna.

Coils are either base, center, top, or continuous-type, and are used primarily on mobiles. The position of the coil on the antenna determines its type, with a continuous load done by spiral winding the conductor along the entire length of the antenna.

These are the most popular with mobile rigs because of their small size and the fact that they usually can be removed when you are parked in high-theft areas, such as parking lots, and are also less an obstacle in campgrounds, gas stations, or out on the trail. They do, however, present the added complication of sometimes having to drill a hole somewhere on your vehicle to install them, rather than mounting them on the bumper, although mounts are available requiring no holes.

Antennas (and loading coils) are usually rated in watts; 100, 300 or whatever; meaning that the antenna can handle an input from the transceiver equal to its rating. To be sure that you are enjoying maximum performance from the antenna itself, look for an antenna with the highest rated coil possible (in your price range), even though relatively low power (4 watts) operation is contemplated. As a practical matter, you probably won't notice the performance difference between a 100 or 300 watt rated antenna, but percentage-wise, the power losses in higher rated coils are usually less resulting in greater signal radiation, thus, greater efficiency.

DO-IT-YOURSELF INSTALLATION

Almost all CB equipment that you will purchase new comes with some sort of owner's manual, set-up instructions, or installation procedures. Installation of standard CB's is not very hard; in the case of emergency units, the only installation is setting the antenna on top of the car and plugging the power source into the vehicle's cigarette lighter. Follow the manufacturer's instructions and supplement them with some ideas here. The hardest part is buying the right pieces to do the job.

Some common hand tools are necessary: electric drill and bits, screwdriver, pliers, soldering gun and resin core solder, assorted wrenches, and wire strippers, etc. You will also need some wire end terminals and a few female spade-type connectors if you are going to go to the fuse block of your vehicle to power your mobile rig. See the section on Tools and Equipment. The foremost problem is deciding where to put the set so that it will fit neartly, be relatively unobtrusive, be within easy reach, and be the least hassle to install. Each factor should be weighed before deciding on a place.

Today's CB's do not present much of a problem because of their small size. Many could fit inside the glove compartment, except that they are hard for the driver to get at. The transceiver should be placed within easy reach of the driver so that operating the set is not distracting. The central engine cover on vans is a natural place, as is the below dash mount in passenger cars. Kits are also available for vans to provide a headliner installation, and one company offers an overhead console. These type installations have the advantage of the speaker facing downward and giving better sound. Other alternatives include transmission hump mount brackets, indash installations, or practically anywhere your imagination deems best.

Motorcycles usually mount the CB on the gas tank in a cradle supported on rubber dampers, as this is about the only possible place. RVs and tractor-trailers usually mount the radio on the lid of the dash console or on the windshield cross-beam preferred by 18-wheelers.

The unit should fit neatly and unobtrusively, with emphasis on the unobtrusive. This is not to say that a careless installation is desirable, but CBs have become a popular item with thieves. Unless you plan to take your set with you or disconnect it every time you leave your vehicle, you had better give some thought to installing

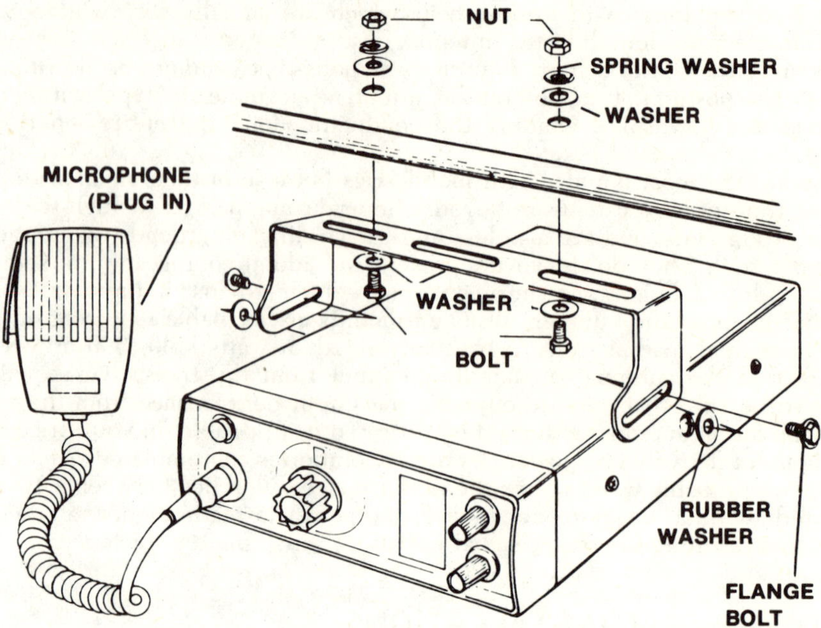

Typical underdash installation. A slide mount can be substituted for a permanently installed bracket

it where it will attract the least attention. Several other options are available here. There are CB lock mounts available to padlock your set to the car, but thieves are generally not too subtle about their work. Most times they will take the CB, lock mount and all, or worse take the whole car. A fairly good solution is to use the slide mounts popular with tape deck enthusiasts to mount your radio. This way you only have to disconnect the antenna lead-in and slide the unit off its mount to stow it in the glove compartment or under the seat. Another simple, but slower, solution to the problem is to use a two-pronged trailer harness to provide a quick-disconnect means for the power and ground leads to your set. After uncoupling the quick-disconnect, simply disconnect the antenna and the 2 or 4 screws holding the set to the bracket and stow the set out of sight and mind.

After spending many agonizing hours deciding where to put your new set, here's how to do it.

• Open the box and lay out all the pieces. Study the instructions and get a mental idea of just how the CB will be installed.

• After satisfying yourself that you have found the ideal mounting place, and you are sure it will fit there, attach the bracket to the radio and hold it up in position.

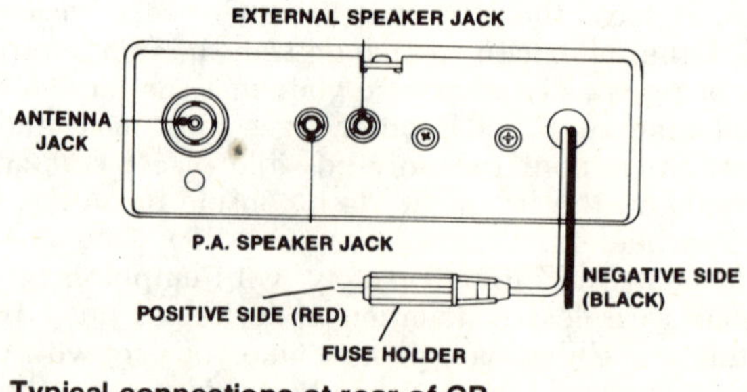

Typical connections at rear of CB

Check that the antenna cable can be easily connected or disconnected, and that the radio does not interfere with any heater or dash-mounted controls. Mark the position of the bracket on the sides or the forward edge.

If you have decided to use a slide mount for easy removal, you may or may not have to mount the normal bracket on the slide mount. It depends on what kind of set you have and what type of slide mount you have. In any case, follow the manufacturer's instructions for installing the slide mount. It is not really different from installing a normal mounting bracket, except that one piece attaches to the vehicle and one to the radio. Electrical contacts are provided so that when the slide mount is engaged, electrical contact is made.

• Take the bracket and set down, and remove the bracket. You're ready to mark and drill the bracket mounting holes. Put the bracket back in place and align it using the marks you just made. Mark the position of the center of the holes with a pencil dot. If you're afraid of scratching your custom paint job with the drill, lay down some small pieces of masking tape prior to marking the holes. Using a center punch and hammer, centerpunch a small hole where the pencil mark is. This will prevent the drill from scratching surrounding metal as you drill the hole. Use a drill stop on your drill bit to avoid drilling through the mounting area when you don't know what's behind it. For most installations, use a drill which is the same diameter as the root diameter of the screw.

• Using the screws or the bolts and nuts provided, securely fasten the mounting bracket in place. If you don't like the screws they gave you, get some you do like.

• Connect the microphone to the set if necessary, and hold the microphone at various places until you have found the best mounting spot. The mike hanger serves two purposes; (1) it keeps the installation neat and the mike out of the way when not in use; and, (2) if the microphone is allowed to hang from the set, it will stretch the cord and connections. Generally, you'll want to mount the mike in a convenient position where, eventually, you won't have to look to hang it up; you'll do it by feel. Likewise, you don't want it in a space where the cord is in the driver's way. You can screw the mike hanger to the dashboard using the same procedure for installing the bracket, or remove one of the screws from the radio housing and attach the hanger to the side of the set. If the idea of drilling more holes in your dash is repugnant, you can use a magnetic mike hanger.

• The next step is to determine battery polarity. You should have done this before you bought the set, but if you didn't, you're probably lucky (or prudent) enough to have bought a negative ground CB set. There are a few sets available which will work with negative or positive ground depending on how they're hooked up, but the vast majority are for 12 volt negative ground systems. If you are working with a 6 volt system, power inverters are available to convert 6 volts to 12 volts.

All modern cars use a 12 volt negative ground electrical system, although some heavy trucks are positive ground, and some older vehicles are 6 volt, positive ground. The battery polarity can be easily identified by seeing which battery terminal is connected to the chassis for ground. This is the ground side and the other side is the "hot" side or power source.

CAUTION: *Never, ever, hook a negative ground set to a positive ground or vice versa. Be sure to check polarity before hooking up a CB.*

• For most negative ground installations there are three popular sources of power, to which the fused lead on the CB set can be connected.

The best source is the positive, or the "hot," side of the battery. This is the best and most stable source of voltage, will lead to the least noise interference, and will provide power whether or not the ignition is "ON." A second source of power, and probably most popular, is the fuse block, usually located under the dashboard. Tapping the fuse block for power will provide a relatively stable voltage source and will enable your set to operate independently of the ignition switch, depending on which accessory terminal of the fuse block you tap. If this method is used, you will

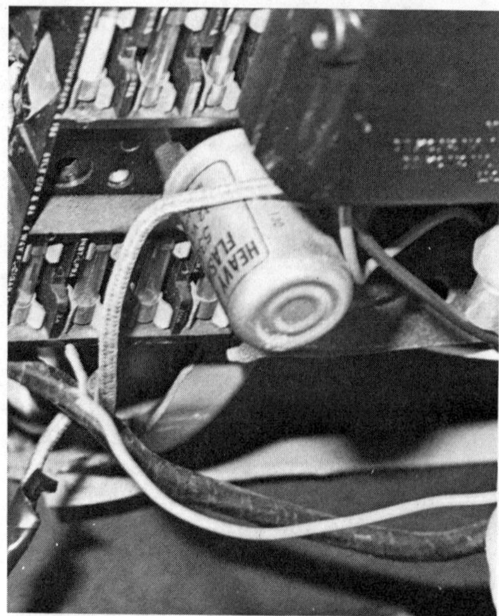

The fuse box under the dash is usually the most convenient power source

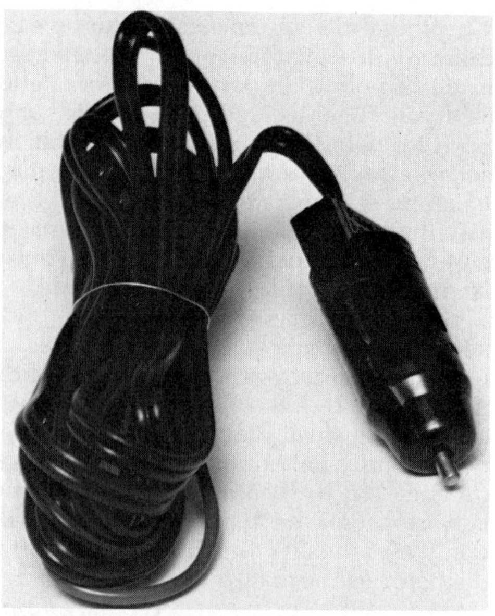

A plug for the cigarette lighter can also be used to power the radio

need to solder a female spade connector onto the end of the transceiver "hot" lead. A third, and least popular, way of getting power to the set is to use the accessory lead or terminal on the ignition switch, which will enable operation of the set only when the ignition switch is in the "ON" or "ACC" position. This method is rarely used since the advent of the steering column-mounted ignition switch.

Whichever method you select, be sure that you have the right polarity and be sure that the fuse clip (usually supplied with the set), is installed between the transceiver and the power source in the "hot" lead. The transceiver "hot" lead is generally fused with a 1.5 amp fuse, available at automotive or electronics stores.

Cigarette lighters adaptor power cords work fine, too, but simply tapping other "hot" wires is not a recommended power source for best performance, as they rarely provide a stable voltage source and can be the source of interference.

Once you've decided on a power source, you will have to install a suitable terminal on the end of the "hot" wire. For fuse box operation, install a female spade lug.

• It is important when installing terminal hardware on wire ends that you get a solid connection, or noise can enter the radio at this point. Cut the wire to length and leave a little slack. It's easiest to use a pair of wire strippers to strip about ½ in. of insulation off the end. Use the groove in the strippers corresponding to the gauge wire you're using. Twist the loose wire strands together tightly and insert them into the lug so that the insulation butts against the barrel of the lug. Crimp the lug around the wire securely, using either the crimpers on the end of the pair of wire strippers or an ordinary pair of pliers. If you use pliers, try to get one side of the lug barrel to go under the other, making them overlap. When this is tightly crimped, finish the job by soldering the connection, after trimming the wire end which protrudes from the lug barrel.

If you're using a slide mount, the same procedures apply for wiring the stationary part of the slide mount as for wiring a CB. The only difference is that you'll have to follow the manufacturer's instructions for wiring the CB to the movable part of the slide mount. Strip a little bit of insulation away from the wire and solder it to the contacts. Make sure that both parts of the mount are using the upper and lower sides of the same contacts, or you'll have no electrical contact.

• The "hot" lead is almost ready to be connected. Before going any further, cut the "hot" lead and install the fuse holder with fuse. After twisting the wire together in a "pigtail" connection, drop some solder on the pigtail and wrap it neatly with electrical tape.

• Decide where you are going to ground the transceiver. This can be almost anywhere—a screw or bolt which is nearby and electrically connected to the frame. If you can't find a screw nearby, drill a hole and use a sheet metal screw, in an out-of-the-way place (for neatness). Crimp and solder a ring or open-type lug onto the ground lead after cutting it to length. Use the same procedure as with the "hot" lead.

If your CB is not equipped with a plug on the rear of the set to disconnect the power and ground leads, you can do this easily. Most automotive stores sell 2-prong trailer connectors which only go together one way. They are inexpensive and solve the problem of disconnecting a ground lead from a bolt every time you want to remove your set from its mount. The 2-prong connector can be spliced into the power and ground leads easily, making sure that the circuits maintain their continuity. The connectors are generally color-coded to make this simple. Pigtail the wires together, apply a drop of solder, and securely tape the connection for a quick and easy disconnect.

• Turn the set "OFF" and route the leads. If it is necessary to route either of the leads through any sheet metal, drill an oversize hole and use a rubber grommet to prevent chafing. Stuff the leads out of the way and secure them with plastic ties salvaged from the kitchen. Connect the "hot" lead and the ground lead. When connecting the ground lead, scrape away a little paint to expose bare metal and use a toothed washer to get a solid ground. Tighten the grounding screw securely.

WARNING: *Do not, under any circumstances, operate the transceiver without connecting the antenna. You could blow out the output transistor.*

The installation of the set is complete; all that remains is to install the antenna.

Installing Mobile Antennas

Before actually going out to get an antenna, look over your car, or truck and decide the best place for your antenna, for this will go a long way to determining what kind of antenna you get. If you have a car or pick-up truck, you can use just about any kind of antenna available—mirror mount co-phase, cowl mount, bumper mount, rooftop, or trunk lid mount. A base-loaded trunk lid mount is probably most popular with passenger cars because it requires no hole drilling in the body. In popularity, these are followed closely by 102 inch whips on bumper mounts and center loaded antennas on rain gutter mounts. More often than not, a van will have a base-loaded antenna installed on the roof to take advantage of the large metal surface area, affording a good ground plane. Pick-up trucks and tractor-trailer operators seem to favor the single or dual mirror mount, usually center-loaded. The reason is that the large expanse of metal on trucks will do a good job of blocking the radiated signal pattern and reflecting a good bit of it back into the antenna. The center-loaded antennas get the radiation pattern up in the air, away from sheet metal.

The basic consideration in antenna installation is height (as far as practicable and legal) but don't overlook the position of the antenna or the type, since both will influence performance to a great extent.

In general it is true that if your whip is not located in the center of the vehicle, the signal will be stronger in a direction diagonally across the vehicle from the antenna. If your antenna is mounted on the right front fender, the signal will be strongest toward the left rear fender. Give the placement of the antenna some consideration before deciding.

The possibilities for mounts and antennas are endless. They run from the simple gutter mount, to the popular trunk lid mount to the co-phased dual mount, known as "twin truckers." Some require hole drilling, some do not. Some can be equipped with quick-disconnect arrangements, others cannot. Naturally, two antennas are better than one, but be warned: they must be at least 78 inches apart to be directional. Some mounts will give better performance than others. You have to be very careful when mounting antennas on pick-up truck bodies or on West Coast-style mirror brackets. Either of these items can easily become electrically isolated from the chassis ground, resulting in an open circuit.

Likewise, you have to be careful locating magnetic mount antennas. SWR can and will vary significantly from one location to another. It's a good idea to mark the location on the car or truck where magnetic mounts were tuned, so that they can be used in the same spot each time.

It's not an easy task to select an antenna; you'll probably agonize over it for hours, trying to balance off all the factors: maximum performance, location, type of antenna, cost, type of mount, length of cable, etc., etc. If at all possible, buy an antenna system, which is, one that comes packaged with the type of mount and antenna you want, the proper length of cable for the antenna, and the hardware. This will save having to buy the pieces separately. Also look for an antenna which has a resonator tip, tunable either by cutting it or by moving it up or down. This will save considerable time and effort.

• Once you have purchased the antenna system (or the antenna and the necessary hardware), lay out all the pieces and see how it goes together. If you bought your antenna system piecemeal, you're basically on your own, except for the recommendations made here which are common to all antennas.

• If you have a co-phased (dual) system, the place to start is at the transceiver by screwing the PL-259 connector into the set. All other installations should begin at the mount.

Do not shorten the coaxial cable supplied with dual antennas. Co-phase cable is RG-59/21 of 72 ohms impedance (net 50 ohm) and single whips use RG-58/21 of 50 ohm impedance. In all other installations, a general rule of thumb is to use the shortest cable possible, although it is not a wise idea to cut the length of the cable supplied with your antenna. It is usually around 18 feet long to accommodate trunk lid mounts, and should be used as it is supplied.

• Install the antenna mount on the vehicle. If you are using a base-loaded antenna with a "no-hole" mount, it is relatively simple, as are bumper mounts. A ball mount or cowl mount will take a little more time. If it is necessary to drill a hole for the mount, drill a small pilot hole first and gradually enlarge the hole with several bits. From here the hole can be reamed to size (after applying a circle of masking tape around the hole to prevent paint chipping), or a metal hole saw can be used. Either way, file the edges of the hole when you're done to remove jagged edges.

• Connect the antenna cable to the antenna at the mount. Depending on the type of mount you're using, there are several ways of doing this. Most base-loaded antennas use a screw-on type mount. The outside insulation is stripped off to about 1 inch back, being careful to leave the coaxial shielding intact. Push the coaxial shield back and carefully remove the foam insulation from the center conductor. Slip the bare center conductor up through the hole in the mount and bend it over in the channel provided. Ground the coaxial shield as specified.

Ball mounts, mirror mounts, bumper mounts and marine deck mounts, usually require that lugs be soldered onto the ends of the cable. Carefully cut away the outer insulation for about 2 inches, leaving the coaxial shield intact. Unbraid the coaxial shield and twist it together. Use the same procedure for attaching a lug of sufficient size, as was used to solder a lug onto the transceiver leads (also in this chapter). Cut away about ½ inch of the foam insulation from the center conductor and attach another lug to it in the same manner as before.

Connect the antenna and ground leads as suggested by the manufacturer. Clamp

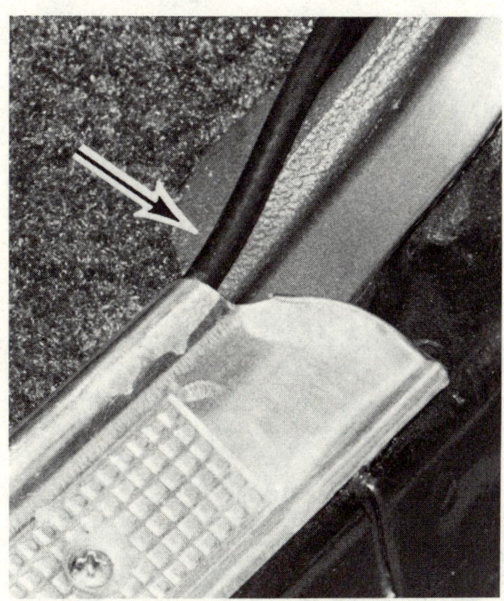

Under the door sill plate is a good place to route CB antenna cables

the wires in place to avoid chafing. Be sure to use all the insulation pieces supplied, and in the proper order of assembly.

• You are ready to route the cable. On trunk lid mounts the cable can be routed through the trunk (leaving enough slack to open the trunk), under the rear seat and along the driveshaft tunnel, coming up under the transceiver. It can also be routed along either side under the door sill threshold plate. Co-phrased harnesses should be routed under the dash and through the body, using a grommet. Sometimes it is easier to route it through each door, since the mirrors are usually on the door. Be sure to leave enough slack in the cable to allow doors to open. For mirror mounts, run the cable along the mirror brackets and secure them with toothed plastic bundling ties. Connect them to the antenna mounts as previously described.

Cowl mounts usually require that the cable run through the firewall at some point. Try to route it away from the fuse box, electrical accessories, etc. Drill an oversize hole and use a grommet to prevent chafing.

Excess cable should be routed so that it is not in a tight loop. It should be in free, loose coils to prevent picking up interference.

• Install the antenna on the mount. At this point you can use any springs you might want, which should be installed now. Fiberglass antennas usually require a spring of some sort to prevent cracking when they hit low tree limbs, etc. Slip a piece of surgical tubing or vacuum hose over a long whip, where it could possibly chafe the body.

A quick disconnect is a good idea at this point, too. It will allow you to push down and turn the antenna to pick it off the mount any time you desire. Base-loaded antennas don't need this as they simply unscrew from the mount.

When you've finished the installation, check it against the following:

1. Don't put any unnecessary strain on the coaxial cable.
2. Avoid kinks and sharp bends.
3. Do not coil excess cable tightly; better to let it lie loose or under the floormats.
4. Keep the cable away from other wiring, especially ignition wiring.
5. Don't feed cable through hood hinges or other places where it could be damaged.

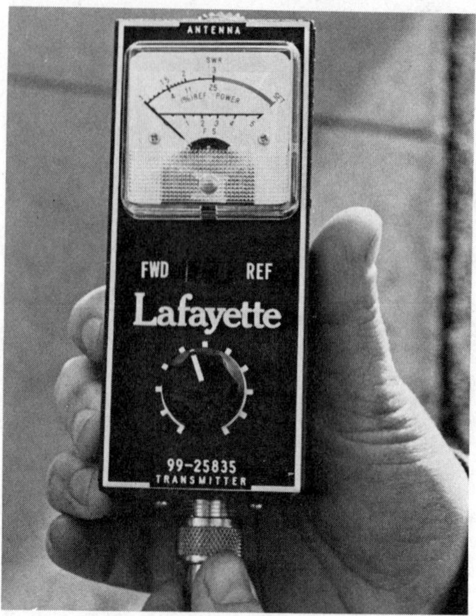

An SWR meter is necessary to properly tune an antenna

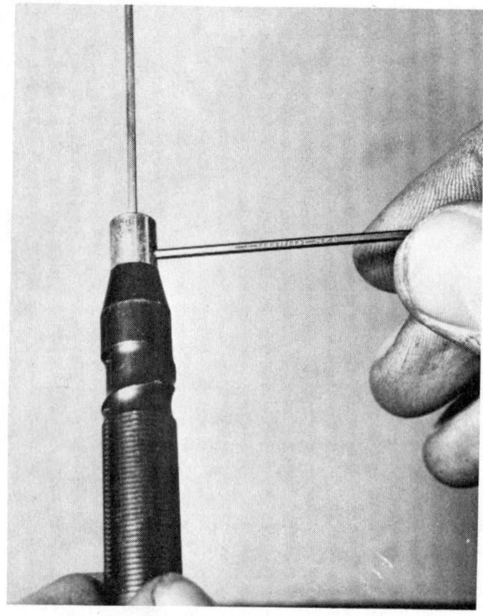

Center loaded antennae are tuned by moving the whip portion up or down. The whip is locked in place with a set screw

Tuning the Antenna

Now that everything is installed and the vehicle is back together, it only remains to tune the antenna. It must be tuned to obtain the lowest possible VSWR (variable standing wave ratio), which is a measure of how much radiated signal power is reflected back into the antenna. Most antennas are factory tuned for 1.5:1 or better, but VSWR of 1.1:1 is considered ideal, but seldom attained, and VSWR of 3:1 or more damage the transmitter.

Antennas are tuned in several ways:

A. Base-Loaded: These are usually equipped with an allen head set screw which is loosened to move the antenna shaft up or down. It may even require a little filing to shorten it.

B. Center-Loaded: These types usually have a resonator tip made of wire held in place by a set screw. They are also tuned by moving the resonator tip up or down or even shortening it slightly.

C. Continuous-Loaded: Continuous-load antennas are tuned either by loosening a thumbscrew and sliding a resonator tip up or down, or by removing the little cap from the antenna and filing a slight amount off the top.

D. Some antennas are tuned by sliding a small ball up or down the resonator.

Check the instructions before attempting to tune your antenna. You will need to buy an SWR meter, and maybe a 2 foot long patch cord equipped with a PL-259 on each end, or install a CB match box, to match antenna and transmitter.

Troubleshooting

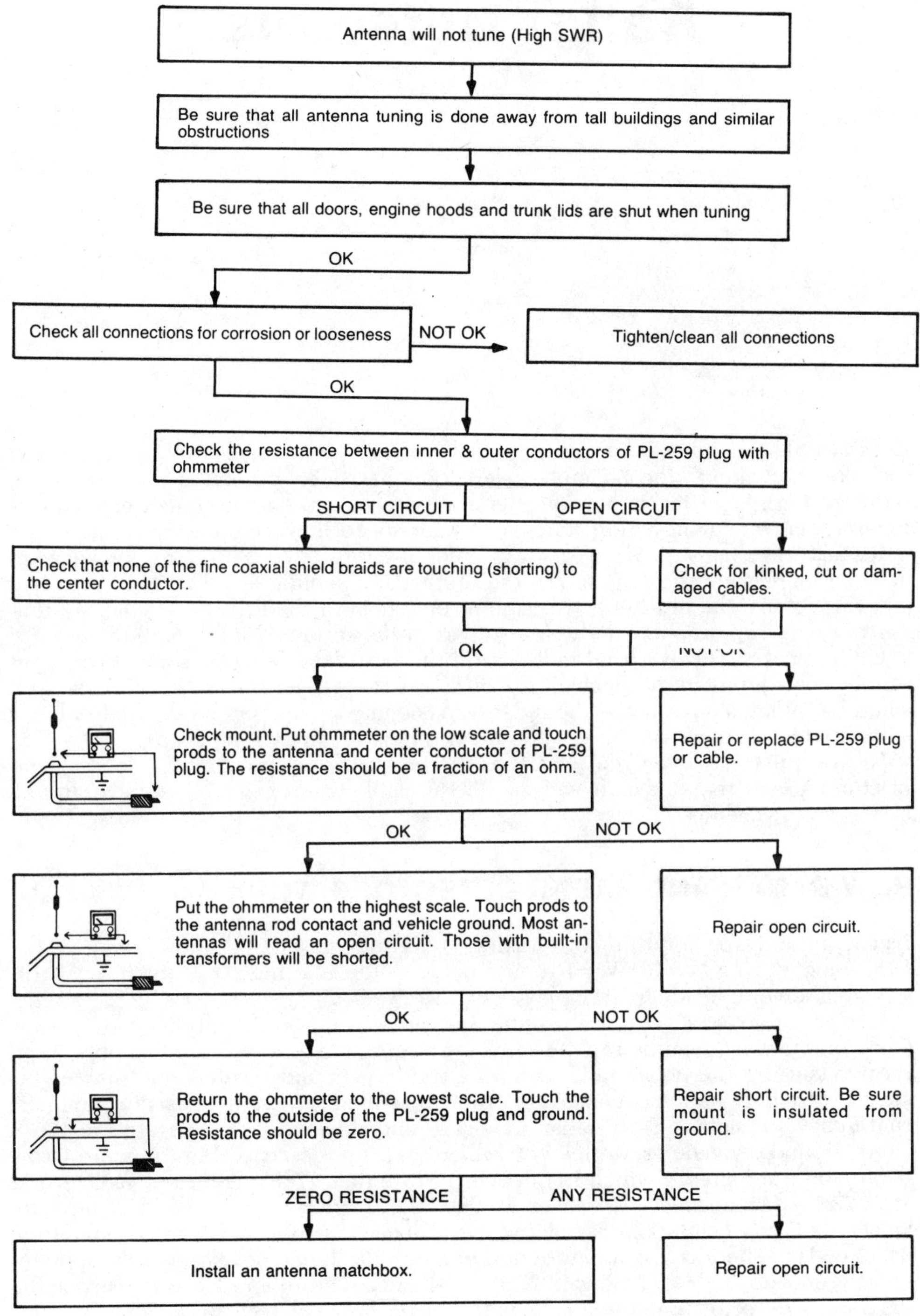

4
Radar Detectors

Let's face it. Regardless of superior visibility, light traffic, or any other excuse you can offer "Smokey," the 55 mph speed limit has been mandated and states are required to enforce it. In fact, the Federal government has thretened to withhold Federal highway money from states with poor speed limit compliance records.

Radar is the states' prime weapon in enforcing the speed limit, and, as radar has become more sophisticated, so are the methods of avoiding it. The radar detector and the CB are the most effective countermeasures in the driver's arsenal. A scanner to eavesdrop on police radio is also part of the serious driver's equipment.

CBers say the citizens band radio is still the best defense against speed traps but serious travellers with a penchant for driving fast, rely on the radar detector. You could be rolling along, just as the radar trap is being set up, and be the first unlucky victim, which is one place where the radar detector can earn its keep.

Newer units may even replace CB as the motorist's early warning defense; manufacturers claim that detectors will soon be available which can pick up radar around curves and over hills.

HOW RADAR AND RADAR DETECTORS WORK

Radar, an acronym for RAdio Detecting and Ranging, was first developed by the U.S. Navy during World War I to accurately determine the range for heavy artillery aboard ship. Traffic radar appeared in 1945.

Just as sound waves bounce around and produce an echo, ultrahigh frequency (UHF) radio waves can be sent out on a set frequency, reflected from an object and received again. The police radar is both a transmitter and receiver and must operate on extremely high frequencies in order to send and receive signals in an almost continuous sequence. Early radar was large and unwieldy and operated in the S band, around 6 gigahertz, or nearly 6 billion cycles per second. Most modern traffic radar works at incredibly high frequencies. More than 95% of all traffic radar works at 10.525 GHz (gigahertz) or over 10,000,000,000 cycles per second. These are known as the X-band. The remaining 5% (K-band) are the newest and operate at 24.150 GHz. There is also a new generation of radar being developed that operates slightly outside the FCC allowed X and K-bands. The difference won't upset the FCC but a detector tuned to a narrow frequency won't detect the radar.

However, all-band scanning detectors are already in the works. The scanning detector scans the entire police microwave frequency area from 9–25 gigahertz

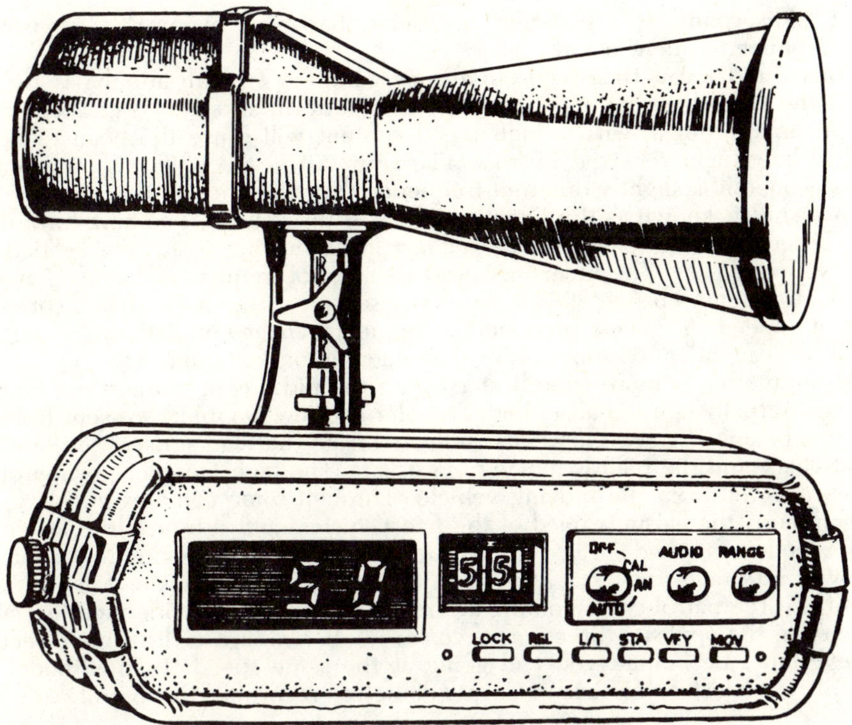

X-Band radar. Can be operated stationary or moving at long range

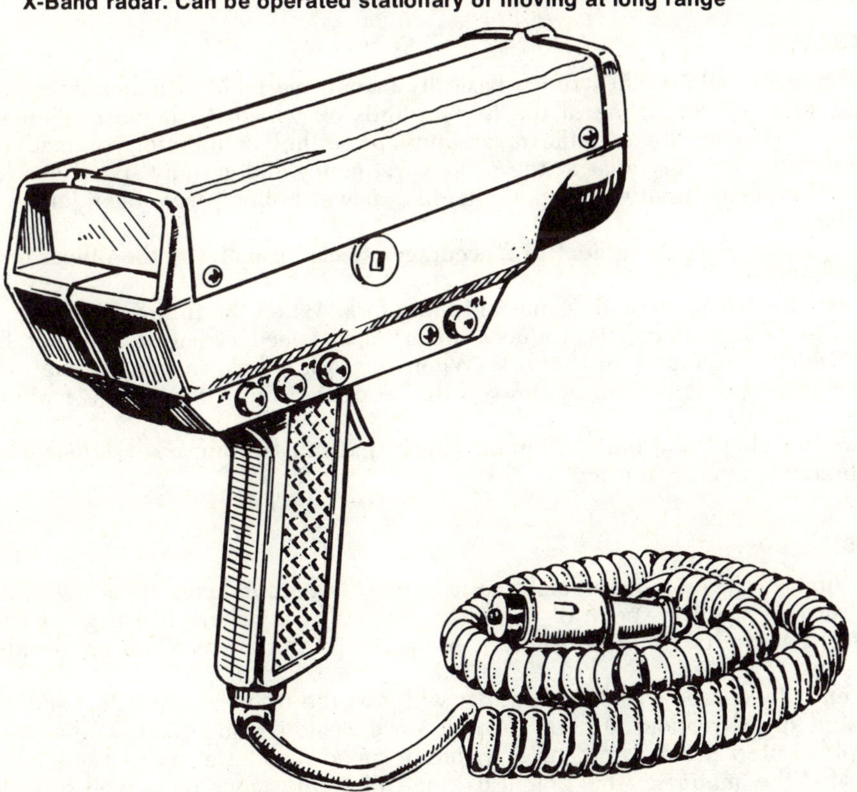

K-Band radar. Hand-held, trigger operated or pulsed, can be operated stationary or moving. Long range, difficult to detect

every 2 milliseconds. It will detect any radar, barring a major FCC revision of allowable police frequencies.

Stationary radar can track you coming or going. A special antenna is used to transmit the radio beam in a narrowly focused pattern, spreading out about 6 degrees. A moving object with a high metal content will cause the bean to be reflected (echoed) and received by the radar unit. Since the object is moving, the signal is echoed at a slightly different frequency than when it was transmitted. This frequency shift is known as the Doppler effect. If the vehicle is coming toward the radar, the echoed frequency will be higher; if it's moving away, the echoed frequency will be lower. The radar measures the rate of frequency change (1 mph is equal to a frequency change of 31.4 cycles per second on the X-band) and computes the target's speed. A vehicle producing a frequency change of 2041 cycles per second will be "caught" at 65 mph, more than enough for a citation.

The computation is more complicated when the radar is in motion in a cruising patrol car. Actually two signals (a high Doppler and low Doppler) are sent from the same radio beam. The low Doppler is reflected from the road surface; to the radar, it is stationary and the road is moving towards it. The high Doppler portion of the beam is reflected from the moving vehicle. Through some complex circuitry, the radar computes the closing speed of the two vehicles, and subtracts the lower frequency speed of the road surface (which the radar believes is moving toward it, but at a slower rate) and arrives at the speed of the oncoming vehicle. Moving radar only works if the patrol car is coming at the target; it will not work once the target has passed in the opposite direction. If you are both heading in the same direction, "Smokey" must be behind you and going at the same speed. In this mode, the radar unit is an extremely accurate speedometer, recording the patrol car's own speed.

Accuracy

Radar is in use in all 50 states and is basically incontrovertable evidence in cases of speeding. Malfunction is one of the few grounds on which it can be challenged. Actually, it's possible for a traffic radar operator, either deliberately or inadvertently to whistle into the radar at the proper frequency and get any speed desired. Relatively simple automotive components, like blower motors, have been known to "fool" radar.

Modern traffic radar is subject to 2 accuracy checks, usually by the officer operating the radar unit.

The first check is made with a special tuning fork. When the tuning fork is struck on a non-metallic surface, it produces an artificial speed signal at a preset frequency, which is stamped on the fork. When the fork is held in front of the radar antenna, the proper speed must show on the readout. If not, the radar is malfunctioning.

The second check is a built-in circuit check that must produce a readout when the calibration button is pushed.

Range

Radar operates only on a line-of-sight basis; it can't see around corners or over hills. But, it can measure the speed of a vehicle practically anywhere it can get a clear line of sight at the target, for instance, just as the target crests a hill or rounds a curve.

It is generally agreed that X-band radar will give the trooper audio alert at about 1 mile, and speed readout at about ¾ mile on a clear, straight road. The newest, most sophisticated K-band units are capable of speed readout at up to a mile. Fortunately for the motorist, the practical range of traffic radar on a well-travelled interstate is about ¼ mile, and, most arrests are clocked within ⅛ mile.

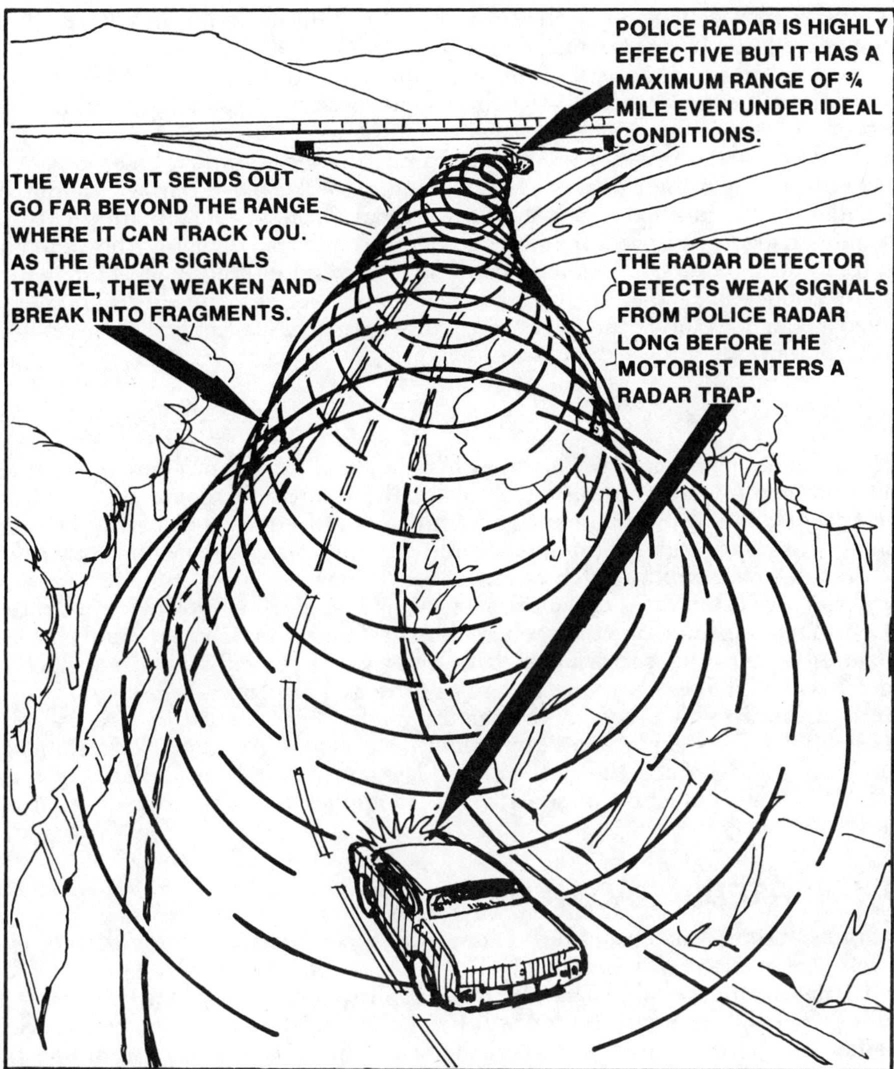

How the radar detector works

Most radar in use today (except for ultrasophisticated models that compute speed instantaneously) require a full second to lock in the target and register speed. But, once it locks onto a target, speed readout is instant. They also have a circuit that rejects inputs where deceleration of the target is more than about three miles per second. It's not hard to figure that if your radar detector goes off, and you can decelerate from 65 to 55 in slightly over three seconds, the radar will reject your speed signal, giving you a chance to get down to the legal limit.

Size is another variable. The smaller the target, the closer it has to be to radar to get a reading. A speeding truck at ¼ mile may give a stronger signal than a closer, slower moving car. Since radar will lock onto the strongest signal, the car could easily pay for the truck's sins. Typically, a large truck will reflect a stationary radar signal at 1200 yards, a full-size car at 800 yards and a small car at 400 yards.

How far away can a detector identify the presence of radar? Depending on conditions, as far as three miles away. Most traffic radar broadcasts its signal at about $^1/_{10}$ watt; the average radar detector can identify a signal with a strength of $^1/_{1,000,000}$

watt. Since it needs to see only the presence of a diffused beam, it will usually give advance warning. Its effectiveness however, is dependent on its sensitivity. Most detectors on an interstate will identify the presence of radar before the radar can get an accurate speed readout. Usually, 5–20 seconds of advance warning will be provided.

Radio waves are reflected from bridge abutments, lines of cars, chain link fences, guard rails, or even the roadway. This "bounce" will be picked up by the detector, and under most conditions, give ample warning. On hills, the situation is roughly the same. Radar waves will bounce off the road surface, enabling the detector to pick them up sooner. On open curves, however, with nothing around for the radar signal to bounce off, radar has the advantage. Since neither can see around corners, the radar can lock onto the car before the driver has a chance to react to the detector's warning.

Falsing

Many radar detectors are so sensitive that they will "false" or sense the presence of another microwave transmitter; actually, the detector is doing its job. Garage door openers, medical equipment and traffic control equipment are authorized to operate near police radar frequencies and will often set off a sensitive radar detector. Most detectors will reject true out-of-band signals.

Sophisticated "superhet" detectors also have a miniature microwave transmitter to maintain their sensitive operating characteristics; unfortunately, the transmitter will also set-off a nearby detector. The distance at which an individual manufacturer's detector will set off another varies from as little as 17″ to over 100 feet.

An odd quirk of all detectors is that the angle of the windshield can affect the units operation. A steeply raked windshield can have a polarizing effect on police radar signals and reduce the detector's efficiency, but only by 1/100ths of a mile. Fortunately, this reduction in sensitivity also applies to "false" signals from other sources.

DO YOU NEED A RADAR DETECTOR?

Most of us, at one time or another, exceed the speed limit, either by design, casual indifference or righteous indignation. Serious speeders figure the most efficient speed (considering penalties) is about 80 mph. Forget the old wives' tales that covering your hubcaps with tin foil will jam police radar. If you regularly cruise the interstates and are inclined to exceed the speed limit, the savings from one ticket for more than 65 mph, coupled with the inevitable court costs, points on your license, inconvenience of a court appearance and resultant high insurance rates, will more than offset the cost of a decent radar detector.

It's estimated that between 70% and 85% of all interstate speeding arrests are made with radar. It's easy to operate, offers practically unbeatable evidence in court, and is versatile. Since inveterate and casual speeders alike are part of the game of psychological warfare, with your driver's license as the prize, you need as many odds as possible in your favor. The CB is still the favorite weapon, but while it provides an overkill of warning for stationary radar traps, it cannot provide much warning for the K-band portable units until an unwary offender is pulled over.

A radar detector offers several advantages:

- No complicated installation,
- No antenna,
- Not subject to weather conditions, interference or inane chatter,
- Works day or night (when a CB is less effective).

However, don't depend totally on the radar detector to protect your wallet. The newest police jewel is a hand-held, portable unit equipped with a hold-button to

The traditional radar detector dashboard mounted

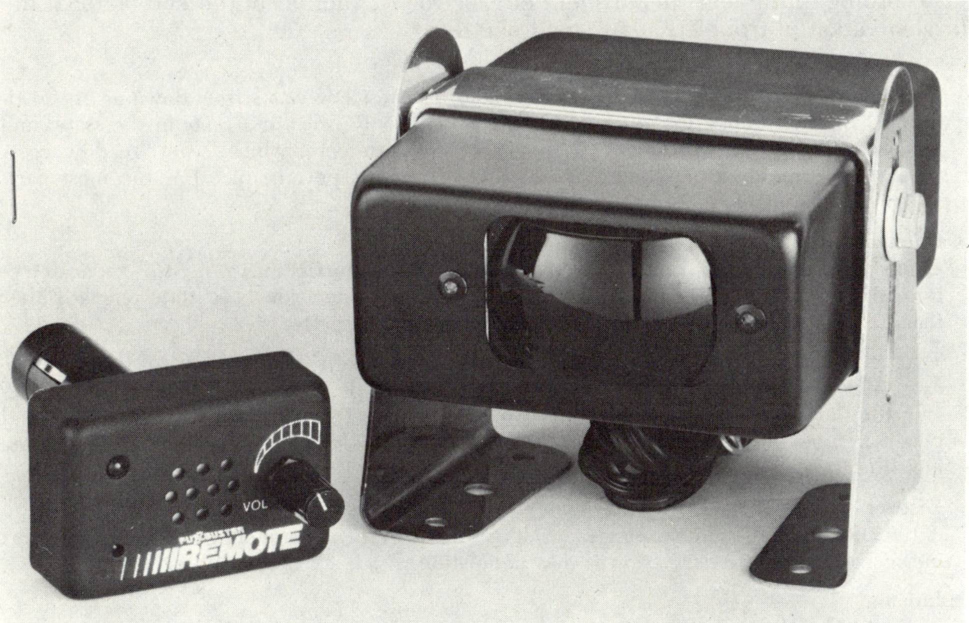

Remote, radar detector uses an alarm panel that plugs into the cigarette lighter

cut off the radar signal until the unit is activated. The trooper waits until he has reason to believe that a vehicle is speeding, aims the gun and releases the trigger. The speed is computed, and displayed in less than 1/100th second. Only the CB will warn you of this fellow when he pulls someone over, unless your detector picks up the signal when the radar is "shot."

In 1979 a Florida judge ruled that radar clockings could not be used as evidence in some 80 cases pending under his jurisdiction. Even though other judges were not bound by his ruling, the judge questioned the reliability of the radar equipment.

Erroneous readings in the radar were apparently caused by interference from billboards, overpasses, car heaters near the radar unit, air conditioning fans in the vehicle, and CB and police radios.

Are Detectors Legal?

Radar detectors are legal in most states, or most states are indifferent to their use since more compliance with 55 mph is the net result. Only 2 states—Michigan and Virginia—had outright laws prohibiting their use. Connecticut prohibited their use by order of the State Police, and New Jersey had an ordinance prohibiting windshield obstruction, a favorite mounting place for detectors. Possession of a detector in Denver or Washington, D.C. got you a fine, and Virginia authorities confiscated a detector, whether it was in use or not.

Since 1975, radar detector manufacturers (in particular Electrolert, manufacturer of the Fuzzbuster®) have spent over $1,000,000.00 waging a successful campaign battling radar detector prohibitions. In 1982, the Michigan State Supreme Court overturned that state's 1929 "police radio" law that was extended to include possession and use of radar detectors, leaving Washington, D.C. with the only regulation in the country prohibiting possession of a radar detector. Similar laws in other states have been struck down or modified to include only the *use* of a radar detector.

According to the legal department of Electrolert, Inc., as of the end of 1982, the legal situation in troubled areas stood like this:

"Virginia:
The enforcement provision of the state's radar detector law was struck down as unconstitutional in 1978. Since that time, there have been only isolated arrests in the state, and no confiscations. The wording of the new law, says a detector which is not "readily accessible" to the motorist or which has no power source is permissible. For the most part, Virginia police have lost their interest in radar detectors.

Connecticut:
Connecticut has a 1962 "police directive" which says motorists may not "use" radar detectors. Because the enforcement measure is an arbitrary decision by a state official rather than a law, the directive has been difficult to attack in court.

Two recent superior court decisions, however, have taken the teeth out of the law. Because the directive specifies that the detector may not be *used*, the simple act of unplugging the device has been sufficient in two appellate decisions to reverse convictions, and police are now under orders not to issue a citation unless it is clear that the unit is plugged in at the time the motorist is pulled over.

District of Columbia:
A 1962 police regulation banning radar detectors was recently upheld by an appellate court in the District. Mere *possession* is now a violation.

Indiana:
In September 1979, Indiana police announced that they were interpreting a 1967 statute (Indiana 3544312) forbidding the use of portable police scanners to include radar detectors.

A favorable decision was recently handed down by the Indiana Court of Appeals (*Lawrence Wallman vs. State of Indiana*) in which it was decided that radar detectors do not apply to this statute."

Legal opinion holds that any or all prohibitions regarding radar detectors may be unconstitutional and that laws regulating their use are contrary to Federal Communications Commission regulations on the theory that a radar detector is simply a radio receiver that sounds a warning when it receives a microwave in the frequency range. The Communications Act of 1934, As Amended, specifically gives the FCC—a Federal agency whose regulations supersede states' rights—the right to regulate interstate radio transmission and reception. The FCC gives the right to "receive telecommunications of any type on any frequency" to all the people of the United States. The only thing illegal is for you to "divulge or publish the existence" of the information which you receive without the permission of the sender (i.e., get on your CB and say that your radar detector uncovered a radar trap at such-and-such a milepost).

DO-IT-YOURSELF INSTALLATION

Installation of a radar detector is the simplest of any automotive electronic accessory. Almost any detector can be permanently wired into the vehicles electrical system, but most come equipped with a cigarette lighter plug that plugs into the cigarette lighter socket in the dash or in the ash tray. Some come equipped with 2 power cords—one for the cigarette lighter and one with clips for connecting directly to the battery.

Depending on the size of your detector it can be mounted anywhere that it has a clear, unobstructed view of the road and does not interfere with the primary task of operating the vehicle.

Some units came in plastic carrying cases, and some come with other ingenious mounting hardware including suction cups and Velcro quick release mounts.

For mounting the detector inside the vehicle, the universal (fits-all) or the made-

Multiple cigarette lighter receptacles can be used to power more than one accessory

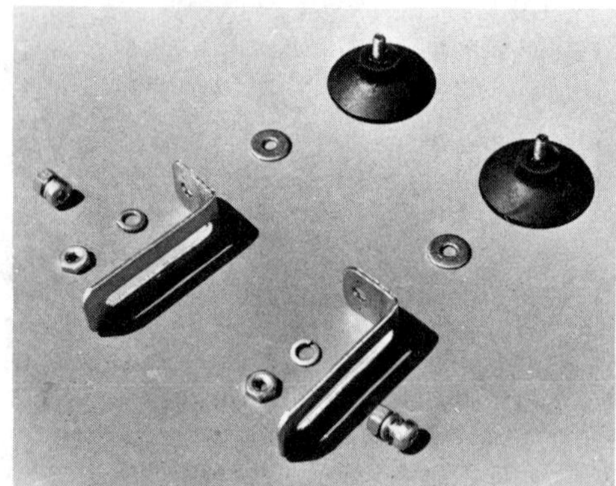
Assemble the pieces shown

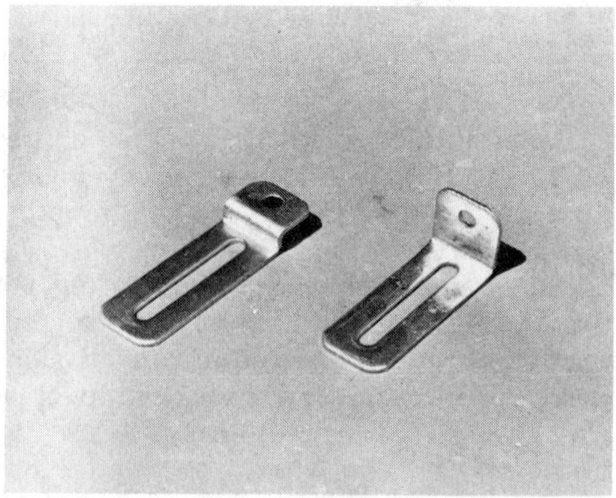
Bend the car stereo mounting brackets into an L-shape

to-fit-one-detector mounting brackets seem to do the job best, especially for those detectors which may be on the heavy side. These brackets are usually available from the manufacturer or from mail order catalogs or retail stores specializing in such things. Most of the brackets are sufficiently versatile to fit almost any dashboard/windshield combination and allow you to use the detector in virtually any car. The detector is secured to the bracket with double faced tape or Velcro spots.

The windshield detector bracket can be made even better for a dollar or two's worth of parts and a few minutes of time. The problem, you'll discover, is that the bracket attached only to the windshield tends to move after a awhile and aim the detector at the wrong place. To make the mounting bracket more sturdy and even more versatile, get the following materials:

- 2 universal mounting brackets of the type commonly sold with car stereos
- 2 rubber suction cups (with threaded ends)
- 2 nuts and lockwashers to fit the threaded ends of the suction cups
- 2 small machine screws with lockwashers and nuts or wingnuts to fit.

Bend the universal mounting brackets into an L-shape with the help of a vise and small hammer as shown. Attach the suction cups to the short leg of the L-bracket with the lockwashers and nuts. Connect these extra "feet" to the detector mounting bracket as required to provide a solid mounting position for the detector. Tilt the detector down a degree or two, and you will sometimes increase the range. The detector will pick up stray radar waves that bounce off the cars hood and road.

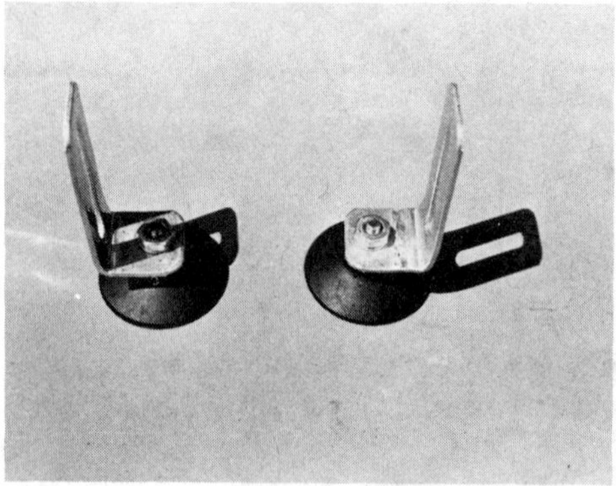
Attach suction cups to the short leg with a nut and lockwasher

A mounting bracket that will fit any vehicle's dashboard

Newer detector units can be disguised as a part of the car of can be mounted on the sun-visor

Run the wire in an out of the way place and plug it into the cigarette lighter. You're ready to go.

The first commandment of radar detector equipped travel states that "Thou shalt not advertise the presence of thy detector". In other words, some minions of the law tend to associate the relative prominence of a detector with the size of one's wallet, and act accordingly. Some detectors can be clipped to the sunvisor, but the power cord becomes a problem. Inventive manufacturers have solved the problem by building remote versions of the detector. The antenna and sensing unit are built into a remotely (and nearly totally invisible) mounted unit. The warning system (buzzer, lights, LEDs, etc.) is plugged into the cigarette lighter on the dash. Nothing is visible to the rest of the world. Other manufacturers have solved the problem by building the detector into a fog light housing or into a rear view mirror housing (yes, a matching mirror is available for the other side). Due to the external location of the antenna, these units offer excellent rear detection as well. The same company also builds a detector into a sunvisor for a limited number of applications. The units are custom designed for each car, and senses radar both in front of and behind the vehicle. It is activated by swinging the visor down, and 2 lights alert the driver to radar signals and the fact that the unit is working.

Three are even companies willing to modify top-of-the-line detectors for remote installation, or provide a kit to the do-it-yourselfer. Kits contain all the parts necessary, but a knowledge of electrical soldering is helpful. Modifications like this have no connection with the original manufacturer of the detector and you'll have to bear full responsibility for the performance of the detector once it's modified.

BEATING THE SYSTEM

In spite of your best efforts, the state trooper with the latest pulse radar equipment nabbed you at 80 mph. All creative excuses have fallen on deaf ears and it's time to pay up. Most states make the decision for you; they simply escort you to the nearest pokey where you pay up or become a guest of the county for a few days. Other states will allow you to go about your business and pay up after you get

	Sends Records to Home State	National Driver License Compact	Nonresident Violators Compact
Alabama	•	•	
Alaska	•	•	
Arizona	•	•	2
Arkansas	•	•	
California	•		
Colorado	•	•	2
Connecticut			•
D.C.	•	•	•
Delaware	•	•	•
Florida	•	•	•
Georgia			•
Hawaii		•	
Idaho	•		2
Illinois	•	•	
Indiana	•	•	•
Iowa	•	•	•
Kansas	•	•	2
Kentucky	•		•
Louisiana	•	•	•
Maine	•	•	
Maryland	•		•
Massachusetts	1		
Michigan	•		
Minnesota	•		•
Mississippi	•	•	•
Missouri	•		•
Montana	•	•	
Nebraska	1	•	2
Nevada	•	•	
New Hampshire	•		
New Jersey	•	•	•
New Mexico	•	•	•
New York		•	•
North Carolina	•		•
North Dakota	•		•
Ohio			
Oklahoma	•	•	
Oregon	•	•	
Pennsylvania			•
Puerto Rico			
Rhode Island	•		
South Carolina	•	•	•
South Dakota	•		•
Tennessee	•	•	
Texas	•		
Utah	•	•	2
Vermont	•		
Virginia	•	•	•
Washington	•	•	
West Virginia	•	•	•
Wisconsin	•		
Wyoming	•		

•Member states
1 sends some records to home state
2 legislation pending
Sources: American Association of Motor Vehicle Administrators; Federal Highway Administration; National Highway Traffic Safety Administration

home and receive the appropriate paperwork. In these instances, the overwhelming urge is to trash the ticket and not venture into the state in question again.

Ignoring out-of-state tickets has become so widespread that states have banded together to recover fines from other states' residents. This is big business. In a typical 12 month period traffic fines will total 125,000,000 dollars nationwide. The Non-Resident Violators Compact includes 22 states and the District of Columbia who will suspend your home state driving license privileges if you fail to pay traffic fines from other members' states.

Many states send records of citations to your home state. If this happens, you may get a reduced penalty, you may have to pay up or nothing may happen. It all depends on the attitude of your home state toward your misbehavior, the manpower available to pursue the matter and the hardware available to the state officials.

A majority of states also belong to the National Drivers License Compact, which was formed to keep track of serious crimes involving motor vehicles. However, member states are campaigning to have all traffic violations entered into this national computer access record.

5
Auto Security Systems

According to the International Association of Auto Theft Investigators, stealing cars is a $4 billion business. Each year a total of 1.1 million vehicles are stolen in the U.S.—one vehicle every 32 seconds. That's an average of one out of every 143 motor vehicles registered nationally. Of all the vehicles stolen, 75% were automobiles, 13% were trucks or busses and 12% were "other" types. And, these statistics do not include vehicles whose contents were burglarized, but the vehicle was not stolen.

Obviously, car theft is a big business these days. Today's car thief knows the laws of supply and demand and specializes in supplying specific car models or accessories that match the demand.

While the popularity of stolen cars varies from city to city and region to region—and even with factors such as whether the car is parked at home or work—the Highway Loss Data Institute has pegged the following cars as those most likely to be stolen:

Chevrolet Caprice Classic
Chevrolet Corvette
Pontiac Bonneville
Ford Thunderbird
Lincoln Continental
Chevrolet Monte Carlo
Chevrolet Camaro
Volkswagen Scirocco
Pontiac Firebird

Those least likely to be stolen include:

Dodge Colt
Plymouth Champ
Plymouth Horizon
Dodge Omni
Ford Fiesta
Chevrolet Chevette
Mazda GLC
Honda Civic
Datsun 210
Toyota Tercel

Police department statistics indicate that in Los Angeles, for instance, Ford Mustangs must be included in the top ten favorites with thieves. In Chicago, thieves' tastes inexplicably run to Buick Regals and Oldsmobile Cutlasses. In New York City, where 300 cars a day are stolen, thieves will apparently take almost anything; and for some reason, their favorite day is Tuesday.

Nearly 40% of all these vehicles will be stripped for parts to supply professional "chop-shop" operations, which supply parts to a variety of auto rebuilding and salvage operations.

PROTECTING YOUR INVESTMENT

Protecting the investment in your vehicle and its contents requires a combination of safeguards and common sense.

Common Sense Protection

Following are a few tips to help prevent vehicle theft and vandalism. Many people wish they had followed these seemingly simple tips. Remember that even if your car is insured and can be replaced you will not be compensated for sales tax, depreciation or inconvenience. These will help to deter the casual thief, but sterner and more sophisticated measures are necessary for the professional thief.

- Close all the windows and lock all the doors when you leave the vehicle. Nearly 2 out of every 10 cars stolen had open windows or the key left in the ignition.
- Leave only the ignition key with a parking lot attendant, if you must leave the keys.
- Stow valuables, packages and other attractive theft items in the trunk or out of sight.
- Don't ever leave the engine running when you are away from the vehicle.
- Hide business cards under the seats, floormats, between windows and doors or behind the seat. They may help identify your car should it be stolen or altered by thieves.
- Keep the owners card and/or title in a safe place, other than in the car.
- Mark accessories (indelibly) with your drivers license number.
- Remember that no device can totally foil the thief that is going to tow your car away. Always try to park in such a way to make towing as difficult as possible.

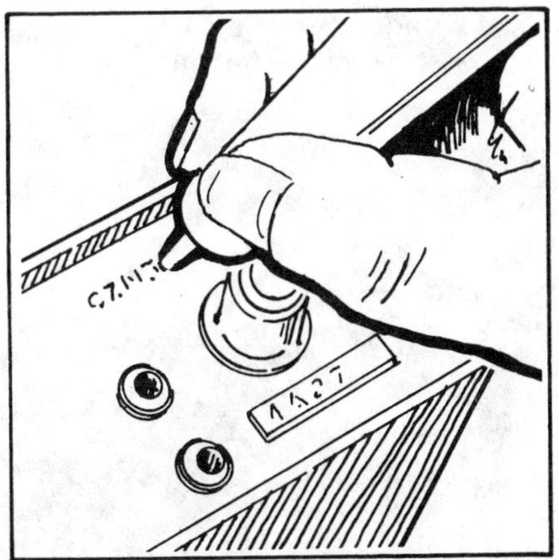

Some police departments will provide an etching tool free of charge to engrave your drivers license or similar easily traceable number on the chassis of your CB or tape deck

If possible, remove attractive theft items and put them in the trunk or out of sight when the car will be unattended

Parallel park between two other cars or objects or with the front end facing a wall or light post and with the wheels turned to fulllock. Consider the possibility of, towing every time you park your vehicle.

• Consider investing in one of the many anti-theft or security devices on the market.

• Always arm or engage the anti-theft devices when you leave the car unattended, even for a short period of time.

• Never tell anyone else how to disarm your security system.

Types of Security Devices

Selecting the right alarm system is the key to protecting your investment. There are literally hundreds of products, ranging from very inexpensive to extremely expensive. Look for protection. It takes an experienced thief less than one minute to enter a locked car, remove the ignition switch, start the car and drive it away, so features are only important in their ability to deliver comprehensive protection from theft or vandalism.

Basically, there are three different types of products available—anti-theft devices, car alarms and vehicle protection systems. Deciding on one type over another requires the answers to some basic questions.

• What are you trying to protect—the vehicle or its contents?

• What mode of operation do you prefer—passive or actively armed?

• What is your budget?

• Are children or pets frequently left in the car? If so, motion sensor systems are ruled out, because of false alarms.

• Do you require a paging system?

The answers to these questions will help you select the right security devices.

Anti-Theft Devices

Locking gas caps, hood locks, and wheel locks are cheap insurance. Locking gas caps are easy to install, and the only sure way to keep that expensive gas in your tank where it belongs and to keep other things from finding their way into your tank. They can be forced open, of course, but most thieves aren't about to take the time.

Hood locks are an excellent way to keep what's under the hood where it's supposed to be and keep thieves from gaining access to theft deterrent systems. In

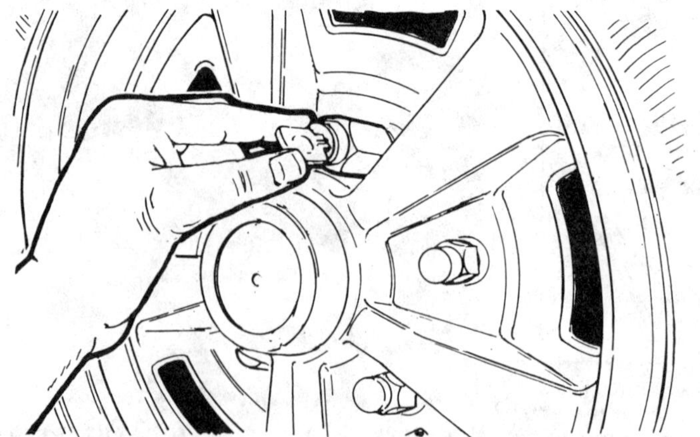

Wheel locks—either keyed or tapered locks designed for use with a unique, individually shaped wrench will protect valuable wheels

Lock the hood with a case hardened chain and lock or hood pins

fact, some vehicle protection systems incorporate a hood lock as an integral part of the system. There are two basic types of hood locks—one uses a strap or length of heavy chain or a dead bolt arrangement and limits the distance the hood can be opened until the lock is released. The other type is just like a trunk lock with a key, and requires that you cut a hole in the hood to install the locks (usually one on each side of the hood).

MOVEMENT INHIBITORS

The most common systems available inhibit the movement of the brake pedal and/or the steering wheel. Of these, the most prevalent (best known by its trade name—Krooklok®) is a locking, telescoping steel bar, with a hook at each end. In use, one hook is positioned around a steering wheel spoke and the other around the brake pedal arm. The steel shaft is then telescoped down and locked into position, preventing movement of the brake pedal and limiting movement of the steering wheel. A similar system utilizes a long steel bar which hooks and locks onto the steering wheel, and prevents it from turning beyond a certain point by wedging against interior components.

Both of these devices have the advantage of being easily visible from outside the car, thereby acting as a visual deterrent to the casual thief. Their main disadvantages are that they are somewhat awkward, they must be removed and installed each time that car is moved and they are relatively easily defeated by a professional.

Fuel Shut-Off Valves

One method of limiting the movement of a vehicle is to install a fuel shut-off valve in an inconspicuous place in the fuel line. Once the valve is installed, simply turn it to the off position whenever you leave the car. The major disadvantage is that

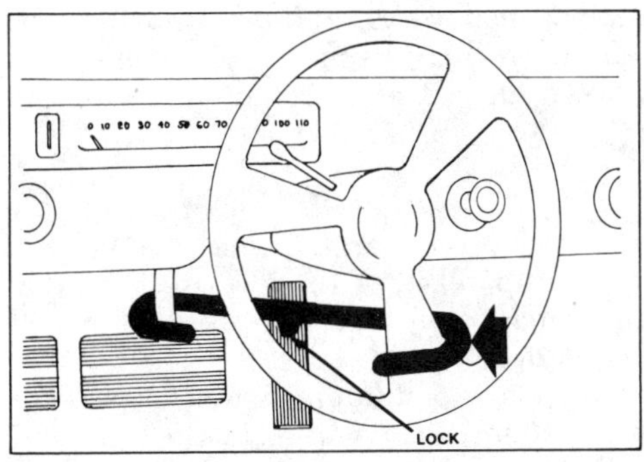

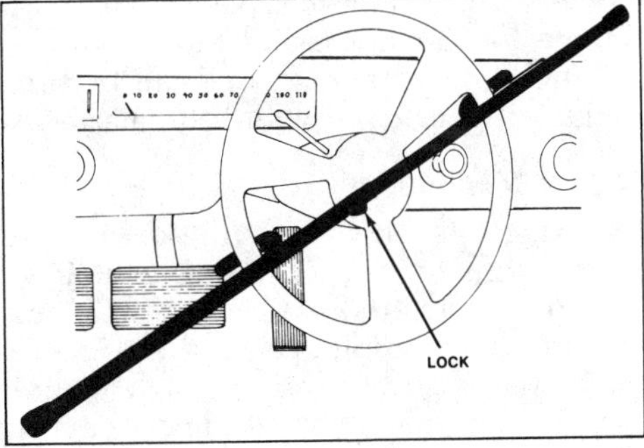

Two types of steering wheel locks installed

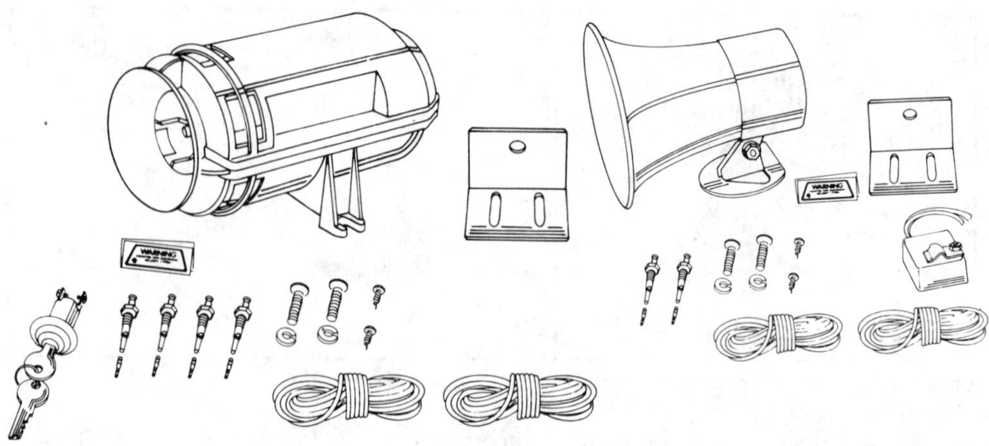

A simple alarm system (left) and a slightly more sophisticated version (right) that also triggers if someone tries to start the ignition if the system is armed

the engine will run until the fuel supply in the float bowl runs out, which means the car can be moved a short distance.

Electrical Cut-Outs

One of the simplest anti-theft devices is an ignition ground switch. A device such as this will prevent the engine from being started when it is activated. A single pole, single throw switch is wired between the distributor primary lead and ground and mounted inconspicuously, preferably in the interior. When the switch is open, the ignition will function normally. When the switch is closed, the engine's ignition-system is grounded and the car will not run.

An alternate method utilizes a switch located in the distributor primary wire. If the car is wired like this, the ignition system will only function when the switch is closed, thereby completing the circuit.

The disadvantage of both these systems is the location of the switch. A professional can easily find or bypass the switch and the system is useless. If the switch is located under the hood, the hood will have to be locked in some manner. Many modern cars have hoods which can only be opened from the car's interior, but a good many of these inside hood latches can be easily broken.

ALARMS

Alarm systems are relatively simple devices that issue a warning when someone tries to get into or (in some cases) move your vehicle. They do not offer anti-theft features.

There are two basic types of burglar alarm systems for automobiles—those which actuate the car horn, and those which set off an auxiliary siren or bell. Regardless of which type it is, each one can be broken down into its separate components: the trigger, trigger control and the alarm itself.

Trigger Mechanisms

The trigger mechanism is the device used to activate the alarm. In most cases, the trigger consists of a switch or switches, and a drop relay. A drop relay is a relay that, once activated, will not recycle until reset manually; therefore, the alarm will not stop functioning even if the trigger switch is deactivated.

Motion sensitive switches such as mercury switches, pendulum switches, etc. are used to detect tampering. The switch may be mounted anywhere in the car, and its sensitivity adjusted to the desired level. The disadvantage of a motion-sensitive

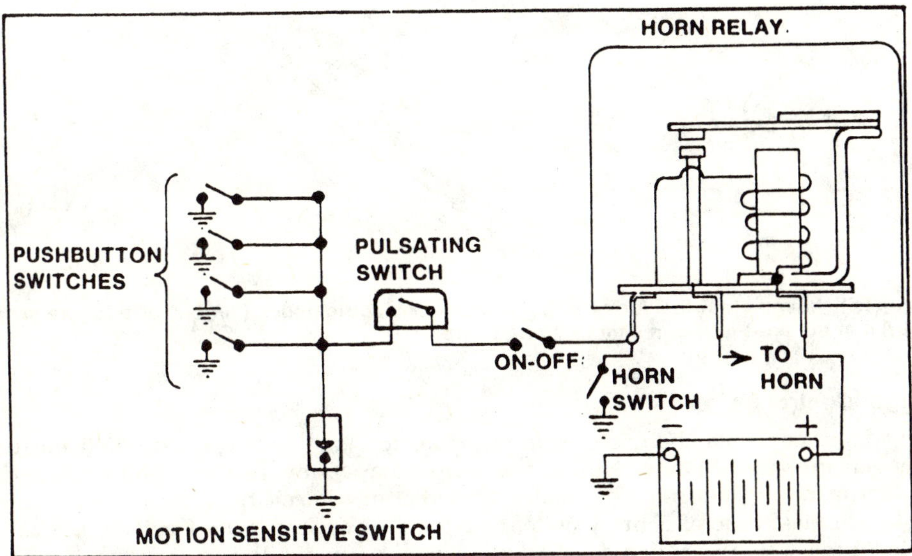

Schematic of an alarm system using the car horn

switch is the accuracy with which it must be adjusted. The switch must respond to the opening of a door, the hood or trunk, but not to such things as parking on an incline, being bumped by a pedestrian, or traffic passing by. Once the proper sensitivity is determined, it is a good idea to include a timer in the trigger circuit, to shut the alarm off after a certain period of time if it is accidentally triggered.

Pushbutton switches (such as interior light doorjamb switches) mounted on all doors and the hood and trunk may also be used to trigger an alarm. These spring-loaded, normally closed switches may be positioned adjacent to the existing switches on the doorjambs and on the hood and trunk latch plates. Mercury switches, used to activate hood and trunk lights, may be used as triggers, in lieu of pushbutton switches, on the hood and trunk.

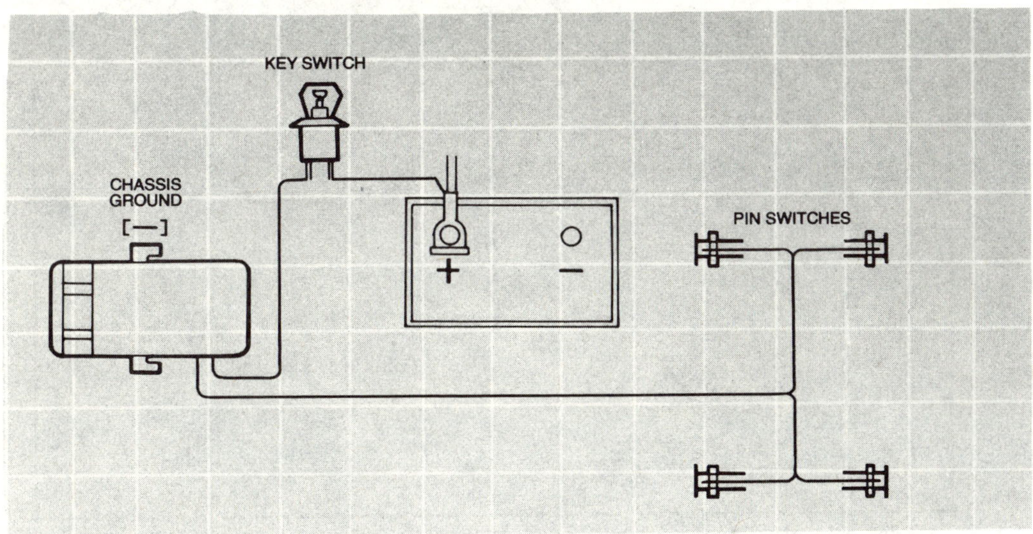

Schematic of an alarm system using an auxiliary siren

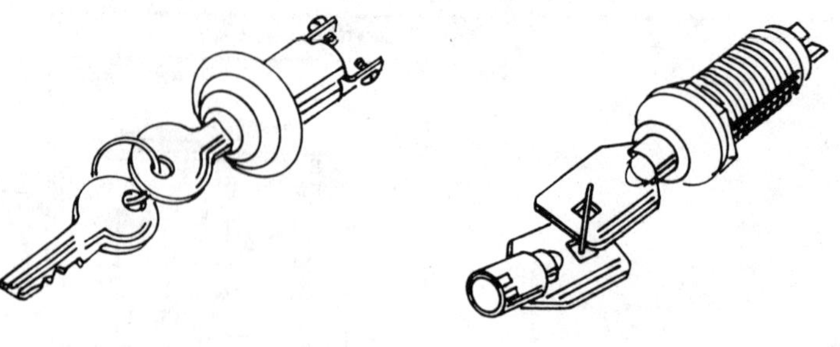

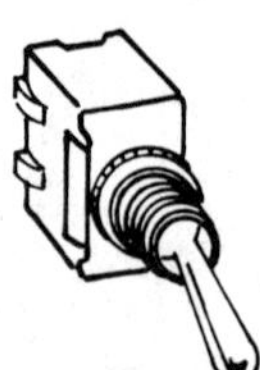

A specially keyed electrical lock (left), a round key electrical lock (center) or a toggle switch (right) can be used to arm a simple alarm system

Trigger Control Switches

The trigger control switch acts as an on-off switch for the alarm system. It must be arranged in such a manner so that the owner may enter the car without triggering the alarm, but a thief must be unable to detect or disarm it.

The simplest type of control switch is a toggle switch mounted outside the car in an inconspicuous place. Inside the fender well or under the rocker panel are two typical places that this type of switch is mounted. The only drawbacks to this type of switch are that the switch and wiring must be waterproofed, and that someone may find the switch and deactivate the alarm.

The most popular type of switch is the locking type which may be mounted anywhere on the outside of the car. These switches use cylindrical locks.

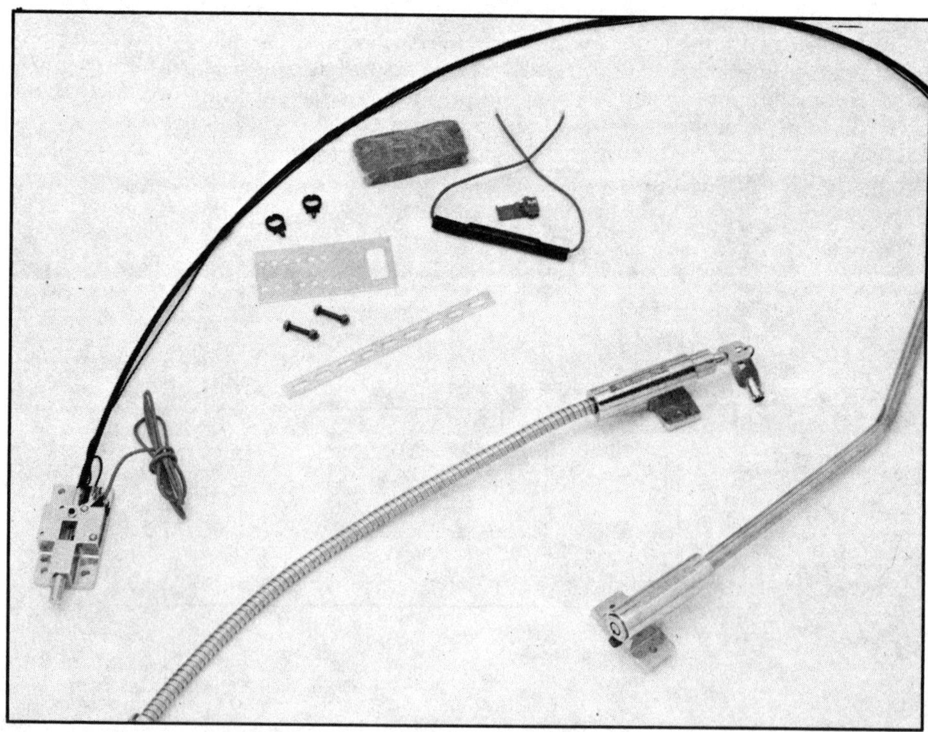

Actively armed security system incorporating a hood lock and ignition "kill" device (Courtesy Monroe Timer Co.)

Passively armed anti-theft system equipped with a paging system (Courtesy Micronics, International)

VEHICLE PROTECTION SYSTEMS

These products usually employ the latest electronic technology and provide not only a warning that someone is tampering with, or trying to steal your vehicle, but also provide a means of preventing the theft. A combination of a visual or audible alarm is used in conjunction with "system interrupters" that shut off the fuel, ignition or other vital automotive system. Many vehicle protection systems also use a sturdy hood lock to prevent access to critical electronic connections.

Standard features of a good quality vehicle protection system often include a siren, motion detector, switches and sensors to detect motion, opened doors or deck lids or current drain, system interrupters, panic switches, hood lock and many are also equipped with auxilliary power packs, paging systems and sophisticated means of deactivating the systems.

There are 2 basic kinds of vehicle protection systems—passive and actively armed.

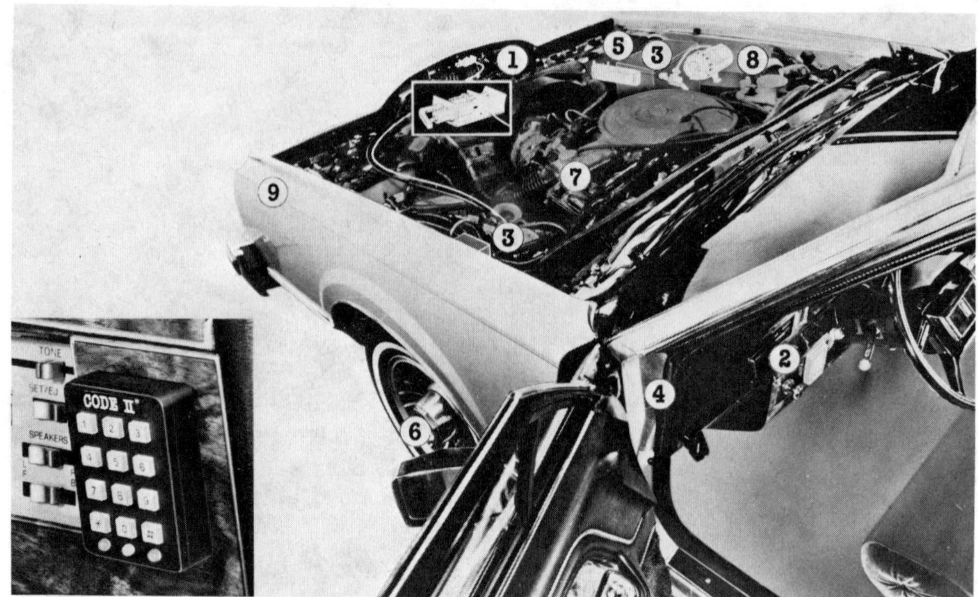

A passively armed security system that features a (1) passive hood-lock and a (2) multi-functional digital keyboard. A four-digit personal code number must be entered to disarm the system and three separate LED displays glow green to indicate that the system is on, glows yellow in the valet mode, or red if the alarm has been triggered. Other features of the system include a (3) control module and current sensor; (4) entry protection at all doors, hood and trunk; (5) a motion sensor; (6) panic switch; (7) digital passive automatic control which automatically sets the alarm when the ignition key is removed; (8) blasting siren; (9) flashing lights

All this means is that a passively armed system is automatically armed when the ignition key is removed from the lock. The driver and occupants then have a predetermined amount of time to vacate the vehicle and close the doors. An actively armed system is armed by a switch on the control unit or by some other deliberate action on the part of the operator.

Regardless of the arming method, there are many ways of disarming the unit. Some manufacturers use a specially coded key that unlocks the device from inside the car. Typically, the operator has a predetermined number of seconds, in which to open the door and disarm the system before it is activated. Other manufacturers use a digitally entered code on a control panel inside the vehicle. Again, the operator has a predetermined number of seconds to open the door and enter the code for that individual unit, in order to disarm the system. Still other manufacturers use a credit card sized device which is equipped with auxilliary power packs, paging systems and sophisticated means of deactivating the systems.

Some really sophisticated, high-tech units use voice synthesizers, in place of sirens or horns, to blare the word "BURGLAR!" over and over. Systems are also available that react to the sound of glass being broken or scratched, or heat sensing devices that react to body heat. It's even possible to use infrared, ultrasonic or microwaves to determine the presence of any unwanted object, and future systems will use voice and fingerprints or the body's magnetic field to identify authorized entrants to the vehicle.

Once activated, a human voice is simulated to shout the word "Burglar!" A siren sounds alternately at 5-second intervals (Courtesy Crimestopper Security Products)

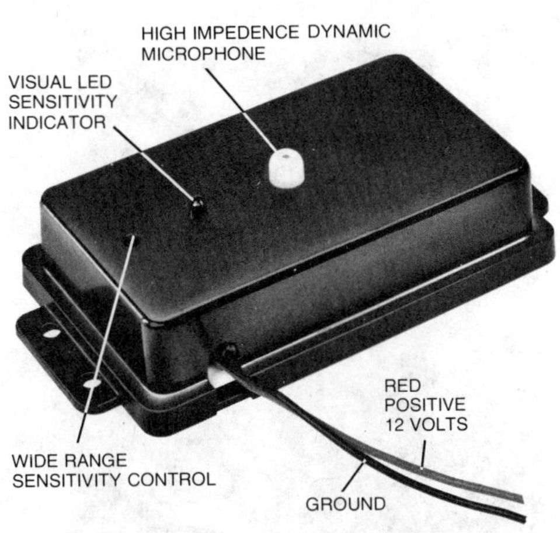

A high technology sensor that distinguishes between an object striking glass and other sounds. It reacts to attempted forced entry through glass only (Courtesy Primary Security)

Protecting Accessories

If you have custom wheels, either factory-installed or after-market items, wheel locks are the best thing you can do for them. Simply take the old lug nuts off, and screw the new ones on. Custom wheels are high on car thieves "most wanted" list, but generally the sight of wheel locks will deter the average thief.

Thefts of CBs and stereos are reaching epidemic proportions, seemingly increasing in direct relation to the number of sets sold.

Is there anything you can do to prevent your precious CB or stereo from becoming a police statistic? The most important item of the system to protect is the set itself, and the best way to protect it is to remove it and take it with you when you leave the vehicle. This can become monotonous and time consuming, unless you had the foresight to install the set on a slide mount, like those used for tape decks. These allow you to slide the set off the stationary part of the mount and stow it out of sight. In-dash combination AM/FM/CB radios are gaining in popularity, but the radio is sometimes just as vulnerable, depending on the accessibility of the dashboard. Likewise, remote-control CB radios are seen with increasing frequency. The set is comprised of several parts: an electronic box housing the transmitting and receiving components, a control box and a microphone. A variation on the theme sometimes eliminates the control housing, putting all the controls in the microphone housing. In any case, everything is compact and can be disconnected from the electronic box and stowed in a pocket or glove compartment, leaving the electronics concealed beneath the dash.

The ideal solution to radio theft is to install it in the dash. A radio hung under the dash is open invitation to thievery.

Most thieves work fast. Once inside a car, prying at the stereo hung under the dash with a stout screwdriver usually frees it in seconds. A couple of snips with the sidecutters and the thief is on his way. Because speed is of the essence, anything that will slow a thief down may be a deterrent. Alarms and mounting brackets are sometimes useful, but alarms can be disabled in seconds (by a professional) and locking mounting brackets are generally pried loose with a stout crowbar, tearing up your dash in the process. Locking barrels over the mounting nuts offer approximately the same resistance, are dealt with in the same crude manner, and gain the

T-Top locks (Courtesy Auto-Safe)

same net result. The simple truth is, if you leave your set in plain sight you're inviting trouble.

IDENTIFY YOUR PROPERTY

Once the CB or stereo or even your car is stolen, it's not lost and gone forever, if you take certain precautions. A lot of property is recovered, but the tragedy is that the owner cannot positively identify it, or the police cannot trace the owner through the serial number because the owner did not send in the warranty card. The "That's my radio! I recognize that little nick on the front," line just doesn't work unless you report the identifying features beforehand.

Police are encouraging people to engrave an identifying number on the CB, stereo, or other component and will often supply the engraver free of charge. Your social security number is not the best number for this purpose, because the social security office in Washington will not release the name and address of the social security number's owner—not even to the police. Use your driver's license number, your name and address, or some other number that can be easily and officially traced to you and no one else.

There are also national computer registration programs, which for a set one-time fee, provide an identifying number (guaranteed yours and yours alone) and a complete kit for engraving it. The number is registered with the computer service. Police can easily trace the number to you through a toll-free phone number to the computer service. No matter what number you use, be sure you have a copy of it, and be sure you can prove the number is used only by you. It is also a good idea to register it with the local police.

Insurance

Auto theft coverage is usually included with the Comprehensive portion of your policy, as is the theft of components or contents. You may find that the insurer has specifically exempted some items (such as CB radios) unless they are installed in the dash or are factory equipment.

You may also find that many insurance companies offer premium reductions for effective anti-theft devices or vehicle protection systems. These discounts could actually pay for the system over the life of the vehicle.

Check your individual policy for fine print, such as:

• Is there a deductible for contents or for the car itself? The higher the deductible (the amount you pay), the lower the premium.

• Does the policy cover CBs, stereos, and tape decks if not installed in the dash or as factory equipment?

• Does the policy cover items stolen along **with** the car, or only **from** the car?

If your car or contents of the car are stolen, be prepared to provide the police with a list of what was stolen, along with any identifying marks.

DO-IT-YOURSELF INSTALLATION

Installation of a vehicle protection system is slightly different from other electronic devices, because the engine of the car is involved at an integral level. However, most quality systems come with explicit instructions designed for foolproof installation by the do-it-yourself mechanic. Most installations instructions also contain easy tests to make along the way to be sure of correct hook-ups and troubleshooting charts to locate malfunctions. You may want to have a manual for your vehicle. The tools needed are no different from those required to do an autosound installation.

Lay out all the pieces and be sure you understand the installation instructions before proceeding

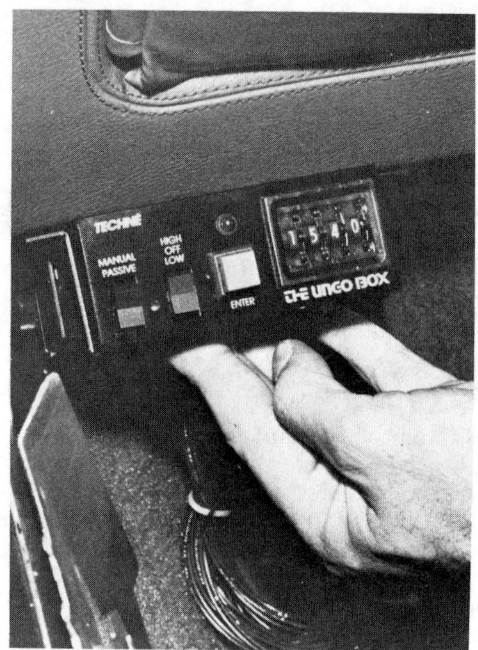

Determine a convenient, but reasonably unobtrusive mounting location for the control

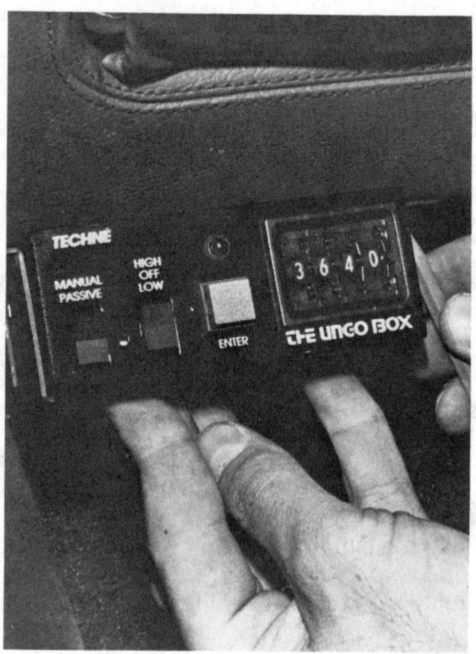

Mark the mounting holes with a pencil

Install the control box with the screws provided

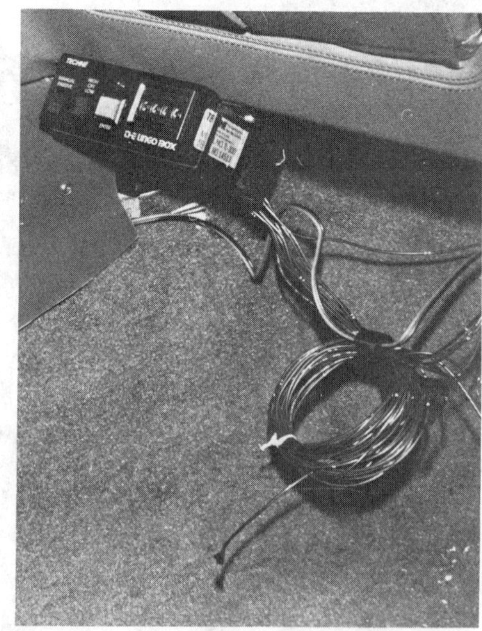

Mount the control unit (right) and the sensor/paging unit

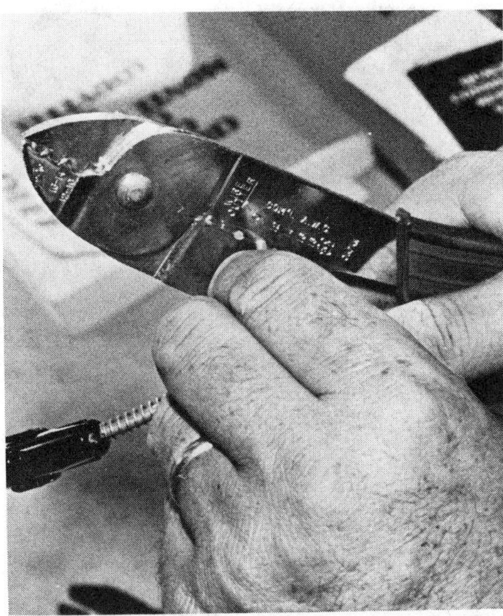

Route the appropriate wires through the fire wall to the engine compartment. Use wire strippers to clean the wire ends if making a pig tail connection. Wrap the connections in electrician's tape

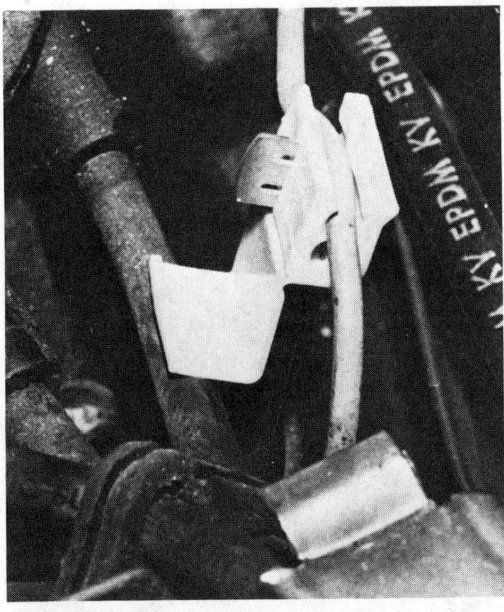

Tap connectors make a convenient method of tapping into another wire without cutting the wire

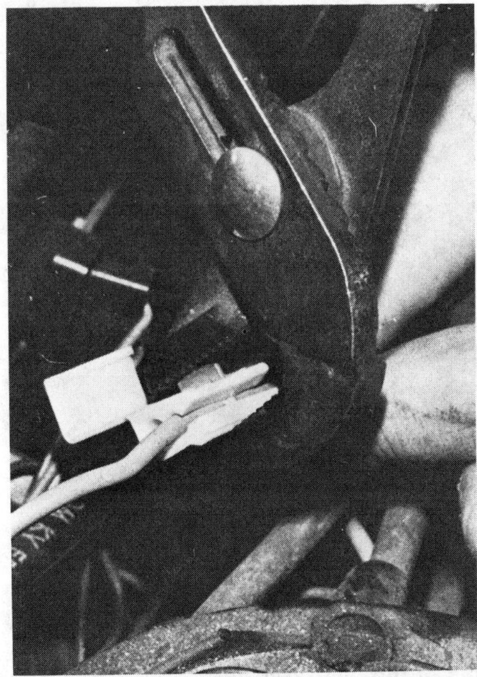

Squeeze the metal blade into the plastic housing to make contact with both wires

The Ungo System uses its own horn, which should be mounted in an inaccessible location, in the engine compartment

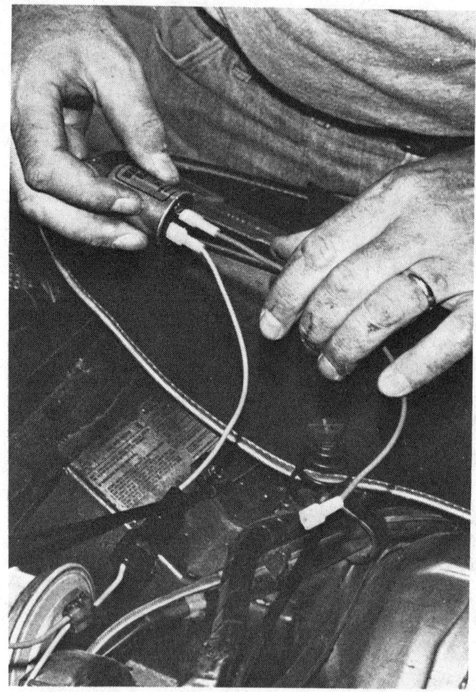

Make the connections to the horn and flasher. The flasher is used to sound the horn at intervals

Make the appropriate electrical connections according to the installation instructions for your car and unit

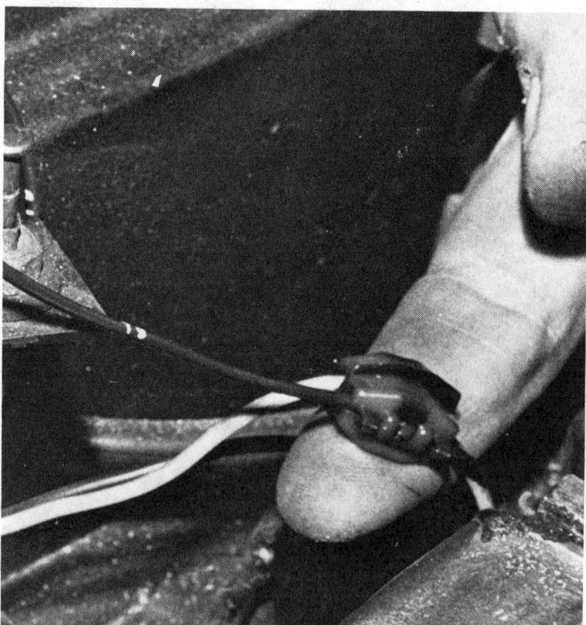

Make the electrical connections at the door switches and hood and trunk switches. Most cars have door switches already installed and wired, but alarm manufacturers supply switches with the kit

Car Stereo Glossary

AC—Alternating current. Electric current whose voltage changes from negative to positive and back again on a regular cycle. House current is usually AC, cycling back and forth 60 times per second in the U.S. and Canada, and 50 times per second in most other countries. See: DC, frequency.

Acid-core—A type of solder having a hollow core filled with acid which cleans metal surfaces to make a better bond. Such solder is NOT to be used in electronic connections, as the acid eventually corrodes the wires.

Acoustics—The pattern of resonances and reflections which affect how a given space or area affects the sound heard within it.

Ad Hoc—(1) A group of car-stereo manufacturers who voluntarily banded together to produce uniform car-stereo specifications; now part of the EIA. (2) The specifications produced by the Ad Hoc group, now the basis of the EIA car-stereo specifications.

Adjacent-channel—A signal on the frequency channel next to the one tuned in, (200 kHz, or 0.2 MHz, away on FM; 20kHz on AM). Adjacent-channel rejection measures the ability of a tuner to reject signals on the next channel.

Alignment—(1) Adjusting radio circuits to respond only to the proper signal frequencies; (2) Adjusting tape heads so that the angle of the head across the tape will match the angle of the recording, to ensure good high-frequency response.

Alternate-channel—A signal two frequency channels away from the one tuned in. Adjacent-channel rejection is commonly quoted in FM specifications; it is always substantially higher than the adjacent-channel specification.

Alternator—An AC generator, commonly used in many modern cars (where its current is turned into DC). Alternators and DC generators create different types of electrical interference, requiring different types of suppressors to cure. See: Generator.

AM—Amplitude Modulation. A system of radio transmission in which the radio station's carrier wave changes its amplitude in response to changes in the audio signal it carries. AM radio can carry greater distances than FM, but is more subject to interference. In the U.S., AM broadcasting occupies a band of frequencies from 540 to 1640 kHz. AM stations overseas may use these and other frequencies.

AM suppression—A measure, in dB, of a tuner's ability to reject signal-amplitude fluctuations, such as those caused by multipath.

Amp—Short for ampere and amplifier.

Ampere—The basic unit of electrical current. See: Power.

Amplifier—A device or circuit used to raise the power of an electrical signal.

Analog—Non-digital. The tapes, amplifiers and radio signals heard in today's car-sound systems are analog. Radio dials with moving pointers are analog dials.

Antenna—The device which picks up a radio signal to feed to a radio or tuner. Antennas work best when designed for specific radio frequencies, as most car antennas are. Whip antennas work better on cars than "invisible" windshield antennas, but are more easily damaged.

Audio—The band of frequencies between 20 and 20,000 Hz, which the human ear can hear; equipment designed to reproduce those frequencies.

Audiophile—Literally, a sound lover; hence, any one particularly interested in and critical of the quality of sound reproduction; by extension, describing recordings and equipment designed to meet those tastes.

Auto-eject—A system which automatically ejects the tape when the player is turned off, either by its own switch or by turning off the circuit it draws its power from. This prevents flat spots developing on the tape or capstan when the tape is left in playing position for long periods.

Auto-load—A system which automatically takes over loading once the tape is partially inserted into the deck: this is a convenience, and also ensures that the user will not shove the tape in so hard as to mis-align the tape heads.

Auto-Reverse—A system which automatically reverses a cassette at the end of play, to play the tape's other side.

Back wave—The wave coming from the back of a speaker. Since the speaker pulls air from the rear as it pushes at the front, and vice versa, the front and back waves are in opposite phases, and will cancel each other if mixed. In practice, this only happens at low frequencies. See: Baffle.

Baffle—A panel or box separating a speaker's front and back waves, to prevent low-frequency cancellation.

Balance Control—A control used to adjust the relative sound levels from a stereo system's speakers, so that both will be heard equally by the passengers in the car.

Band—A defined range of frequencies. Examples include the AM and FM broadcast bands (540 to 1640 kHz and 80 to 108 MHz, respectively) and the frequency bands of an equalizer. In car stereo, the latter are generally one or two octaves wide, with center frequencies which are either multiples or sub-multiples of 1,000 Hz. The audio band is generally considered to be from 20 to 20,000 Hz.

Bass—The low end of the audio frequency range, usually from about 500 Hz on down.

Bi-amplification—The use of separate amplifiers to power the low and high frequency speakers in a system. This results in cleaner sound but also, since it involves extra amplifiers and an electronic crossover, in higher cost.

Booster—(1) an auxilliary amplifier placed between a car stereo's output section and the loudspeakers, to increase the power available to the speakers. (2) An auxilliary amplifier placed between an antenna and the input of an FM tuner, to provide a stronger signal to the latter.

Capstan—A constantly-rotating shaft in a tape deck, which drives the tape. During playback or recording, the tape is held against the capstan by a soft pinch roller, for steady, controlled speed. During fast winding, the pinch roller is released, so the tape can move freely.

Capture ratio—The smallest difference (in dB) which must exist between two FM signals on the same frequency, in order for a specific tuner to distinguish between them. The smaller this ratio, the better the tuner will perform.

Carrier—A radio frequency which is modulated by another signal, carrying that signal to radio receivers. In AM, the carrier frequency remains constant, but its amplitude, or volume, changes in accordance with the signal; in FM, the carrier's amplitude stays constant, but its frequency varies above and below its nominal frequency.

Cartridge—See Eight-track

Cassette—See Compact cassette

CB, Citizens Bank—A two-way radio service for the use or ordinary prople. No license is currently required, and the radios are available for use in the car, for portable use, and for use at fixed locations. The radios have limited power, and operate on 40 channels in the 27-MHz band. Channel 9 is legally reserved for emergency messages. Channels 19 and 12 are among those commonly used for sharing information about highway hazards and traffic, directions, and so on.

CD—Compact Disc. A digitally recorded disc, 4.7 inches in diameter, turning at 1,800 rpm, and played by scanning it with a laser system. Compact-disc players are not yet available for use in the car, but such players should come within a few years. The size of the disc was chosen with that idea in mind.

Channel—(1), in a stereo system, that part of the system carrying signals to be heard through only the right or the left speakers. (2) In radio or television broadcasting, a range of frequencies allocated for particular stations.

Chrome, Chromium Dioxide—Colloquial and technical terms for a type of premium tape requiring a playback equalization setting of 70 uS (labelled "metal" on many car-stereo players), and corresponding to IEC tape Type II. Most premium tapes are Type II, and may be colloquially called "chrome" even when they use other formulations which mimic (and sometimes surpass) chrome's performance.

Coaxial—Having a common axis. Coaxial speakers have the small tweeter mounted within the larger woofer, usually at the latter's center-point. Coaxial cable used for antenna and signal connections has an inner conductor surrounded by a concentric outer one which serves as a shield against electrical interference.

Compact Cassette—A plastic cassette containing a length of tape, 1/7 inch wide, which is wound back and forth between two hubs built into the cassette. When the cassette is loaded into a suitable tape deck, the deck's heads contact the tape through windows in one side of the cassette, while the deck's motors grip the inside of the cassette hubs, to move the tape.

Compandor—A device which can be made to work as either a compressor or expander.

Compressor—A device which reduces a signal's dynamic range, either so it can more easily be recorded or so that it can more easily be heard in a noisy environment.

Continuity tester—A device which quickly shows whether two points in a circuit are connected or not.

Crimping tool—A tool used to crimp connectors such as spade lugs onto wires, without soldering.

Crossover—A circuit which divides frequencies between the drivers in a loudspeaker system, so that high, low and middle frequencies go only to the drivers designed to handle them. Crossovers built into a speaker system are "passive" crossovers. "electronic crossovers" divide frequencies between amplifiers which then power the separate drivers.

Current—The flow of electrons in a circuit, measured in amperes.

DAD—Digital Audio Disc; see: CD, Compact Disc.

dB, decibel—The standard measure of relative sound or signal power. One dB is about the smallest signal difference most ears can consistently detect on immediate comparison. The dB scale is logarithmic: If two signals differ by 3 dB, the larger is twice as powerful as the smaller. If they differ by 10 dB, the larger is ten times as powerful; if by 20 dB, the larger is 100 times more powerful, and so on. This logarithmic scale corresponds to our hearing: doubling the power (+3 dB) yields a difference just large enough to be noted when time elapses between signals; it takes a change of 10 dB to make a signal sound "twice as loud."

dBf—An increasingly common unit for measuring FM signal power in rating tuner performance. Since it measures signal power, not just signal voltage, this specification will be the same whether applied to the 75-ohm antenna circuits common in car tuners or the 300-ohm circuits most common in home systems. The dBf stands for decibels referred to one femtowatt, or 0.000000000000001 watt. See: Microvolts, Impedance.

dBA—Decibels, weighted per the standard "A" weighting curve. See: Weighted.

dbx—A noise-reduction system offering a very wide dynamic range. The system works by compressing the signal during recording, and expanding it again in playback. The tapes are designed to be heard only when expanded by a dbx decoder. Otherwise, because of the strong compression used, the tapes sound unpleasant.

DC, direct current—Electric current whose voltage does not fluctuate cyclically, like AC's, and which moves constantly in one direction. The current from automobile and other batteries is always DC.

Delay Circuit—A circuit which delays a signal by a small fraction of a second before sending it to loudspeakers. The purpose is to simulate the delayed echoes which give large spaces their characteristic reverberance.

Digital—By the numbers. More and more car stereo systems have digital tuners, which jump in precise steps between station frequencies, rather than sliding from one to another, through all the non-station frequencies which lie between. Digital recording stores sound as a numerical record of its levels at more than 40,000 intervals each second, which solves many sonic problems. The "digital" recordings now sold for use in the car are actually analog copies made from digital masters; true digital recordings are now reaching the home as Compact Discs, which should be playable in the car in a few years.

Distortion—An undesired change in the signal, usually by the addition of frequencies not belonging to it. See: IM, Multipath, THD.

DNR—Dynamic Noise Reduction. A noise reduction system which limits the system's high-frequency response when the high-frequency levels in the signal get uncomfortably close to the noise level in the system. DNR does not reduce noise as effectively as Dolby or dbx; but it also does not require specially-encoded signals, as the others do, so it can be used on any tape or broadcast, and can even be used in conjunction with the other two systems.

Dolby noise reduction—A system of reducing noise and increasing dynamic range, in which high (and some middle) frequencies are compressed in recording and expanded in playback. Dolby B, the original (and now almost universal) home noise reduction system, reduces noise by about 10 dB; Dolby C, a new variation, reduces it by about 20 dB.

Tapes made with either Dolby system sound shrill if played back without proper decoding. However, it is possible to play Dolby C tapes through a Dolby B decoder, or Dolby B tapes with no decoder, if the sound system's treble control is turned down. Some FM stations use Dolby B encoding in their broadcasts, and the Dolby B decoders in a very few car-stereo systems work on FM, too, for best reception of those stations.

Driver—A single loudspeaker, usually one of several used in a loudspeaker system. Such a system will typically have a large "woofer" for lower frequencies, and a small "tweeter" to handle the highs.

Dynamic Range—The range (usually stated in dB) between the loudest signal a system or component can handle before distorting it more than some stated amount, and the softest signal the system can handle without burying it in noise, roughly equivalent to the signal-to-noise ratio (S/N). The higher the dynamic range, the better.

DX—Distant. Abbreviation, common on local/distant (LO/DX) switches.

Efficiency—A measure of how well a system transforms one form of energy into another. For example, the common Class-AB amplifiers are more efficient than the Class-A ones now appearing for mobile use, because they consume less battery power for the same output to the speaker. Similarly, one speaker is more efficient than another when it requires less amplifier power to produce the same sound output.

EIA—Electronic Industries Association of America. The EIA, among its other duties, sets uniform standards for measuring and stating car and home stereo specifications; however, not all car-stereo makers follow them.

Eight-track cartridge—A tape system using quarter-inch tape wound in an endless loop, and carrying eight signal tracks. Most 8-track tapes are stereo, having four pairs of signal tracks, with the tape head moving down to the next pair at the end of each complete tape run-through. At one time, four-channel tapes were also made, with two pairs of four tracks each; these required special players, no longer made, for the four-channel effect to be heard. Eight-track cartridges are larger than cassettes; and for that and other reasons, are less popular.

Electronic Crossover—A crossover designed to go between a preamplifier, receiver or tape deck and two or more amplifiers, feeding each amplifier a different portion of the audio band. See: Bi-amplification.

Enclosure—A box used as a baffle for a speaker. For best results the enclosure's volume and shape, and the size and shape of any ports permitting sound to escape, should be carefully calculated. In the car, where the enclosure may be any handy cavity, this is rarely possible, unless the speakers come with enclosures of their own (in which case, fitting them in becomes a problem).

Equalization—(1) In tape playback, a standard alteration of frequency response, applied to a tape to cancel the effects of another, standard alteration made in recording; this permits wider dynamic range and frequency response. "Normal" (Ferric, or Type I) tapes require a "120-uS" curve for playback; premium ("Metal," "Chrome" or Type II, III and IV) tapes require a "70-uS" curve. Playing back with the wrong curve does not harm the tape, but does alter the frequency response slightly.

(2) The process of adjusting an equalizer to obtain flat response from the sound system as a whole.

Equalizer—A device for altering a system's frequency response, usually to compensate for response variations elsewhere in the system. See: Graphic, Paragraphic, Parametric.

ETR—Electronically-Tuned Radio. Trade term for a radio using digital frequency synthesis tuning.

Expander—A device which expands a signal's dynamic range, by amplifying loud signals more than soft ones. Mild expanders may be used to "liven up" the sound; strong ones are usually used in conjunction with equal and opposite compressors, as in the dbx noise-reduction system.

Fader—A control used to balance the sound levels between front and rear speakers

Femtowatt—See: dBf.

Filter—A circuit to separate desired from undesired sounds. Filters are used to reduce interference from a car's ignition and electrical system; in the tuner to separate the desired station from others on the dial, and in equalizers to separate the frequency bands affected by each control.

Flat—Accurate in frequency response. A sound component's output for a given input signal level should be constant for all frequencies it's rated to handle. A graph of its output level vs. signal frequency should therefore be a straight, flat, horizontal line.

Flush-mount—Of a car-stereo speaker: Designed to be mounted in a hole cut into a car's interior bodywork, so as not to project more than a fraction of an inch from the surface it is mounted in. See: Surface-mount.

Flutter—Rapid, cyclic variations in the speed of a tape or tape deck, causing a gargly, "underwater" sound if extreme. See: Wow.

Frequency—Sound or radio waves are usually cyclical, rising and falling at more or less regular intervals. The frequency at which these oscillations occur governs the pitch of sound waves, and the tuning frequency of radio ones. Frequency is usually measured in "hertz"

(abbreviated "Hz"). One Hz corresponds to one cycle per second. Sound waves are generally audible from about 20 to 20,000 Hz (the precise limits depend upon the listener's ear). The North American AM radio band uses frequencies of 540 to 1640 kHz (1 kHz = 1,000 Hz); FM uses 88-108 MHz (1 MHz = 1,000,000 Hz).

Frequency response—The specification for the way a system or component responds to different frequencies. The clearest and most detailed way to show this is by a graph depicting all peaks and dips in the response. However, it can also be summarized by a indicating the limits (in dB) of those peaks and dips over a given frequency range (e.g.: "20–20,000 Hz, ± 3 dB"). The smaller the limits, the flatter the response over the designated range. See: Flat.

Frequency-Synthesizer—A type of tuner circuit whose internal oscillator is controlled by a digital circuit. This allows it to step directly from one legal station frequency to another, without moving through the in-between frequencies at which stations can't be received. A properly-made synthesizer tuner needs no fine-tuning—quite convenient when you're trying to tune and drive at the same time.

Fundamental—The lowest frequency of a musical note, and the one which gives that note its pitch. See: Harmonic.

Generator—A DC generator, used in cars to provide electricity for ignition, lights, and such accessories as the car stereo system, and to recharge the battery. See: Alternator.

Grommet—A rubber or brass ring used to line or reinforce a hole. Rubber grommets should be used where wires go through holes in metal panels, so that the edges of the holes won't cut the wires or insulation.

Harmonic—A frequency which is a multiple of some other frequency. Harmonics are a natural part of sounds, and give them their characteristic tone, or timbre—without them, a violin and oboe playing the same note would sound alike. However, undesired harmonics can be generated by a sound system; see: THD.

Heat-shrink tubing—A form of plastic tubing which shrinks to a smaller diameter when heated; excellent for insulating wires and connections, when a non-hazardous heat source is available to shrink them.

Hertz—The unit of frequency measurement. One Hertz equals one cycle per second. See: Frequency.

Hiss—A random mix of frequencies, especially high frequencies, appearing as noise in recordings, broadcasts and electronic circuits.

I.F.—Intermediate Frequency. Tuners are basically filters to screen out undesired signals from the one tuned in. It's hard to re-tune filters (especially multiple ones) to each new station frequency; so in most modern radios, the filters are tuned to a fixed "intermediate frequency" (usually 10.7 MHz in FM tuners, for example). The jumble of station frequencies coming into the antenna terminals is then mixed with another, variable frequency (the "local oscillator"); this frequency is varied till the difference between it and that of the desired station equals the intermediate frequency. That difference in signal then passes through the i.f. filters.

I.F. Rejection—Ability of a tuner to reject outside signals which happen to have the same frequency as the i.f.

Ignition—The circuits in a gasoline engine which ignite the fuel. This constant source of high-voltage sparks just a few inches from the radio is a potent interference source, but one which can be tamed.

Image-rejection—A measure of a tuner's ability to reject signals in the aircraft band.

Intermodulation Distortion (IM)—A type of distortion in which two frequencies which belong in a sound signal mix to produce other, sum and difference frequencies, which do not.

Impedance—Resistance to alternating currents of a given frequency. (Resistance which is the same at all frequencies is known simply as "resistance.") Electronic devices are usually designed to work best with other devices of specific impedances, such as 75 ohms for antennas, and 4–8 ohms for speakers.

Key-Off Eject—See: Automatic Eject.

Keyhole Saw—A small saw with a stiff, finely-serrated blade supported at one end by a tubular or pistol-shaped grip. Useful for cutting odd-shaped shaped holes.

Kilohertz, kHz—Thousands of hertz; a measure of frequency. See: Hertz.

Kick Panel—A low-placed interior body panel in a car. Speakers may be mounted in kick panels, provided that: the rear of the panel is not exposed to weather or flying pebbles; the high frequencies (if the speaker is not just a woofer) will be able to reach the listeners' ears from that location, and the speaker's grille is reasonably resistant to scuffs and kicks.

LCD—Liquid Crystal Display. A type of display, common on calculators and watches, in which numbers and symbols darken against a light background. LCD dials are easy to read in bright ambient light, but must be illuminated to be seen in dim light.

LED—Light-Emitting Diode. A self-illuminated device, used in numerical dial displays and small indicator lights. It is easy to see in dim ight, but sometimes hard to see or read when ambient light is bright.

Local/Distant Switch—A switch which adjusts a tuner's sensitivity for strong (local) or weak (distant) stations. Not all radios need this switch (nor do all radios which need it have it), due to differences in their basic adaptability. On some radios, it may not adjust sensivity, but only select how strong or weak a station the automatic tuning circuits will stop at. See: Scan, Seek.

Lockwasher—A springy washer with a serrated edge or a split to grip at the underside of a bolt head and the surface beneath it. This lessens the chance of the bolt's vibrating loose.

Loudness Control—A control which adds more bass (and, sometimes, treble) as the volume is lowered, to compensate for the ear's lower sensitivity to those frequencies at low volumes. This prevents low-volume sound from seeming thin and distant. A loudness switch turns this compensation on or off. See: Volume control.

Loudspeaker—A device to convert an electrical signal into sound with enough power to be heard clearly more than a few inches away.

Memory—Like the memory of a computer, that of an electronically-tuned car radio stores information. In this case, the frequencies of the stations to be pre-selected by each button (and, in at least one case, such other parameters as whether or not the station broadcasts Dolby).

Metal Tape—A fairly new type of tape, capable of exceptionally high recording quality, and requiring 70-uS playback equalization. Only recorders made within the past few years can record it properly; cashing in on this prestige, car-stereo makers often label their 70-uS positions "Metal," even though it will more often be used for the far more common chrome and chrome-equivalent tapes.

mHz—Megahertz, a unit of frequency corresponding to one million hertz. The FM band runs from 88 to 108 MHz.

Microcassette—A very small tape cassette, for which car stereo players will probably be available very soon, if not already. The fidelity is less than that of standard cassette, and the availability of pre-recorded tapes in this format is likely to be limited for some time to come; but the size is most convenient on long trips.

Microvolt—Millionths of a volt; unit commonly used in measuring radio signal strengths as received at or from the antenna, and therefore in measuring tuner performance.

Modulation—Information imposed upon a carrier by changing one of its characteristics, such as its amplitude (AM) or frequency (FM).

Monophonic—Having only one channel of information (as opposed to stereo, which has two, and quadraphonic, which had four). A single channel remains monophonic, even if delivered over several speakers. FM tuners switch from stereo to mono under difficult reception conditions, as mono FM is less sensitive to noise, multipath and other problems; some tuners also let the user switch, for marginal conditions.

Multipath—simultaneous reception of a signal and slightly-delayed reflections of that signal. In FM, this causes distortion; in TV, it causes "ghosts."

Multiplex—The FM stereo broadcast system, or any other system for putting several channels of information onto one carrier.

Muting—A circuit to switch off a tuner's sound output when the R.F. signal falls below a certain level. This prevents noise blasts when tuning through frequencies where no station is currently being received. It also prevents reception of very weak stations, whose signals would be noisy; some tuners let you switch muting off when you want to hear such stations.

MW—Medium Wave; European designation for the AM broadcast band.

Neon Tester—A simple, inexpensive tester, commonly used to determine which wires do and do not carry power in a car or other electrical system.

Noise—Any undesired signal added to a signal and usually unrelated to it. (Undesired additions related to the signal are generally forms of distortion.)

Noise Reduction—Any system for reducing noise in audio systems. See: dbx, DNR, Dolby.

Octave—The musical interval between two frequencies whose ratio is 2:1. Tones spaced octaves apart are perceived as different versions of the same note, e.g., 220, 440 and 880 Hz are all perceived as "A." The audio band is approximately 10 octaves wide.

Equalizer bands are sometimes specified in terms of how many octaves they cover. A ten-band model is an "octave equalizer," while 5-band models cover two octaves per band, and 31-band models are "third-octave equalizers."

Ohm—The unit of measurement for resistance or impedance. See: impedance.

Ohmmeter—A meter used for measuring DC resistance; it can also be used as a continuity tester. It does not, however accurately measure impedance.

Overdriving, overloading—In practice, the same: trying to feed more signal through an audio component than it can take without distortion or, in extreme cases, damage.

Overtone—A harmonic occuring as a natural component of a sound. Overtones give musical notes the timbre which helps the ear distinguish between instruments playing the same pitch.

Paragraphic—A type of equalizer having several bands of equalization (like the graphic), but with provision for shifting the frequencies covered by each band (like the parametric).

Parametric—A type of equalizer having fewer bands than the graphic, but gaining versatility by allowing the width of these bands to be varied and the frequency range shifted up and down.

Peak—The maximum voltage, current or power of a wave over a period of time. Music often contains brief peaks 10 or more times as large as the average sound level of the passage being heard.

Phase—Signals are said to be in phase if they rise and fall in unison, completely out of phase if one rises while the other falls. These differences are measured in degrees, from 0 (perfectly in phase) to 180 (completely out of phase), and beyond. Out of phase signals cancel each other, in proportion to their phase angle and relative strength.

Pinch-roller—The soft rubber or plastic roller which holds the tape against the captstan during play or recording. If it stays pressed against the tape when the tape is no longer moving, flat spots will develop in the roller, which will later cause wow and flutter. Some car-stereo units therefore have auto ejection, to ensure the roller is released if the tape ends or the power is cut off.

Player—A tape unit which can play but not record tapes. The vast majority of car tape decks fall into this category.

Polarity—The property of having opposite poles, as most electrical circuits do. Stereo components will not usually work, and may be damaged, if their power connections have the wrong polarity. Speakers must be wired with the same polarity in each channel, or bass will be lost (due to cancellation by one speaker pushing while the other pulls), and the stereo image may seem diffuse, or wandering in space.

Power—The ability to do work; in car stereo, usually referring to an amplifer's output, or its ability to make a speaker work. Amplifer power measurements, to be truly valid, should include the distortion level at which that power level is attained, and the range of frequencies overwhich it is attainable.

Preamp-level—A signal level of minimal power, intended solely as input for a power amplifier. Expensive car-stereo units may have only preamp-level outputs, on the assumption that the user will want power enough to justify a large amplifier, and may choose to bi-amplify his system. Mid-priced units may have both speaker-level and preamp-level outputs, so as to be immediately usable by themselves, but ready for installation of a higher-powered amplifier later.

Radio—(1) A system of communication involving wireless transmission of electrical signals. (2) A receiver for that system.

Rain-shield—A waterproof device designed to shield the back of a loudspeaker from water drips; recommended for installations in doors with window channels down which rain can drip.

Range—(1) The set of frequencies covered by a device; e.g., a tweeter might cover the range from 5,000 to 15,000 Hz. (2) The distance over which a radio signal can be received.

Receiver—A device consisting of a tuner section for selecting and demodulating radio signals, and an amplifier section to render those signals capable of driving a loudspeaker. Most car-sound receivers include tape players as well; those which don't, are usually just called "radios."

Recorder—A device which can record (and usually play back) tape or some other medium. Recorders are comparatively rare in car-stereo systems, which usually just play tapes.

Relay—An electrically operated switch, allowing a small voltage or current to turn a larger one on and off.

Resonance—The quality of being unusually sensitive to a particular frequency, so much as to amplify or prolong vibrations at that frequency; the frequency at which a body or circuit resonates.

Reverberation—(1) Multiple sound reflections, which help give a room or other space its sonic character. (2) Electronic or electro-mechanical simulation of such reflections, so as to change the sonic character of the listening space, usually by making it sound larger.

R.F.—Radio Frequency. The range of frequencies used as carriers by radio or television transmitters, and to which receivers are tuned. Usually used to describe circuits handling these frequencies, as opposed to those handling the audio frequencies from 20–20,000 Hz. (Radio frequencies are higher.)

rms—Root Mean Square. A mathematical term describing the process used to measure the average, as opposed to peak, level of a signal; sometimes used interchangeably with "average."

Rosin-core—A type of solder having a core of a rosin which cleans surfaces, for a tighter solder bond, without corroding them. This is the only kind of solder to be used in electrical or electronic soldering. (See: Acid-Core.)

Saber Saw—An electric saw having a short, thin blade projecting and moving at right angles to the motor housing. Useful in cutting speaker holes, and for similar tasks.

Scan—A tuner feature which automatically plays a few seconds of each station signal it encounters, then moves on to the next unless commanded to stop. See: Seek.

Seek—A tuner feature which automatically finds the next station signal on the dial and stops there. See: Scan.

Selectivity—A measure of a tuner's ability to distinguish between signals (usually FM) on closely-spaced frequencies. See: Adjacent-Channel, Alternate-Channel.

Sensitivity—A measure of a tuner's ability to handle weak signals. Usually stated in terms of the minimum signal level necessary to achieve a given degree of performance.

Shielding—Metal cabinets, screens, etc., used to prevent signals from leaking into or out of an electronic system.

Signal—An audio or radio wave carrying information. In radio, an audio signal is used to modulate an r.f. carrier to form the broadcast radio signal; the tuner then demodulates this signal to extract the audio signal.

Slider—A control which slides rather than turning. Sliders are most commonly found in graphic equalizers.

S/N—Signal-to-noise ratio. The ratio between the level of a signal and that of the noise it contains. The higher the ratio, the less noisy (and therefore more listenable) the signal.

Socket Wrench—A wrench having a ratchet handle which accepts interchangable sockets of different sizes.

Soldering—A process of joinging metals by melting a lead/tin alloy ("solder") over them. The alloy has a comparatively low melting point; the heat is supplied by a small torch or (far more practical, in the car) an electrical "soldering iron."

Sound—Vibrations in the air which fall within the range of hearing, or audio frequency range; the sensation of hearing those sounds.

Spade Lug—A metal connector, having a tubular section which is crimped or soldered to a wire, and a flat, forked section which goes around a terminal screw.

Speaker—Short for loudspeaker. The device in a sound system which translates electrical vibrations from the amplifier into sound vibrations.

Speaker-level—Signals at the level normally fed to loudspeakers. "Booster" amplifiers have only speaker-level inputs, designed to accept such signals. Power amplifiers may have only preamp-level and speaker-level inputs, or only preamp-level ones.

Specifications—A manufacturer's statement of his products' features and performance.

Spurious Response Rejection—Basically, a measure of a tuner's resistance to strong-signal overload.

Static—Radio-frequency interference, chiefly in AM radio.

Stereo, Stereophonic—Having two channels carrying signals picked up from different microphones, in order to create an illusion of music being performed in space.

Subcarrier—A frequency modulated by another signal, the whole then being used to modulate a radio frequency for transmission. In FM stereo braodcasting, the stereo information (i.e., the difference between the left and right channels) is used to modulate a 38-kHz subcarrier, which is then added to the monophonic signal (the sum of the left and right channels) to make a composite signal which, in turn, modulates the station's carrier. Without this technique, the sum and difference signals would be at the same frequency, and would interfere with one another.

Subwoofer—A speaker devoted to the lowest audio frequencies, usually below 100 or 200 Hz.

Suppressor—A circuit or device used to suppress interference or keep it from reaching a system sensitive to it.

Surface-Mount—Of a speaker: Designed to mount on an interior surface of the car, rather than being sunk into a hole in that surface. (See: Flush-Mount.)

SW—Short Wave. The frequency bands (receivable on a few car radios, either directly or with adapters) from 5.95 to 26.1 MHz, chiefly used for long-distance AM communications.

Tape Head—In a tape player, the device which "reads" the changing magnetic signals on the tape and converts them into electrical signals which are then fed through the rest of the sound system. Tape recorders have at least one other head, to erase the tape before new recordings are laid down on it; the recording head may be a separate head, or the playback head may be used to make the recording, too.

Template—A full-sized diagram of mounting holes, used as tool to show where such holes must be cut or drilled.

Terminal—The mechanical point at which an electrical connection is made. Terminals may be screws holding spade lugs or bare wires, or may take other forms accepting special connectors.

THD—Total Harmonic Distortion. The sum of all illegitimate harmonics in a signal, expressed as their percentage of the total.

Three-way—Of a speaker: having a separate woofer, tweeter and mid-range. See: Tweeter, Two-Way, Woofer.

TIM—Transient Intermodulation Distortion. A type of distortion which chiefly effects or is triggered by, brief, transient signals.

Tone Control—A control which alters the frequency balance of a signal. Those labelled "Tone" usually cut the high frequencies when turned down, but otherwise leave the signal unaffected. Separate bass, treble and midrange tone controls usually can be set either to raise or lower the level of the frequencies they affect.

Transient—A brief signal, usually a peak.

Transmitter—The part of a broadcast station which generates and modulates the carrier before feeding it to the transmitting antenna.

Treble—The upper end of the audio frequency range.

Tweeter—A driver used only to handle treble frequencies.

Two-Way—A speaker with a woofer and tweeter, but no mid-range driver.

Unweighted—See: Weighted

Usable Sensitivity—The signal level necessary for a tuner or receiver to achieve the modest goal of 30 dB S/N. The term is a misnomer, as few listeners, today, would consider such a noisy signal "usable"; for historical reasons, however, it is still the most commonly quoted specification for sensitivity.

Volt—A unit of electrical force.

Volume—(1) the internal dimension of an enclosed space. (2) Sound level.

Volume Control—A control which varies signal (and hence sound) level in an audio system. Technically speaking, one which varies only sound level, without shifting frequency balance as a "loudness" control does; however, some systems have controls which may be switched to operate as either type, and may bear either label (though more commonly called "volume" controls to distinguish them from the "loudness switch."

VHF—The radio-frequency band from 30 to 300 MHz, containing TV channels 2 through 13, and the FM broadcast band (which lies between channels 5 and 6, in the U.S.). Some radios therefore label their dials "VHF" instead of "FM."

Watt—The unit of electrical power, equal to one ampere of current at one volt (or such equivalents as two amperes at 0.5 volt, etc.).

Wave—A physical vibration travelling through air (sound) or an electrical one travelling through the air (radio) or a wire.

Waveform—The shape of a wave, usually as seen on an instrument called an "oscillosocope."

Wavelength—The length of one cycle of a wave, which is determined by its frequency and its speed in the medium through which it is passing.

Weighted measurements—Those whose components are counted more or less heavily, according to a pre-determined rule. Noise measurements, for example, are usually weighted to count most heavily those frequencies to which the human ear is most sensitive, while counting other frequencies less heavily. A weighted noise measurement may therefore be either less or more than an unweighted one, depending on the frequencies of the noise in question.

Whizzer—A small, stiff cone attached to a larger speaker, to improve its high-frequency output. Not to be confused with a "tweeter," which is a complete and independent driver.

Whip—An upright or quasi-upright antenna.

Woofer—A driver designed to handle the lower frequencies in a speaker system.

Wow—Slow, periodic speed changes. See: Flutter.

wrms—Weighted Root Mean Square. A weighted average. See: rms, Weighted.